EXPAT FAQs
Moving To and Living in The Dominican Republic

All of the things you always wanted to know about becoming an expat in the Dominican Republic. Plus a few of the things you didn't!

Ginnie Bedggood
Ilana Benady

First Published in Great Britain 2011
by Summertime Publishing

© Copyright Ginnie Bedggood and Ilana Benady

All rights reserved. No part of this publication may be reproduced, stored in or introduced into a retrieval system, or transmitted, in any form, or by any means (electronic, mechanical, photocopying recording or otherwise) without the prior written permission of the publisher.

This book is sold subject to the condition that it shall not, by way of trade or otherwise, be lent, resold, hired out, or otherwise circulated without the publishers prior consent in any form of binding or cover other than that in which it is published and without a similar condition including this condition being imposed on the subsequent purchaser.

All photographs © Copyright
Pedro Guzmán used with permission.
www.flickr.com/pedritoguzman

This book is dedicated to the memory of Ginnie Bedggood, who passed away unexpectedly in July 2010, the same week we sent the text to the publishers.

Acknowledgements

Every single Dominican whom the authors have met in their combined thirty-year experience of living in the Dominican Republic has provided inspiration for this book in one way or another. However, two in particular have devoted hours to examining the text for any bloopers, which could offend the host population, and to José Sánchez and Himilce Tejada we extend our grateful thanks. This is the second time their patience has been tested as they performed a similar service in relation to our previous book: *Dominican Republic - Culture Smart! The Essential Guide to Customs & Culture*.

Just as many Dominicans have left their imprint on this book, so, too, have a number of expatriates. Again four in particular, two British, one American and one Canadian, have offered a number of helpful suggestions from their differing perspectives of 'recent expat' and 'experienced expat'. To John R Evans, Elizabeth Eames Roebling and Sylvie Normand, thank you for spotting our omissions and adding fresh insights and special thanks to Eve Hayes de Kalaf for her invaluable help with the history section.

Ilana Benady's husband is the well-known Dominican photographer Pedro Guzmán and it is he who has provided both the cover photograph and those within the book.

Both he and Ginnie Bedggood's partner, Grahame Bush, are owed thanks for their patience and support.

Finally, thanks to our editors, Joe Gregory of Bookshaker and Jo Parfitt of Summertime Publishing for their support, understanding and encouragement.

About the Authors

Ginnie Bedggood arrived into this world as the air raid siren sounded an alarm - June 1943 in London UK and World War II was in progress.

Following expulsion from a Roman Catholic convent grammar school (!) she graduated from London University (Queen Mary College) with a degree in history. During her university years she became interested in social work and taught drama in a Boys' Club in the East End of London. Her failure to graduate on her first attempt led to a year working in a girls' remand home in Sussex and a period of four months living in Ohio, US, while she awaited the results of her second attempt. This was her first experience as an expat, one where she encountered racism for the first time up front and personal through her relationship with an African-American. She also experienced working as a waitress in a drive-in and a go-go dancer in a singles bar.

On returning to UK she undertook a postgraduate Diploma in Social Administration at LSE and professional training as a probation officer at the University of Southampton whence she emerged with her professional qualification in 1966. At the age of 23 she was appointed one of London's youngest probation officers, attached to Marlborough Street Magistrates' Court and covering the areas of Carnaby Street and Soho. Her work was mainly with prostitutes from whom she says she probably learned more than she taught! She also specialised in the transient and young drug addict population of Earls Court.

During her long vacations from this post she had her second experience of being an expat driving across the Sahara desert and in West Africa in places such as Timbuktu. After three years she moved to the NSPCC as a social work tutor. Here she taught and supervised students working with cases of physical and sexual abuse of children. In 1973 she met her future husband, Ginger Bedggood, an airline pilot, whilst she was learning to get her Private Pilot's Licence at Denham airfield in Buckinghamshire. By now she was commuting daily from Bucks to London and so in 1975 she began working as a social work teacher at High Wycombe College of Art and Technology in the county. She remained with this college for 17 years. During that time she taught countless students to be social workers and probation officers as well as herself completing an MA in Public and Social Administration at Brunel University.

She divorced her husband in 1982 and after wild oats' sowing for eight years met her current partner Grahame Bush in 1990. That same year she travelled across Russia, Mongolia and China on the Trans-Siberian Railway and saw life from the inside of a Mongolian yurt.

In 1992 Grahame and Ginnie moved to the Dominican Republic where Ginnie taught English, was a freelance journalist and tour guide, ran a B&B and eventually 'retired' to reinvent herself as an author. Her first book was published in 2007.

Unfortunately, Ginnie passed away suddenly when this book was in its final stages, in early July 2010. She is greatly missed by all who knew her personally and many more who didn't – all the readers and correspondents she advised via email and internet forums. This book is just the latest example of her enduring legacy to the Dominican Republic and foreign residents there – her down-to-earth advice, her perceptive and sympathetic understanding of the Dominican Republic and its people and the way she conveyed all this to her readers.

Ilana Benady is a Gibraltarian who studied and lived in the UK for more than fifteen years, graduating in Politics and Social Anthropology from the University of Kent at Canterbury.

Initial notions of a career in journalism led to her working for a BBC local radio community programme in Bristol and a long spell of travel and work in South, Central and North America, Europe and the Middle East. This was followed by a year spent in Gibraltar working as a radio, newspaper and magazine contributor and founding and coordinating the local Friends of the Earth group.

At some point in her mid 20s she decided that journalism wasn't for her, moved back to the UK and took up a career in international development. Her work at the Oxfam headquarters in Oxford led her to several countries in the Middle East, Latin America and the Caribbean. One such assignment was a six-week stint in the Dominican Republic and Haiti in early 1996. Ilana's instant love affair with the Dominican Republic was sealed by a relationship with one of its citizens, photographer

Pedro Guzmán, who she met during her third visit to the country, in 1998.

She settled there and married Pedro in 1999. At first, she lived in the central province of Cotui, working as a fundraising and communications advisor to *campesino* groups in Cotui and Salcedo as a *cooperante* (skills sharing volunteer) for British agency ICD (now Progressio), before moving to the capital, Santo Domingo, where they lived for nine years. Initially she went back to working for Oxfam GB, as Communications Officer for Central America and the Caribbean based in the Santo Domingo office.

After the Oxfam GB regional office moved to Mexico City and her son was born in 2000 she took a career break and did not return to full-time work until the 2004 crisis in Haiti, when she spent several months working as Oxfam GB's communications officer. Since then, she has worked as a freelance consultant for Oxfam and a number of other international organisations (including Plan International and Unicef), Dominican media in English like DR1.com and several PR agencies and private clients, providing research, communications, fundraising, translating and editing services.

Ilana and Pedro and their son Lucas now live in Punta Cana on the east coast.

Ilana is the co-author of Dominican Republic - *Culture Smart!: The Essential Guide to Customs & Culture* (also with Ginnie Bedggood) and *Aunt Clara's Dominican Cookbook and Traditional Dominican Cookery*, with Clara González.

Ilana Benady and Ginnie Bedggood

Foreword

You returned from a two-week vacation here in the Caribbean to the bleak cold of winter. You find yourself humming a merengue tune on your daily commute. The dark days of winter now bring on an increased sadness. You long for the warmth of the sunshine, the bright blue of the sea, the happy smiles of the Dominican people. Your retirement options in your home country are looking grey and depressing. You start asking yourself:

"Could I do it? Move to a tropical island? Adapt to a new culture? Have an affordable retirement offshore? Create a new life for myself? What would it take?"

Between them, the authors, Ilana Benady and Ginnie Bedggood, have lived 30 years in the Dominican Republic. They are not speculating about a country that they do not know. Nor are they trying to sell you anything.

In fact, you may read this and decide that you simply will not be able to cope because they do not sugar coat the realities of living here, in the "developing" world. They describe all the pitfalls that one is likely to encounter. If you finish this guide and say "No, not for me", you will have saved yourself thousands of dollars and months of heartache.

If, however, at the end of the book, you can say, "Yes, I can do that," then you may be one of the lucky ones who will join us here in our land of constant sunshine.

Inside this guide you will find most of what you will need to know, descriptions of various towns, lists of schools and hospital, historical facts, local customs, and pitfalls to avoid.

I wish I had had this book when I moved here seven years ago.

Elizabeth Eames Roebling
Santo Domingo, Dominican Republic
www.elizabetheames.blogspot.com

Contents

Foreword
Contents
Why?   1
  Why the Dominican Republic?   1
  General background   *1*
  Pros and cons: is this country for me?   *2*
  Culture shock   *4*
  Quality of life   *13*

Where?   17
  Geographical Areas   17
  North Coast: Puerto Plata, Sosúa and Cabarete   *17*
  North East Coast: The Samaná Peninsula   *23*
  East Coast: Punta Cana/Bávaro   *27*
  South Coast: East of Santo Domingo   *31*
  Capital: Santo Domingo   *35*
  Santiago   *40*
  Other Cities   *44*
  South West   *50*
  The Mountains: Jarabacoa and Constanza   *53*
  Constanza   *55*

What?   59
  Practical Information   59
  Cost of living   *59*
  Renting accommodation   *60*
  Food   *63*
  Utilities   *66*
  Health care   *68*

Education	78
Pre-school	82
Higher education	83
Spanish lessons	83
Some useful contacts/resources	84
Immigration and visas	94
Finance and taxes	100
Real estate	109
Safety and security	115
Politics and legal	125
Consular and Embassy assistance	134
Transport and driving	141
Driving licences	144
Telecommunications	149
Employment	153
Expat employers	159
Leisure pursuits	174
Sports and pastimes	183
Animal companions	184
Voluntary work	185
Volunteer work opportunities on the north coast	189
Getting involved in local community activities: cultural issues	192
The hazards of handouts	196
Some charities and international organisations in the DR	197
Shopping	203
Online shopping	217
Weather	221
Environmental issues	234
Wildlife	236
Forest cover	238
Plants	238
National parks	239
South west	240
Eco-Tourism	241

Who?	**245**
The Expat As…	245
The single male	*246*
The single female	*247*
The expatriate couple	*248*
Bi-national couples	*249*
Mixed couples where one is a returning Dominican	*250*
Couples with children	*250*
Single parents	*251*
Registering a child born in the DR to foreign parents	*252*
Retired people	*253*
Dying in the DR	*254*
Overseas students at DR universities	*256*
Lesbian/Gay	*257*
Disabled	*259*
Freedom seekers	*259*
How?	**261**
Cultural Context	261
History	*261*
People	*274*
Customs	*278*
Demographics	*284*
Culture	*287*
Language	*294*
What The…?	**303**
'Only in the Dominican Republic'	303
Understanding DR bureaucracy	*313*
Resources	335
Non-Fiction Books	*335*
Fiction Books	*335*
Video/DVD	*336*
Reports	*336*
Articles by Ginnie Bedggood	*337*

Why?

Why the Dominican Republic?

General background

The Dominican Republic (DR) is the second largest country in the Caribbean after Cuba. It is situated on the eastern two thirds of the island of Hispaniola in the Greater Antilles, between Puerto Rico and Cuba, and is bordered to the west by Haiti, which takes up the remaining part of the island. The Dominican Republic's many geographical contrasts include tropical forests, semi-arid regions, agricultural valleys, several mountain ranges and 1600 kilometres of coastline. The highest and lowest points in the Caribbean can be found within its borders: Pico Duarte at 3175 metres and Lago Enriquillo at 40 metres below sea level.

And that is pretty much a metaphor for living in the Dominican Republic. Chances are you will either love it or you will scratch your head wondering what on earth these crazy expats are wittering on about.

Pros and cons: is this country for me?

Non-residents of the DR have been heard to say wistfully 'It must be really great to live in the Dominican Republic'. For many, that rhetorical statement is very true, but it is not a great place to live for everyone! If you are a confirmed individualist who can think outside the box, if you don't expect anyone else to look after you, if you welcome the challenges of what some have called the 'wild west', or what Dominicans ironically call 'Wonderland', if you can cope with things like power outages and water shortages and are naturally streetwise, then the Dominican Republic is a great place to live. If you expect a good standard of paved roads, sane driving skills, City Hall to provide services, and if you want to live in an expat bubble with other like-minded expats… then choose another destination. Have we put you off yet?

Yes we have great beaches, a wonderful climate (when we're not having hurricanes or tropical storms), a local population which will humble you with their irrepressible optimism, indomitable spirit and generosity of soul, inexpensive labour costs, and, if you're smart, inexpensive property. But, if you're not cut out for life here, you will be unhappy. So do your homework carefully. There is no shame in concluding that the DR is not the place for you.

And it isn't the place for everyone. As DR residents with 30 years here between us we have seen enough expats come (and go!) to be able to hazard a fairly educated guess at the personality types that will feel at home in the DR. For the dependent, the timorous, the clock-watchers, the dedicated rulebook followers *et al.* the DR will not provide a happy fit. Those who are independent, even to the point of obstinacy (!), those who have a 'can-do' spirit, those adept at finding work-arounds when presented with seemingly intractable problems, and those who have an inbuilt ability to be laid back; those are the people who thrive and flourish here.

One absolute requirement for contented living in the DR is flexibility, being able to go with the flow, having a positive outlook on life and not reflecting on every little setback as a catastrophe. Perhaps, above all, learning the skill of tolerating uncertainty and being able to predict when the goalposts will move.

In this book the reader will find much in the way of factual information. We can tell you what the law says about taxation and real estate for example. However there can be a gulf between what the law says and how a particular official interprets it. Sometimes this gulf is a chasm. Sometimes a law is on the statute book but it has not been promulgated by the President so it is not yet in effect. Sometimes laws are both on the statute book and have been promulgated yet they are not implemented. So, although the law says 'a' what happens in practice is 'b'. Very few things are cut and dried in the Dominican Republic, except perhaps the newbie expat who, presenting as wet behind the ears, can be hung out to dry! Tolerating uncertainty in a country where political corruption flourishes takes quiet self-confidence and a certain level of skill, not to mention cash. But it is a skill that can be learned, and it is certainly one where experience breeds improvement.

However, there is a whole world in the DR quite apart from bureaucratic anarchy and mayhem. A good reason to move here is if you want to do something worthwhile. Here you can make a difference. This is a third world country with poverty, educational disadvantage and corrupt politicians. If you have money it is paradise; for the disadvantaged every day can be a struggle. So, if you want to do something other than vegetate in an expat watering hole, if you want to volunteer your services and talents, the DR is the place for you. Senior citizens need not feel their days of contributing to society are over; not only does this make you feel good, it's a great way to forget about the ageing process.

Culture shock

As stated above, for the disadvantaged every day in the DR can be a struggle. For the disadvantaged expat, those without a certain level of finance to fall back on, life will certainly be hard. However, many volunteers come to work in the DR; frequently they have limited financial resources but enormous psychological resources of enthusiasm, dedication and service. Expats such as these are able to cope with physical privations seemingly without noticing, so it is possible. Most expats, however, will require a standard of living similar to that experienced in their countries of origin and for this a certain level of finance is required as insurance against normal occurrences such as power outages and water shortages.

Part of the colourful cast of carnival characters

A certain level of income will purchase a generator or inverter to provide power or a cistern or *tinaco* to store water, but money alone cannot buttress against things that will inevitably be experienced as 'different'. Here is where the expat's sense of humour is crucial, the ability to laugh at oneself as one struggles to adjust to the vagaries of the new adopted country.

Possibly the first shock is how friendly the inhabitants of the DR are. Walk down a street and perfect strangers smile and offer greetings. They are not 'after' anything (other than in tourist areas where they might be) and you don't need to turn round to see if they are greeting the person behind you! Dominicans are courteous and hospitable and after a few years here the expat too will take the initiative in greeting perfect strangers.

Life in the DR is lived at a different decibel level than in sleepy old Vermont or sedate Twickenham. Everything is louder: the merengue music, the political campaigning, the *motoconchos* without exhaust systems, the roosters, or the neighbours' matrimonial disputes. Probably the single most useful item to bring is a box of earplugs until you learn to adjust.

Not only is life louder but it is more exuberant at every level. You will know when a Dominican is happy or sad. If you do not speak the language (Spanish) it is very easy to mistake an animated discussion for a bellicose argument. Subtlety does exist in the DR but it isn't the same as in Henley-on-Thames, and of all the expats here, it is probably the Brits who notice this the most.

Life for many Dominicans is focussed on surviving day-to-day: forward planning is thus a luxury for many. If water comes through your tap one day in fifteen then that will be the day you do the washing regardless of what other appointments you had 'planned'. There is usually a reason for behaviour that the expat finds annoying, and part of the process of becoming an expat is taking the time to discover those reasons.

There is an initial temptation to make judgements based on one's country of origin and the way things are done there, as if that was the right way of doing things and everything else was wrong. Intellectually we can see how this elicits the worst of a colonialist, imperialist attitude and we are usually quick to protest that we are not one of 'those' expats, but put us in a situation of stress and it does not take long for that attitude to surface again. The aware expat will be monitoring this for her or himself and asking their life partners to do the same.

Along with a different sense of forward planning there is also a far more laid-back attitude to time and time-keeping in the DR than in most developed countries. Whoever told you *mañana* means tomorrow? It might, or it might not mean the day after tomorrow, sometime next week or never. Dominicans, along with many other inhabitants of tropical countries, do not understand the punctuality obsession displayed by most foreigners; in their view it almost equates to a neurosis. Foreigners, on the other hand, start out believing that 11am means 11am. It doesn't take long to broaden one's understanding to 'anytime before 3pm'. Likewise *ahora* or *ahorita* do not mean 'now' but 'soon', or 'some time later'. It is said that *ahorita* is like *mañana*, but without the same sense of urgency!

It is never a good idea for the new expat to make a big song and dance about such issues. It will not change the outcome. All it will do is invite a list of increasingly improbable 'explanations'- good for a laugh perhaps, but at times like these your sense of humour will not be at its most accessible level.

Alongside the attitude to time is a similarly relaxed attitude to 'taking one's turn'. Queueing is recognised in institutions such as banks, and many supermarkets have a numbered ticket system for the delicatessen counter, but life is far more informal in the smaller corner stores known as *colmados*. This can mean that the shopkeeper responds to the most recent interruption while other customers who had arrived earlier are left hanging. Although tempting to make a song and dance about this, too, it is far more effective to recapture the shopkeeper's attention by making yourself the 'most recent interruption'.

It is said that travel broadens the mind. Living in the Dominican Republic certainly widens the eyeballs! There are some sights that will strike the new expat as… different: how many people can be crammed into a public bus or taxi, or onto a *motoconcho* the ubiquitous motorcycle taxi peculiar to the DR; the 'roller-blade snake-dance' (a scooter or motorbike with a string of roller-skaters or skate-boarders attached behind); 'any spark you can make I can make better' (a *motoconcho* passenger trailing a handful of steel bars along the street several yards behind the *concho*); a pair of scooters driving side by side, the driver of one with a foot on the other; in wet weather in flooded areas, a scooter with a scrunched up driver (the driver's feet resting on the handlebars to avoid getting wet!); in a busy shopping area a driver suddenly seeing an old friend driving in the opposite direction and stopping in the middle of the road for a chat and when the inevitable traffic-jam gets well developed, a cacophony of honking from cars fifteen back even though it is perfectly obvious that the car in front has nowhere to go.

As the reader will have gathered by now, driving in the DR takes a while to adjust to! But it can be pretty: witness the sheaves of leaves and twigs tastefully arranged to stick up from a hole in the road (just where you were about to drive). This is not a municipal beautification campaign: it is to warn you that someone has stolen the manhole cover.

There are other scenarios, which can extend the new expat's adjustment skills. For example, being given candy or chewing gum in lieu of small coin change in a supermarket or *colmado*. Sometimes this is because there really is a shortage of small coin change; sometimes the store will keep the small change for Dominican customers and give the sweeties to the tourists. Think of it as delayed revenge for the beads and mirrors that foreign invaders swapped for the DR's gold five hundred years ago! The expat can decide for himself whether to make an issue out of this. Sometimes a look is enough.

Dominicans take pride in their appearance and hygiene, and it is common to see local men with well-groomed hands, clear varnished nails, and plucked eyebrows. Businesses that provide these services might include as standard some which the new expat is not expecting: the male expat at a barber's shop should not be surprised that ear hair is razored away nor that eyebrows are tidied up. Men and women having a shampoo, cut and blow dry might want to check for the ferocity of the hairdryer. Sometimes they might be required to act as the stylist's electrical assistant by holding the two wires from the dryer into the wall socket...

When travelling on public transport in the DR one's nostrils are not assailed with the sort of odours that can be experienced in certain other parts of the world. Dominicans, no matter how poor, use deodorant. If that familiar perspiration smell wafts over you in a shop or on the beach it is far more likely to come from a *gringo*.

If the above information has not put you off from pursuing your dream of living in the DR, rest assured that adjusting to living here is a process – and one that every new expat goes through. One way of understanding this process is to describe the offshore resident as moving through stages from unconscious incompetence, to conscious incompetence, to conscious competence, and finally unconscious competence. (See *Culture Shock Revisited - Groping Towards A More Useful Conceptual Framework - by Ginnie Bedggood March 19, 2007 OffshoreWave.com*).

At the stage of 'unconscious incompetence' you don't know what it is that you don't know. This would explain the early euphoria or honeymoon phase before the reality of one's new lifestyle strikes home. This stage may be drastically curtailed or even removed by careful preparation, research and the acquisition of realistic information before the move is made. Vasco da Gama, for example, had no *Expat FAQs: Moving To and Living In The DR* to consult! Not that he was actually coming here…

So potential offshore dwellers should read, ask, read some more, ask some more and visit their intended new home several times before making the move. That reading should include books about the history and culture of the DR. These will be far more enlightening than all the internet real estate websites! Having said that, some people will be able to adjust and adapt no matter how little preparation they do. For the potential expat there are plenty of existing expats living in the DR who can be consulted (some better than others); the days of the pioneer have long since gone.

At the 'conscious incompetence' stage the new offshore resident becomes aware of how much they do not know and how much there is to learn about the new environment. This can be a fairly debilitating phase because of the feeling of being permanently wet behind the ears, and it is how one handles this phase which shapes the future development, well being and happiness of the expat. But this phase can also be life changing. This is the phase for focusing on the positives, not concentrating on the negatives, whether that is enhancing one's sense of humour (sometimes of the gallows variety), drawing strength from one's relationships, or really concentrating on the new opportunities which the different lifestyle provides.

Motivation is an important factor here: very few volunteer workers, whether missionaries, Peace Corps, Habitat for Humanity or those not attached to any NGO (Non-Governmental Organisations working with poor people or the environment in the DR) seem to focus on feeling 'wet behind the ears'. They are doubtless aware that there is much to learn, but they do not focus on themselves so much as the people they have come to help. So expats going through the 'conscious incompetence' stage could well be advised to spend less time berating themselves and more time helping the less fortunate.

The third phase, that of 'conscious competence', is when expats can work out the solution to most issues confronting them if they sit and think about it long enough. This is the phase of having knowledge of one's surroundings at the intellectual level but not at the heart level. At this stage people know the 'what', they do not, however feel the 'how' instinctively. Frequently at this phase we notice that the offshore resident is tempted to set up relocation services for other new expats (one of ourselves included). Maybe something to do with the pecking order in the barnyard? Or maybe something to do with shoring up an ego which has taken a bit of a bashing in the preceding stage, by surrounding oneself with people who think you are an expert and know less than you do? Either way, many expats remain at this stage for the rest of their offshore life, because although they are knowledgeable about their new country they do not feel it, they merely know it.

The fourth stage of the process, 'unconscious competence', you really won't know you have arrived at until quite some time after you have got there. This is where an understanding of the 'new' culture becomes instinctive; you can, for example, predict reactions to given situations with the same degree of accuracy as you would have had in your country of origin. You don't have to 'think about it' anymore, you just do it naturally. For that reason you will not be aware you are doing it unless you stop to think about it. This does not mean you have nothing left to learn about the new culture; there is always masses left to learn. But because you instinctively know how to handle a situation, the 'what' or factual data or knowledge becomes less important because you know how to get it; or rather you feel how to get it. So knowing how much you don't know stops being debilitating; it is no more debilitating than it would be in your country of origin where you knew the ropes.

Stay long enough in the DR, and all those quirky, seemingly off-the-wall occurrences outlined above will become second nature. You will actually grow very fond of some of them and miss them enormously if you visit that strange country from where you moved to live here!

Quality of life

Once you have learned to live with some of the quirks and the unpredictable bureaucracy of the Dominican Republic there are quality of life issues that are of profound importance. For those coming from countries that have 'rule and regulation constipation' perhaps the most noticeable difference is the amount of freedom here. You can design your house the way you want it, it does not have to be painted a certain colour, nor does the garden have to measure a certain depth. You can run a business from home, no need to commute. You can enjoy consistent temperatures within a low differential range year round. You can buy fruit and vegetables, which do not have to comply with European directives over, for example, the size and shape of a banana. Your neighbours will not complain if you throw the occasional exuberant party although they might think it strange if they were not invited!

In the Dominican Republic there seems to be a level of tolerance that is perhaps missing from some of the more developed parts of the world. Sometimes that means that the less good is tolerated along with the good (variable driving practices, for example). Likewise, you will hear repeated use of car and scooter horns, but it is frequently not intended as an instruction to 'get out of my way' so much as an indication that 'I am here and I have seen you', or even a helpful reminder, in case you may have failed to notice, that the light has changed to green: a cause for celebration, not an aggressive act. Overall the more laid back attitude redolent of Caribbean nations manifests itself not just in the tolerance of fellow human beings, but also in a genuine interest in them.

Dominican coffee is usually taken black, strong and very sweet

Of course the foreigner, coming from a 'little boxes' society can interpret this interest as nosiness. It is certainly true that there are no secrets in Puerto Plata for example. Dominicans are by nature hospitable and generous people and they will generously share any secret with which you have entrusted them! Most things will get from one end of the street to the other in a matter of hours. But the other side of the coin is that Dominicans have *time* for you. The simple pleasure of a conversation, an art lost in the hurly burly of the more developed world, is alive and well in the DR.

Most expats employ some type of domestic assistance such as a maid, gardener, nanny or handyman, and salary rates make such assistance very affordable. Thus the majority of expats will find themselves doing fewer of the heavy domestic tasks and will have more time for what they want to do. This sort of luxury was probably not available to them in their countries of origin. The open-minded expat will also use the opportunity to learn more about how 'it' is done in the DR from their domestic staff – anything from where to get the freshest vegetables, to how to make a medicinal tea, to whether a price quoted is in the realms of reality or insanity!

Domestic staff might also be the expats' first consistent experience of the subtleties of body language in the DR. If you don't understand the gesture, ASK! Everything from eyebrow movements to shoulder movements or hand gestures means something. The measurement of *'un chin'* (a little bit) with finger and thumb is different to the measurement of *'un chin-chin'*, or a tiny little bit.

What most expats can offer their domestic staff in return is modelling in, for example, assertion – such as not believing everything they are told by a doctor or other 'expert' if it doesn't pass the common sense test. There is a tendency in the DR, partly as a result of the poor public education system, to swallow whole the opinions of 'experts' without question or challenge. Those of us who have had the advantage of a good education tend to know when something should at least be questioned.

There will also be those beliefs, which no amount of reasoning will alter: some based on old wives' tales. If you come home from jogging, for example, and go straight to the refrigerator for cold water your maid will most likely have conniptions. It is not done here to open the fridge and expose yourself to cold air when you are hot. If you put the air conditioning on she'll probably start praying for your wellbeing! Likewise you will need to tolerate your every ache or pain being interpreted as 'gripe' (a cold) and treatable by using Vicks Vapour Rub!

For some expats much of the interaction will be lost in the early days due to language issues (see separate section: Language). Like everything else about the new lifestyle, stick with it and understanding will dawn. You will probably end up even knowing what all the acronyms used in the DR mean.

As indicated earlier, the frustrations of living in the Dominican Republic are not for everyone, but the joys more than compensate. So let us start by telling you about the different geographical areas and what they have to offer.

Where?

Geographical Areas

North Coast: Puerto Plata, Sosúa and Cabarete

The north coast of the Dominican Republic is probably home to the longest established expat communities in the whole country. Having said that, it should be remembered that all of these are much smaller than expat communities in places such as San Miguel de Allende in Mexico, Boquete, Bocas de Toro or Panama City in Panama.

Christopher Columbus was probably Puerto Plata's very first 'cruise tourist' and although there is disagreement among historians as to exactly when it was founded, the general consensus is that in 1496, Columbus's brother Bartholomew officially founded the city naming it San Felipe de Puerto Plata. The natural harbour aided the development of shipping and trade but as other locations in the New World were discovered and assumed greater importance, Puerto Plata port became the hub of the substitute commercial activity, smuggling. This was also a 'tourist' enhanced activity; Sir John Hawkins the chief architect of the British Elizabethan navy brought a cargo of slaves from Sierra Leone in 1563 and traded them with the Spanish of Puerto Plata for pearls, hides, sugar and gold. The French and the Dutch also became involved in the buccaneering business until word of all this reached the Spanish Crown and Ferdinand III ordered the city to be destroyed in 1605.

One hundred years later the city was repopulated and rebuilt mostly by immigrants from the Canaries who came from farming stock. In the nineteenth century as a maritime centre Puerto Plata enjoyed prosperity as evidenced in the building of large Victorian style homes. Many of these are still in existence albeit not in very good condition; community groups persist in pressurising the Dominican Government to restore these buildings so that history is not lost forever.

European immigrants were of similar significance in the development of Sosúa whose first expats were some 600 Jewish refugees fleeing Nazi Germany during the Second World War – they set up a dairy community and inter-married with the local population so that their descendants are for the greater part considered to be locals.

In the 1970s and 1980s tourism took off in Sosúa and many of what were the then tourists returned as residents resulting in large expat communities of Americans, Germans and later Canadians and British nationals. As a result residential communities were built to accommodate the influx and in the last few years Sosúa has been expanding towards Cabarete, which is primarily known for having excellent conditions for the sports of windsurfing and kite boarding. Recently Cabarete has seen an explosion in construction, both condominiums and villas, as expats attracted by sea and sun make it their home. Indeed the construction boom is now spreading further down the coast to Rio San Juan, Gaspar Hernandez and Cabrera.

The upside of all this is that it is not difficult to find other expats living on the north coast of the Dominican Republic. The downside is that heavy concentrations of foreigners in one location can alter those locations in ways that are not always pre-planned, thought through, or for the best. The increasing numbers of expats will, of course, ensure that the goods and services they seek are made available, sometimes by expats themselves. This can improve life for the local population as well and provide jobs for locals, but if that employment is purely in a service capacity such as maids, gardeners, and construction labourers, the question is raised of tourism leading on to expatriate relocation being as much a form of exploitation as any other activity which relies on cheap labour.

For some potential expats the towns of Sosúa and Cabarete may already appear to have reached saturation point as far as the relative percentages of expats to Dominicans are concerned. Puerto Plata town itself is not in that category since the vast majority of its inhabitants are locals and most of the expats live in communities just outside Puerto Plata, like Costambar and Cofresi. Those thinking of moving to the north coast should investigate areas away from the coast and/or which have not yet been affected by the concentration of foreigners, leading to increases in property prices.

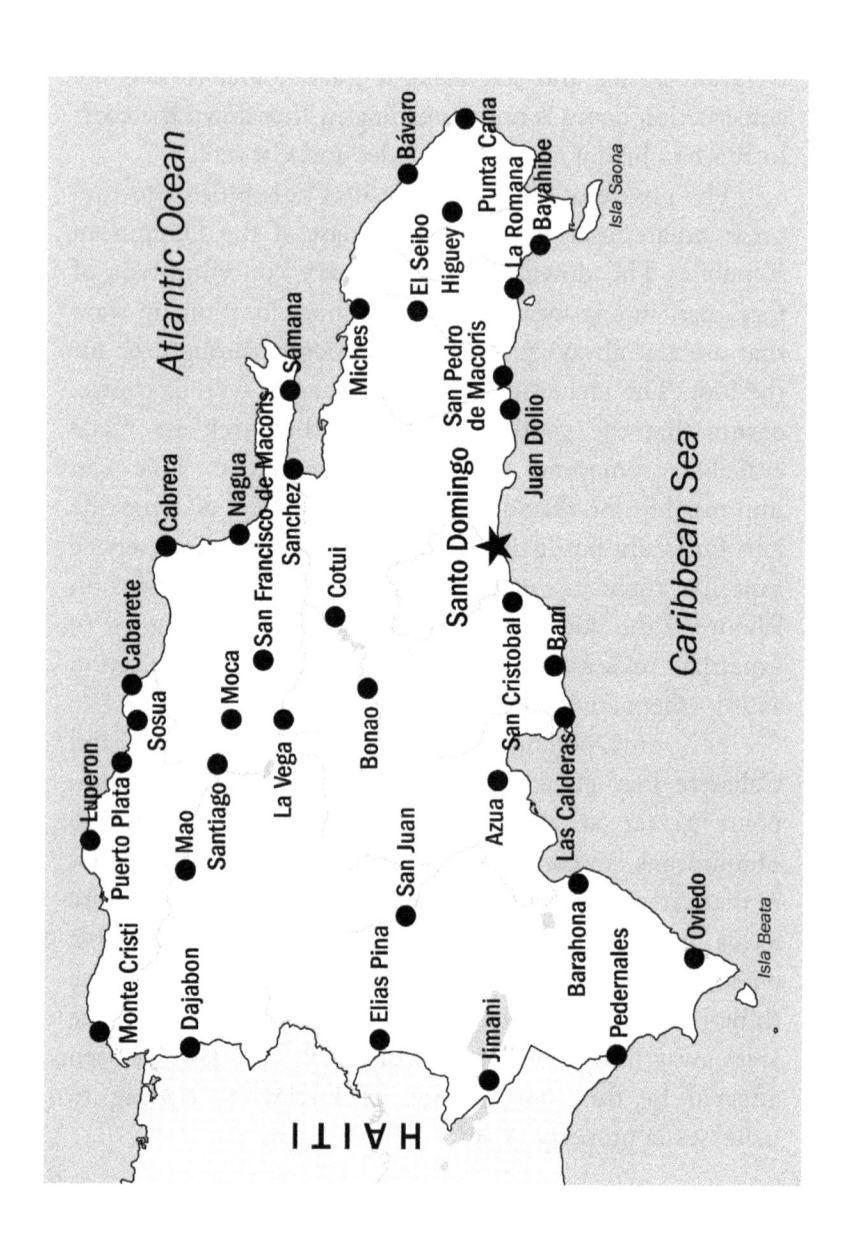

WHERE?

To the west, for example, Luperon has a small expat community that grew from the sailing fraternity visiting Luperon harbour; to the east Cabrera is a small town, which does not rely on tourism for its income. Cabrera's main source of income is cattle, meat, and milk alongside agriculture such as rice farming and coconuts. However, due in part to the work of a former Mayor of Cabrera, Jorge Cavoli, foreign investment has recently been attracted to the area, which is described as the 'Dominican Hamptons' due to the number of luxury style villas that have been built. Gaspar Hernandez has not developed in the same way but retains much of the charm of a north coast town prior to the arrival of tourism. Playa Grande is probably best known for its world famous golf course and stunning beaches. Those looking to live a quiet existence in property which is not overpriced (at present!) would also be advised to venture a little off the beaten track to Playa Caleton.

Punta Rucia beach on the northwest coast

Shopping

Even the smallest hamlet in the DR will have a corner store or *colmado* where residents can do their grocery shopping. These are open from very early to very late and in many areas double up as entertainment centres, snack bars, bars, social centres, gossip-hubs and at election times, campaigning events. Each tourist centre will have a number of supermarkets or minimarkets such as Playero, Super Super in Sosúa, and Janet's in Cabarete. Colmados are much more fun and great places to get to know your Dominican neighbours but will not, generally speaking, be places where English is spoken. In Puerto Plata most locals and expats shop at either Tropical Supermarket, the newly opened Multicentro La Sirena or Supermercado Jose Luis; in fact many Sosúa and Cabarete residents venture to Puerto Plata for shopping since prices tend to be lower.

There is one hypermarket on the north coast, Multicentro La Sirena on the *Malecón* (seafront promenade) in Puerto Plata, although many residents still visit the shopping malls of Santiago for a collection of stores such as Nacional, Price Smart, Ochoa or Haché. Shopping for furniture, household items, electronics and even vehicles tends to be more competitive in Santiago.

Schools

For expats with school aged children there are a number of schools on the north coast where teaching is in English, bilingual or even trilingual. In Sosúa, Garden Kids and the International School of Sosúa, in Puerto Plata Alic New

World School, O&M Hostos, Achievers International and a Montessori school for pre-school aged children, in Rio San Juan the French language L'École Française de la Costa Verde, and the International Academy in Cabrera.

HEALTH CARE

Likewise there are private health facilities like Servi-Med in Cabarete, Centro Medico Bournigal in Puerto Plata and the very new Centro Medico Cabarete just outside Sosúa. Most expats would expect to travel to Santiago or Santo Domingo's medical facilities for more specialised treatment.

The tourism focus of much of the north coast ensures plenty of leisure pursuits are available for expat residents – golf, horseback riding and water sports are among the most popular. Likewise there are many bars, restaurants and discos and other nocturnal pursuits of a less salubrious nature!

North East Coast: The Samaná Peninsula

Wealthy Dominicans have had holiday homes on the beaches of Samaná for many years now, in areas like Portillo, and a significant expatriate population, mainly French, but also German, Italian, Canadian and others has taken root in the last two or three decades, predominantly in the seaside resort towns of Las Terrenas and the quieter Las Galeras.

The Samaná peninsula, an area of truly outstanding natural beauty on the far north-eastern corner of the Dominican Republic, remained a relatively well-kept secret until fairly recently. The virgin, white sand, palm fringed beaches – especially Playa Rincón, ranked by Conde Nast Traveller as one of the Top Ten beaches in the Caribbean (or in the world, depending on who you choose to believe) – are arguably the most beautiful in the DR, and the landscape is dominated by hills of coconut palms and small traditional villages with bijou pastel coloured wooden houses. Samaná is perhaps most famous for its whale-watching season (roughly mid-February to the end of March) when humpback whales migrate from the north Atlantic to mate in the waters of the Bay of Samaná.

The provincial capital, Santa Bárbara de Samaná (founded in 1756 and initially settled by immigrants from the Canary Islands) overlooks the bay, formerly named *Bahía de las Flechas* – the Bay of Arrows – after the hail of arrows that met the Spaniards in 1493 during Christopher Columbus's second voyage, when they sailed into the bay and encountered the local indigenous *Taíno*s, who were clearly not too impressed by those first would-be expatriates. Over the next few centuries the area remained more or less a backwater, although for many years the town of Sánchez in the south west of the peninsula was an important port, linked by rail to the heart of the country's main agricultural production centre, La Vega in the fertile Cibao Valley. Today the port is a shadow of its former self, the railway no longer exists, and the town's long-lost glory is only hinted at in few remaining 'Victorian' wooden houses. Today, Sánchez is mainly known for its small-scale fishing industries and its delicious shrimps.

The present-day population of the peninsula is partly made up of the descendants of freed American slaves who settled on the peninsula in the 19th century. Although only a few still speak English, their origins are revealed in the predominance of English-sounding surnames (Kelly, Robinson, and so on.) and Protestant churches like 'La Churcha' in Samaná city. At one stage the peninsula was almost sold to the US during the nineteenth century, but the plan was abandoned.

The Dominican government started developing tourism in the area in the 1970s and 1980s with projects like the Hotel Gran Cayacoa (now a fully revamped Bahia Principe property) and the 'bridge to nowhere' linking the islets in the Bay. Then President Joaquín Balaguer made the spectacular blunder of razing Samaná city's charming wooden houses and replacing them with modernist concrete blocks. More recently the *Malecón* area has been refurbished and replicas of the old wooden houses built as part of a new shopping centre aimed at tourists. On the whole, though, up until the last few years, tourism on the peninsula was mainly small-scale and expat-owned and run, but large hotel companies like Gran Bahia Principe are changing that, combined with the improvement in road links with the capital (cutting down driving time from four to two hours) and the opening of the international airport at El Catey.

Even with this change of pace that threatens its small-scale character, the Samaná peninsula is still an attractive option for expats in search of idyllic surroundings, and who don't mind the relatively remote location.

Shopping

Shopping facilities are limited, but on the bright side, you can get some good French baguettes, patisserie and cuisine, as well as the delicious local fare, invariably dominated by the ubiquitous coconut.

Schools

There are bilingual schools in Samaná city and Las Terrenas, but the main health facilities are farther afield in Nagua or San Francisco de Macorís. The nearest large supermarket is La Sirena in San Francisco, a two-hour drive.

Las Terrenas

The main schools catering for expat children in Las Terrenas are the Ecole Francaise Théodore Chasseriau (named after the French 19th century Romantic painter who was born in nearby El Limón), Colegio Alianza and Colegio Nuevo Despertar.

Samaná City

Colegio Arcoiris is a bilingual pre-school and primary school in the city.

Las Galeras

There is a small French-run private primary school in Las Galeras.

HEALTH CARE

Health facilities are relatively limited. In Las Galeras, the *Guariquen* project runs a community health clinic, and there is one private doctor, Dr Khira Hiche in Plaza Lusitania. Dr Rodriguez and the Cuban Clinic are two options recommended by expats living in Las Terrenas. There is a small public hospital in Samaná city, as well as several small private clinics, but the nearest large-scale medical facilities are in the cities of Nagua, San Francisco and beyond.

Property is going up in value as a result of the improved road and air links, meaning that the Samaná area is more accessible to both domestic and international tourists.

A very important consideration for potential residents is that Samaná is one of the few areas in the Dominican Republic, along with the east coast, that has it own private electricity company, Compania de Luz y Fuerza de Las Terrenas. Power is expensive, but in contrast with the rest of the country the supply is more or less constant, so you save yourself the expense of running back-up generators and inverters.

East Coast: Punta Cana/Bávaro

Punta Cana/Bávaro with its palm-fringed coastline is a sensational Dominican success story. Up until the late 1960s or early 1970s the area was all but cut off from the rest of the country. While residents from nearby cities like Higuey used to take a bumpy ride to enjoy the beaches there on weekends, this spectacular stretch of white sand was mainly deserted until a group of investors happened to fly over, spotting its potential as a world class tourist destination. These first developers built what is now Punta Cana International Airport to make it accessible to tourism.

Today road connections with the rest of the country are much better. Punta Cana International (PUJ) has grown from a rough airstrip to the busiest airport in the country in terms of passenger numbers. The forty kilometre coastal strip from Uvero Alto in the north to Cap Cana in the south is now a thriving tourism area with dozens of hotels.

For a couple of decades that's all there was in Punta Cana/Bávaro – large, all-inclusive resort hotels hosting tourists from the US, Canada and Europe – but in recent years the area has started to develop a life of its own with many young professionals, businesspeople, expatriates and retirees choosing the area as their home. New nationalities are entering the tourist and expatriate demographic, most notably Russians.

Sugar cane cultivation is still labour intensive and lo-tech

Residential options in the Punta Cana/Bávaro area range from high-end luxury mansions to middle-market condominium complexes. Cap Cana is perhaps the ultimate expression of exclusive, privileged living, along with the pioneering Punta Cana. Big names are associated with these areas: Donald Trump is linked with Cap Cana, and Mikhail Baryshnikov, Oscar de la Renta and Julio Iglesias have homes in Punta Cana.

There was a strong sense of a boomtown in the area, although there is no 'town' as such and the 2008 financial crisis slowed the pace down somewhat. The area consists of commercial, residential and tourism developments along a section of the coast, some better planned and controlled than others, with nothing that could be described as an urban centre. As well as expats and professionals flocking to the east, the workforce that services this population is also largely made up of migrants. There was only a tiny rural population before the area started to develop, so most of the labour force needed to service this growing, dynamic economy has had to be brought in. Dominican and Haitian workers have populated areas like the town of Verón and El Hoyo de Friusa.

SHOPPING

There is glitzy shopping and nightlife in the Palma Real Mall, San Juan Shopping Center, Galerias Puntacana and many smaller malls and shopping centres. The area has several outstanding golf courses to suit most pockets and abilities, and, of course, some of the best beaches the country can offer - the reason the area was developed in the first place.

SCHOOLS

Two excellent international schools – Puntacana International and Heritage Cap Cana cater for children of expats and Dominicans in the area, as well as several other smaller options in the Bávaro area, including Colegio Calasanz.

HEALTH CARE

There are top-class health facilities – Hospiten Bávaro (in Verón) and Centro Medico Punta Cana between Cortecito and Friusa.

The downside for some is the distance from the country's main urban centres and all that these have to offer. The capital is an arduous three to four-hour drive away, and the highway that will bypass the cities of Higuey and La Romana sometime in the future is still under construction. As remote areas go, though, Punta Cana/Bávaro is rapidly catching up on most counts, in response to the needs of the growing residential population.

Another limitation is that much of the coastal strip has been effectively 'privatised' even though in theory all beaches in the Dominican Republic must have public access, so the best beaches 'belong' to seafront hotels and resorts. Some – but not all – residential complexes have access to these beaches. There are, however, several exceptions: beaches that are fully accessible to the public include Bibijagua, Cabeza de Toro, Cortecito and Macao.

A very important consideration for potential residents is that in contrast to the rest of the country, the Punta Cana/Bávaro area has it own private electricity company. Power is expensive but almost 100% constant, so you save yourself the expense of running back-up generators and inverters.

South Coast: East of Santo Domingo

In the Dominican Republic, the south coast east of the capital is officially and commonly called 'the east' as in *La Sultana del Este* (the nickname for the city of San Pedro de Macorís) and La Romana's baseball team *Los Azucareros del Este*.

The main tourist centres in this part of the country are Boca Chica, Juan Dolio, La Romana and Bayahibe, and the main cities are San Pedro de Macorís and La Romana on the coast, and inland cities Hato Mayor, El Seibo and Higuey.

The landscape ranges from semi-arid plains near the coast to scenic rolling hills inland, with large expanses of sugar cane fields and cattle ranches and the mountains of Los Haitises, a national park, visible on the horizon.

Bateyes, or cane-cutter settlements, received their name from the indigenous *Taíno* name for a central square surrounded by dwellings, and are where the poorest and most socially excluded residents of the Dominican Republic live. Mainly Haitians or Dominicans of Haitian origin, cane-cutters are paid very low wages; when they are paid at all. State sugar company workers generally endure poorer working and living conditions than private sugar company workers.

The east is also famous for producing world-class baseball players, and many a poor boy from the *bateyes* around San Pedro (like Sammy Sosa) has gone on to fame and fortune in the US Major Leagues. As a result many US baseball teams have training academies in the area.

Boca Chica has a beach, several good restaurants and is close (twenty-minute drive) to the capital, and that, dear readers, just about sums up its advantages. On the downside (depending on your perspective) it has a thriving sex-tourism scene and all the crime and problems that accompany this. It is an option for expatriates who need to be near the capital yet want to live on the beach, but proceed with caution: Boca Chica is really not for the faint-hearted. Before its decline, it was one of the DR's first tourist areas, where wealthy families from the capital had holiday homes. There are still several good restaurants (Neptuno, Pelicano and Boca Marina) with private beach access, making for a pleasant day trip from the capital. There are several large hotels in Boca Chica, the most famous being the Hamaca, built in the resort's belle époque the 1950s by then dictator Rafael Trujillo. In a further brush with infamy it was the place where Trujillo granted asylum to the Cuban dictator in exile, Fulgencio Batista, when he fled his country after the 1959 revolution.

Juan Dolio is being touted as the next big thing. For many years a small beach town with holiday homes, including that of the President, popular with day-trippers from the capital (a forty-minute drive), and nearby San Pedro de Macorís, as well as home to several all-inclusive resorts, it is now the scene of large-scale luxury residential developments. Its beach was recently given a new lease of life with many tons of white sand. Juan Dolio's proximity to San Pedro de Macorís (of baseball fame) puts it within the reach of good supermarkets, health facilities and a university (UCE). Juan Dolio itself has an international school (Villas del Mar) but San Pedro is near enough for other options, and is close to several good golf courses like Guavaberry and Metro Country Club.

Bayahibe: a resort town that conserves its fishing village charm

La Romana is a bustling provincial capital, home to the Casa de Campo tourism and luxury residential complex and Teeth of the Dog golf course, originally developed to provide Gulf and Western employees with an incentive to live in this booming sugar town. La Romana is good for shopping, health facilities, a yacht marina and occasional big name cultural events at the amphitheatre in the artists' village of Altos de Chavón, and one of the country's top bi-lingual schools – Abraham Lincoln. The city is strongly influenced by its history as a company town – it grew around the sugar industry since its foundation in the early twentieth century. Many of La Romana's institutions, such as the school, were developed by Gulf and Western that eventually sold its shares to the Central Romana Company in the 1980s.

Like most of the Dominican Republic, these areas are prone to blackouts, so anyone considering a move needs to be prepared to use a back-up power inverter or a generator.

Bayahibe is a short drive from La Romana and its international airport. It is mainly a resort town that nonetheless retains some of its former fishing village charm, and has a prominent Italian expatriate presence. Its proximity to La Romana (approximately twenty-minute drive) with its cultural, educational and retail facilities means that Bayahibe is another option for expatriates, with its many new residential developments. A branch of New Horizons School is due to open in La Estancia, a new residential development between Bayahibe and La Romana, for the 2011-2012 school year.

As well as attractive beaches (which have received European Union Blue Flag certification thanks to the efforts of an active local hoteliers association), Bayahibe is on the edge of the National Park of the East that includes the so far unspoilt island Isla Saona. The Romana-Bayahibe Hoteliers' Association has pioneered nature conservation initiatives and has created eco-trails highlighting the area's natural treasures, such as the endemic *Rosa de Bayahibe* (*Pereskia quisqueyana*) flowering cactus. The area is also popular with scuba divers and snorkelers.

Compared to its neighbours along the coast to the west, Bayahibe has the added advantage of being one of the few parts in the country, along with Punta Cana-Bávaro and the Samaná peninsula, with its own private electricity company. Power is more expensive than in the rest of the country, but supplies are almost completely constant, eliminating the expense of running back-up generators and inverters.

Capital: Santo Domingo

Santo Domingo is a brash, modern city with a swaggering seafront avenue known as the *Malecón* that stretches for a good 15 kilometres (Sans Souci to Manresa); it is a city which President Leonel Fernández has famously pledged to transform into a 'Mini New York' with a tropical flavour. It is still a long way from pulling that off, but if you don't look beyond the broad avenues, expensive vehicles, shiny high-rises and the impressive system of underpasses and overpasses in the modern city centre, you would get the impression you were in a first world metropolis. Scratch beyond the bling though, and the third world is never far away: urban decay, poverty, and chaos, are all part of this energetic, fascinating and vibrant mix.

The city's feel is more American than European, apart from in the Colonial Zone: this is the spot where the continent's first European city, grandly named Santo Domingo de Guzmán, was founded by Spanish explorers in the fifteenth century and many of the old buildings and their ruins remain.

Until the mid-twentieth century, Santo Domingo was still a very small city. Following the devastating San Xenon hurricane in 1930, the then dictator, Rafael Trujillo, went about modernising the capital, expanding it beyond the old limits of the Colonial Zone and Ciudad Nueva. Many of his megalomaniac legacies survive, from the name 'Ciudad Trujillo' (as the city was renamed in the dictator's honour) on the old manhole covers, to the Mussolini-esque neo-classical public buildings in La Feria and the Telecommunications Palace in the Colonial Zone. Well into the 1960s places like La Feria and the El Embajador hotel were outside the main urban area.

Whether or not they choose Santo Domingo as their home, every expatriate in the country will have to visit the city occasionally for bureaucratic, cultural, health or shopping purposes, and it's certainly not everyone's cup of tea. If you're in the Dominican Republic to escape the rat race, you will not be wooed by a city notable for traffic congestion, poor planning and security issues. However, as Latin American mega-cities go, it has its good points. The Colonial Zone is charming and oozes history, and there are several pleasant suburbs offering safe residential options.

Shopping, culture, recreation, health and education facilities are far more complete, varied, and accessible, than most other parts of the country.

The controversial Metro project set to transform Santo Domingo

The city has a large expatriate population, including some retirees, but foreigners tend to be mostly in the younger bracket and in employment, whether in embassies, international organisations, bi-lingual schools or private companies, or as independent entrepreneurs. The call-centre sector has grown in recent years, attracting English speaking Dominicans at floor level, and expats at managerial level.

The sheer size of the city means that expatriates are not a particularly visible presence, although there are some areas or venues where you are more likely to spot this species: jogging or cycling on Avenida de la Salud in Parque Mirador Sur, in the supermarket at Bella Vista Mall, on Plaza España at night, and at certain cultural and sports events.

The better residential neighbourhoods are on the western side of the Ozama river, starting with the Colonial Zone which is undergoing serious gentrification. The days are over when a colonial ruin or a rundown art-deco apartment could be bought for a song and remodelled. Gazcue, Zona Universitaria, La Esperilla, La Julia, Evaristo Morales, Naco, Piantini, Serralles, Julieta, Urbanización Fernandez, Paraíso, Mirador Norte, Mirador Sur, Bella Vista, Los Cacicazgos and Arroyo Hondo are all good places to live.

All these neighbourhoods have better and worse areas so always check the exact location, especially for noise levels. The Oriental Zone on the east side of the river has some suitable areas, and property prices there are much lower. As well as the quality of the neighbourhood and location within, a resident's typical routine needs to be taken into account when choosing where to live, work and send the kids to school, if applicable.

The capital is not a pedestrian-friendly city, with the exceptions perhaps of the Colonial Zone, Ciudad Nueva or Gazcue where a reasonable amount can be done on foot. Public transport consists of *conchos* or *carros públicos* – ramshackle shared taxis that travel set routes, or buses known as *guaguas* or *OMSA*s. Private cabs are reasonable and rapid, giving the luxury of a chauffeur without the stress. Flat rate fares means there is no stress when stuck in traffic. The first Metro underground train line was launched in early 2009 in an attempt to ease traffic problems, but the full-scale Metro network serving the rest of the city will take a good few more years to complete.

Driving may seem daunting at first but is not so bad once attempted... drivers just need to remember to be on the defensive, and expect absolutely anything.

Culture and entertainment are definitely the high point of life in the capital: Teatro Nacional, Plaza de la Cultura, Casa de Teatro, Monumento al Son, nightclubs and discos, art galleries, cinemas, public art on Parque Independencia, the Helen Kellogg Library for books in English, and so on.

SHOPPING

For shopping you have Price Smart, Carrefour, Nacional, Bravo, Pola and Cadena Supermarket chains, Malls like Plaza Central, Bella Vista, Diamond Mall, Blue Mall and Acropolis, Department Stores like Ferreteria Americana and Plaza Lama, and the recently opened IKEA. There are also specialist food stores like Omaha Steaks and Omaha Gourmet, Orgánica, and L'epicier de l'orient. Local grocery stores (*colmados*), pharmacies and many other businesses deliver your purchases home for no extra charge, although it is customary to tip the deliveryman.

SCHOOLS

The best international-type schools popular with expatriates include Carol Morgan, New Horizons, St George and the Community for Learning, but there are about a dozen others worth considering for location, price and educational methodology.

HEALTH CARE

Good health centres include Plaza de la Salud/Cedimat, Abel González, Abreu, Corazones Unidos and many others.

Santiago

Santiago de los Caballeros received its grand old name from the thirty Spanish noblemen who founded it in 1495 during the first wave of European colonisation. The original colony was in Jacagua, but after it was destroyed by an earthquake it was rebuilt in 1506. It was devastated by another earthquake in 1562 and was again rebuilt, this time on the Yaque del Norte river. Throughout the seventeenth, eighteenth and nineteenth centuries, Santiago suffered earthquakes, destruction through fire, a hurricane, invasion by first Haitian troops, and then Spaniards. In fact this second metropolis of the Dominican Republic took whatever was thrown at it and still thrived. Even as late as 2007 parts of Santiago were flooded when the Tavera Dam was opened following tropical storm Olga.

The Santiago monument was built by Trujillo as a monument to himself

Santiago de los Caballeros in the fertile Cibao Valley has at times throughout history been the capital of the country, and was an important strategic city in the Dominican War of Independence in 1844. Santiago is not a tourist town in the sense that it does not derive its income from tourism although it does have a number of attractions that draw visitors, including the ruins of the original colony. *Santiagueros* have the reputation of being more affluent and industrious than *capitaleños*. Known as *La Cuidad Corazón* (the heart city) for its location at the centre of the country, Santiago has historically generated an important part of the country's agricultural riches, and is home to several old families who made their fortunes growing tobacco and distilling rum.

Manufacturing has likewise played its part and Santiago had a prosperous Free Zone up until fairly recently when the export of textile manufacturing faced severe competition from Chinese products. An attempt has been made to develop the telecommunications industry and Santiago has many outsourced call-centres, which provide employment. Both these, and the Free Zone factories, are not helped by the DR's precarious supply of electricity.

Many of the expats who move to Santiago are younger families of working age rather than the retiree population. Such expats may have moved to teach or study at one of the city's many schools, colleges or universities. Other expats have moved to Santiago to be with their Dominican spouse or to set up a business. These, therefore, will be working families, not usually working in the field of tourism and therefore much less easy to spot for the new expat.

Santiago has no shortage of cultural centres. The Centro Cultural Eduardo León Jimenes, known as the Centro León, periodically hosts art exhibitions of both Dominican and international artists as well as having permanent displays dedicated to Dominican culture and history. In the historic city centre the Museo Folklórico Yoryi Morel houses carnival displays and the Museo del Tabaco gives insight into manufacturing methods and historical developments. A monument very difficult to miss is the sixty-seven metre *Monumento a los Heroes de la Restauración*. Trujillo had the monument constructed in his own honour, but after his death it was renamed to honour those who lost their lives in the War of Restoration. Those fit enough to climb the stairs of the monument will be rewarded with amazing views of Santiago and the surrounding area.

SHOPPING

Santiago has an abundance of shopping opportunities and north coast expat residents frequently make the seventy-five minute drive to avail themselves of wider selection and more competitive pricing on a range of household and electrical items. There are chain stores such as Plaza Lama and La Sirena, 'everything for the home' stores such as Ochoa Hogar and even international chains such as Price Smart. The city also offers good restaurants and an active nightlife.

SCHOOLS

Educational facilities in Santiago, which attract expat residents range from pre-kindergarten to University. Whilst Garabatos Pre-school is for the very young, New Horizons has a bilingual programme currently up to seventh grade but is developing to add a grade each year. Other schools to which expats send their children are La Salle, Holy Trinity and Santiago Christian School where about a quarter of all students are from foreign families. As the name indicates bible classes are required.

Perhaps Santiago's most famed seat of learning is its University – *Pontificia Universidad Católica Madre y Maestra* (PUCMM), popularly known by the phonetic rendition of its acronym, *Pucamaima*, which was the first private, Roman Catholic, coeducational university located in the DR. The university grants undergraduate, graduate, doctoral, and professional degrees as well as dual degrees with associated universities in the United States and France.

HEALTH CARE

As indicated in the North Coast section, expat residents would expect to travel to either Santiago or Santo Domingo for more extensive health facilities and *Santiago* boasts some first rate clinics and hospitals such as Clínica Unión Médica del Norte, Clínica Corominas and the new state-of-the-art HOMS (Hospital Metropolitano de Santiago) which is the largest hospital in the DR and one of the most modern hospitals in Latin America and the Caribbean, with 300 doctors' offices, 400 beds, sixteen operating rooms, a hotel, and other specialized units. It is likely to become a focal point for health tourism whereby foreigners will have the opportunity to receive high-quality health care at low prices.

Other Cities

This section covers the parts of the DR that are/might be considered less obvious choices for expatriates to choose as their home. There are, however, several reasons that might lead a minority of foreigners to decide to live in one of these cities, towns or surrounding rural areas, the very absence of other *gringos* being among the attractions for some.

Another reason is that in provincial towns the economy is not tourism or foreigner orientated, wages are generally much lower and this is reflected in the cost of living. In some cases the foreign resident might have some personal connection to the area via marriage to a local, a business venture, development work, or employment in one of the industrial, agricultural or commercial sectors in the area.

SHOPPING

The downside of living in these areas will always be the lack of anything but the basics; supermarkets (if they exist) and restaurants will cater for local tastes only, and there will be very little in the way of high culture or to some extent intellectual stimulation, but be prepared for surprises and seek out the exceptions.

HEALTH CARE AND SCHOOLS

Health and education facilities are usually inadequate or limited. Unless otherwise stated, assume that this will be the case in all of the cities outlined below. With some exceptions, many of these towns are subject to lengthy power outages, reportedly even worse than in the country's main cities.

Because of the decline of the agricultural sector, many provincial towns' *raison d'être* has all but disappeared. A large proportion of their population has had to migrate, either to the DR's larger cities or to the US and other countries, and their dependents live on the remittances they send home. This is evidenced by a noticeable lack of obvious economic activity alongside the trappings of relative prosperity such as imported clothes and designer sneakers, the latest electronic gadgets, newly built houses, and new vehicles. Attempts have been made to restore provincial economies with the installation of Free Trade Zone industrial parks as an alternative source of employment, but the low wages offered do not provide sufficient incentive for many remittance recipients.

Most Dominican provincial town centres are not particularly attractive in themselves, mainly due to haphazard planning and excessive traffic – small motorbikes in particular – but the residential areas tend to be cleaner than many parts of the big cities. Many municipalities have made efforts to beautify their *Parque Central* as the central square found in all Dominican towns and villages is known, often with the help of collective donations from Dominican émigré communities.

Cotuí in the central region is a case in point. It has a small foreign population associated with the gold mining industry in the adjacent mountains. A nearby attraction is the large artificial lake created by the construction of the Hatillo Dam, and the city itself has several pleasant residential areas (Los Españoles, Los Mineros and El Dorado).

Another central region mining town, **Bonao**, has facilities that cater for more international needs, including a residential complex, social club and at least one good school, legacy of the ferronickel mining company. However, the *Falconbridge* mine shut down most of its operations as a result of the economic slump in 2008, with serious economic and social consequences for the city and surrounding areas. It is due to re-open in 2011.

San Juan de la Maguana is a large and prosperous city in the south west, a three hour drive from the capital. Located an hour's drive inland from the coast just a few kilometres south west of Azua, San Juan sits in an eponymous fertile valley also known as *el granero del sur* (the breadbasket of the south), producing beans and other Dominican staple crops. The relatively high altitude makes for a fresh, comfortable climate, and the landscape, especially the outlying parts of San Juan province like Vallejuelo and Hondo Valle is breathtaking and completely unexploited.

Santiago Rodriguez, Mao and **Monción** are quiet cities in the rural north, all within an hour or so from Santiago and near areas of notable natural beauty like the Monción dam. **Montecristi** is further out, in the semi-arid northwest, on the coast. **Dajabón** on the Haitian border is famous for the colourful spectacle that is its twice-weekly bi-national market with traders from Haiti.

To the east of Santiago, **Moca** is the small capital of a province where agricultural production is dominated by coffee and cacao, but this is not how it got its name, which dates back to *Taíno* times like many other place-names in the country. The hills and mountains offer an escape from the heat of the valley lowlands, and are near enough to Santiago for access to more cosmopolitan products and services.

Salcedo is another attractive provincial capital, best known as the home of the Mirabal Sisters, three national heroines who were killed for their opposition to Trujillo, and who grew up in nearby Ojo de Agua. An interesting and well-run house-museum dedicated to their memory is just down the road in the village of Conuco, and provides an intriguing glimpse into the everyday lives of privileged Dominican landowners in the 1950s as well as a vivid testament to the sisters' own heroic story. In fact, the province itself, also formerly known as Salcedo was renamed Hermanas Mirabal in 2007.

San Francisco de Macorís is a large modern city in the north east of the Cibao region whose prosperity derives from large-scale agriculture, mainly rice farming and processing, but reputedly also from less savoury activities. Its many mansions are built in a gaudy style dubbed 'narco-deco' by the *Washington Post* in an article about the DR's links to the drug trade; the number of luxury car dealerships one encounters in San Francisco is only rivalled by **Higuey**, a bustling city in the eastern region and capital of La Altagracia province. Higuey is also notable for its vast Basilica built in honour of the virgin, Our Lady of Altagracia who is revered by Catholic Dominicans as the protector of the Dominican Republic. The basilica is the site of a mass-pilgrimage in the run-up to her saint's day in January. Higuey is the nearest urban centre for residents of the east coast region.

Smaller cities further inland include the provincial capital of **El Seibo,** famous for its traditional drink *mabí* the recipe of which dates back to pre-Columbian times, and for being the only place in the DR where bullfights are held. The eastern region is cattle-ranching country, which goes hand-in-hand (or hoof-in-hoof) with horse riding. Higuey even has its own *paso fino* equestrian breed and many towns in the region hold competitions and rodeos. Another inland eastern cattle-ranching town is Hato Mayor.

Many towns, especially in the poorer areas of the country like the south west or the east will also have some foreign aid workers, Peace Corps volunteers or missionaries.

The clock tower – Montecristi landmark

South West

The south western peninsula is commonly and officially known as 'the south'. Considered the DR's poorest region, it has never been a mass-tourism area. Its very remoteness and relatively unspoilt natural beauty is helping the south west make a name for itself as an ecotourim destination. A number of small hotels and businesses, some of them foreign-run, have sprung up in the area, mainly along the scenic coastline southwest of Barahona and the remote, sparsely populated but starkly stunning province of Pedernales.

The area has its own special semi-arid natural beauty as well as the more typical tropical landscape, and even some cool highlands in the coffee growing areas of *Sierra de Neyba* and the *Sierra de Bahoruco*, and on the coast, the *Bahía de las Aguilas* National Park. The largest lake in the Caribbean, *Lago Enriquillo*, with its reptilian inhabitants (crocodiles and iguanas) is also at the lowest point in the archipelago.

Barahona, the main city in the region, has its own airport named after the city's most famous modern-day daughter, 1940s Hollywood diva Maria Montez. The airport was built in anticipation of the south western region's development as a tourist destination, which never happened on a large scale, and so it remained closed until the Haiti earthquake of January 2010, when it re-opened to receive disaster relief flights.

Bahoruco, a few kilometres to the south west, is the site of an underwater mine where locals risk life and limb diving for *'larimar'*, a semi-precious pale blue stone said to be unique to the DR. To the west of Barahona, travelling past

Cabral to the mountain town of Polo is a spot known as *El Polo Magnetico*, where objects appear to roll uphill. Despite the stories you will hear from the locals, it is worth remembering that it is an optical illusion; what appears to be a slight incline upwards is in fact a slight downward slope. In fact the whole area has its myth and legend even in the present day; a humanitarian mission of US troops in 2006 sent to rebuild clinics and hospitals was assumed to be a front for spying on Venezuela and as a result 'Yanqui go home' graffiti sprung up throughout the province. Even more curiously, the village of Salinas in the lowlands near Cabral has been the subject of scientific studies and *National Geographic* articles because of the uncommonly high incidence of pseudo-hermaphrodites (also known as intersex individuals) among its population, attributed to in-breeding.

Generally agreed to be the poorest part of the country, with a large population of undocumented Haitian migrants, many international and national organisations are active in community development and emergency work, so a number of foreigners linked to this sector, like Peace Corps volunteers and other expatriate aid workers are based in the south west. Other foreigners living in the area are linked to the sugar, mining and cement manufacturing industries, as well as small-scale tourism, as mentioned above. The south west has suffered a series of natural disasters in recent years, most notably Hurricane Georges in 1998 and tropical storms Noel and Olga in 2007. In 2004 the border town of Jimaní was engulfed by mudslides, which killed hundreds of people. In early 2010 the town served as a staging post for aid convoys headed for the devastated Haitian capital, Port-au-Prince in the aftermath of the January 12th earthquake.

Apart from Barahona the other main coastal cities are Azua and Baní, and larger towns include Jimaní and the extreme south western outpost of Pedernales.

Although some foreigners in search of solitude might choose to live in the south west, it has to be stressed that living in these remote towns, and more so in the rural areas, will involve going almost totally native in terms of health facilities, shopping and education.

The capital is a full three-hour drive from Barahona, approximately one-and-a-half hours from Azua and about one-hour by car from Baní. None of these towns have much to offer in terms of clinics, schools or supermarket shopping. Road links are fairly good and *CaribeTours* buses serve the main inter-urban route.

Azua is a bustling provincial capital self-dubbed 'cradle of culture' and 'the Dominican Athens' because it gave the nation several writers, thinkers and poets. The city is surrounded by a fertile plain, the Valley of Azua, where tomatoes, melons and other crops are cultivated. Baní is mainly famous for its luscious *banilejo* mangoes, as well as its astute small-scale entrepreneurs, many of whom have migrated to run successful *colmados* in the capital and overseas. Nearby Salinas (not the same as the village of the same name near Barahona, mentioned above) is becoming famous as a windsurfing and kite-surfing resort, not on the scale of Cabarete in the north, but certainly offering a more conveniently located option for water sports enthusiasts from the capital.

The south west may not be most people's choice for a place to live unless you are a writer or artist seeking solitude, but it is still well worth a visit. It is also likely to be one of the next development locations as Canadian hoteliers are viewing the area with interest, so those seeking moderately priced land would be advised to investigate sooner rather than post-development when all pricing will doubtless skyrocket.

The Mountains: Jarabacoa and Constanza

Whilst most expats are attracted by the lure of the sea and coastline, a growing number are looking inland where property prices are considerably less expensive. The so-called *Dominican Alps* of the *Cordillera Central*, the tallest mountain range in the Caribbean, offers a cooler temperature and a different pace of life than coastal tourist resorts. Jarabacoa sits about 525 metres above sea level and enjoys a 16^0C to 22^0C degree temperature all year round, though in winter it can be as low as 7^0C.

Jarabacoa was born as a refuge from war when in 1805, during the Haitian invasion of the Cibao, survivors from the massacres of Santiago de los Caballeros and La Vega escaped to the mountains of the Central Cordillera and settled in the valley of Jarabacoa. In 1854, a military post was installed and in 1858 the town was incorporated as a municipality and celebrated its 150th birthday in 2008.

The local economy is traditionally based upon agriculture – it is known for its strawberries, coffee and pimento. This town has been a popular summer retreat for wealthy Dominicans for some time but adventure-sports tourism and ecotourism have recently made it more so. It is a natural hub for those wanting to enjoy these types of activities – the surrounding nature offering mountain fresh air, tall pines, huge waterfalls and many river rapids as well as being a starting point for those wanting to hike Pico Duarte, highest peak in the Caribbean, at 3187 metres (10,128 feet). Families with young children should note that Rancho Baiguate Adventure Centre does not restrict itself to tourist activities but also provides development courses and summer camps focussed on communication skills, leadership and team work for children.

SHOPPING

Like most Dominican towns, Jarabacoa is easy to navigate. The main road entering the town is Avenida Independencia (one-way until you enter the town, and then becomes a two-way street.) The centres of activity in Jarabacoa are the main crossroads and around the *Parque Central*, with restaurants, a popular pool hall and a bank with a twenty-four hour ATM. On the busy corner to the right leaving town to the south is a convenience store (good coffee, pastries, and fresh fruit, along with Spanish-language newspapers). The Shell gas station opposite the convenience store marks the start of the road to Constanza and the route to many of the area attractions and accommodations outside of town.

Santiago and La Vega provide what local stores do not in the way of shopping items. Jarabacoa has become home to many Dominican artists and their works can be viewed and bought in the town's galleries.

SCHOOLS

Educational facilities such as the Doulos Discovery School in Jarabacoa have a mix of local and expat children and local and expat teachers. It is based on Christian principles but seeks to accommodate a range of religious beliefs and economic backgrounds. There is also a Roman Catholic Salesian College – the Colegio y Liceo Salesiano Santo Domingo Savio. For older students the Universidad Agroforestal Fernando Arturo de Meriño provides courses in Humanities, Agronomy and Computer Sciences.

HEALTH CARE

Emergency health services are provided at clinics such as Centro Médico Jarabacoa, the recently inaugurated Clinica Dr Federico Cabrera González and the municipal Hospital Octavia Gautier de Vidal but for more extensive health care expats make the 45 minute journey to Santiago.

Constanza

Constanza like much of the DR was populated by the indigenous residents long before colonisation and acquired its name from the daughter of a *Taíno* Chief. Despite access difficulty due to lack of roads several explorers found this valley in colonial times: a Spanish settler named Victoriano Velano brought in the first cows and mares in

1750. Something must have happened to these animals during their adaptation process to the new environment because Cayetano Armado stated in his work on the geography of the DR published in 1915, that 'in the valley of Constanza grows a dwarfed race of cattle and equine, similar to the size of a goat.'

The British consul in Santo Domingo, Robert Schomburgk, visited Constanza in 1851 and found only one inhabited hut. Twenty years later the North American palaeontologist, William Gabb who carried out a geological survey of the DR, found twelve huts. In 1887, Danish botanist Baron Henrik Franz Alexander von Eggers visited the Central Cordillera and found 100 residents inhabiting thirty huts scattered in the valley of Constanza. By 1894 these huts had become a town that grew very slowly in the following 50 years.

Nor were the explorers the only expats to set foot in Constanza. Dictator Rafael Trujillo, who was constantly trying to transform the economy of the DR throughout his regime, brought about 200 Japanese families over to the area to improve farming production. The old Japanese Colony – now mostly a collection of tumbledown shacks – can still be seen there, though most of the Japanese who remained have moved to more upscale dwellings. It was the Japanese who introduced the economical irrigation system used in the area.

June 14th 1959 saw an invasion by Dominican exiles from Cuba, when the then-new Castro regime tried to help the Dominican opposition in exile overthrow Trujillo in an attempt to bring a more Cuba-friendly government to the DR. A Cuban force landed in Constanza only to be routed by Trujillo's forces; all but four of the Cubans were later executed but this feat became the inspiration for a clandestine group that would seek to continue undermining Trujillo's power and would be called the '*Movimiento Catorce de Junio*' (14th of June Movement). In fact Constanza's airport refurbished in 2006 was renamed *Aeropuerto Héroes del 14 de Junio* when it was inaugurated in July 2007.

Like Jarabacoa the economy is based on agriculture, specifically the growing of fruit, vegetables and flowers and the early expats in this area, the Spanish, Japanese and Lebanese, made a significant contribution to this. Adventure tourism and eco-tourism also make an important contribution to the local economy. Constanza is the base for much of the mountain trekking in the *Ébano Verde* and the *Valle Nuevo* Scientific Reserves. Invariably tourism means some incursion into the natural beauty but the Dominican Government and the Cluster Movement are working hard to keep this a protected area, while at the same time developing new types of tourism; for example the recent fly-in in light aircraft by US eco-tourists.

The trails through the 37 square kilometres of the *Ébano Verde* Reserve where more than 687 plant species can be observed are well-kept and the trees are labelled. The pine forests are also home to indigenous bird life seen only in this area. So for the expat who is an outdoor enthusiast this area is truly Paradise. It is frequently visited by national and international scientists who have tried to understand how the typical vegetation of the European Alps can be found in a Caribbean country

Likewise the *Piedras Letreadas*, (Carved Stones) Natural Monument is a focal point for students of *Taino* culture. Constanza would be an ideal location for expats who want to farm: the current crop of potatoes, garlic, carrots, strawberries, cilantro, onions, tomatoes, beans, corn, broccoli, peppers, cucumbers, lettuce, leeks, celery, beets, cabbages, and flowers, supplies not only the DR's population of nine million, but also its tourist hotels and a growing export business.

Constanza is also home to poets and celebrates an annual poetry festival as well as artists inspired by the local sights, such as *Aguas Blancas* by Rosario de Valdez. The road to Constanza was repaired in late 2010, which has made access much easier for visitors as well as for residents and farmers transporting their produce to the rest of the country.

SCHOOLS

Testament to the local interest in poetry is the fact that a Constanza school, the Liceo Gastón Fernando Deligne was renamed after the fall of Trujillo whose name it then bore, to honour one of the DR's greatest poets and writers. In January 2008 wireless internet connectivity was made available to schools in the Constanza area.

HEALTH CARE

Constanza has two hospitals for emergency treatment, the Hospital Pedro A Cespedes and the Hospital Constanza but more specialised medical services would be sought in Santiago.

What?

Practical Information

Cost of living

Inevitably, the cost of living will depend very much on the lifestyle chosen. Go 'native' and you will get by on US$1000 per month for one person – many Dominicans live comfortably on far less. At the other end of the scale, eat out in upmarket restaurants every night and you will probably find you can spend US$5000 per month. Assuming your house and car is paid for, US$2000 per month should provide a very comfortable lifestyle for a couple with no children. An average food shopping bill per month for an expat couple living in Puerto Plata is around US$400, for example. US$140 per month will cover employment of a maid for four hours a day, three days a week. US$200 a month will obtain the services of a gardener for two full days a week. Labour is inexpensive, cars, fuel and electricity are not.

The currency is the Dominican Peso, and the rate of exchange at the time of publication (July 2011) is just over 38 Dominican pesos to the US dollar. Dominican pesos are written RD$, so RD$37 is what you will get for US$1. However, for ease of recognition prices in this section will be referred to in US dollars. Gasoline is currently US$4.60 a gallon for Regular and US$4.94 for Premium whilst Premium diesel (called gasoil in the DR) is $4.40 and Regular diesel is US$4.24. If you keep your electricity bill just under 700 kilowatt hours per month your bill will be just over US$100; go above the magical 700 kilowatt hours and the whole tariff doubles! The installation of a solar powered water heater can combat this ruse. Local foodstuffs are inexpensive, imported items still seem to be an arm and a leg job even in spite of the Free Trade Agreement known as DR-CAFTA. Prices and things can and do change here, rapidly! Shop around for items such as electrical products for the home and negotiate for almost everything! You are expected to negotiate and your respect rating as a foreigner will go up if you do. Services such as Cable TV and fast internet connection are available in all but the more remote areas. Those remote areas do not have piped electricity or water either but such utilities can be self-provided.

Renting accommodation

The cost of renting a property will vary greatly depending on location. A decent two-bedroomed apartment in a truly Dominican locality will go from US$200 to US$400 per month. In a more tourist oriented or resident expat locality the cost could be as much as US$700-US$1000 per month. To illustrate the extreme ends of the scale, a room in a

Dominican rooming house in Puerto Plata costs US$34 per month, whereas an upscale tourist villa in Cabarete can cost between US$500-US$1000 *per night*. So asking the question "how much to rent?" is a bit like asking the length of a piece of string.

Renting property is to be preferred over purchasing until the new expat is absolutely convinced that the DR is the right country for him or her. Selling one's property is not always easy or rapid: the north coast building frenzy of recent years means that there is more supply than demand. As a result some developments have come to a grinding halt as developers have run out of money or pre-construction sales did not go according to plan. Other developers leave completed homes empty because they cannot achieve the asking price.

Expats renting in different locations of the Dominican Republic in 2010 were paying the following amounts per month: for a one-bedroom apartment in Bella Vista, Santo Domingo US$600, for a three-bedroom apartment in Mirador Sur, Santo Domingo US$1000, for a three-bedroom apartment in Santiago US$300, for a three-bedroom apartment in Gaspar Hernandez (north coast but outside the tourist location) US$250, for a three-bedroom detached house in Puerto Plata US$750, for a two-bedroom apartment in Puerto Plata US$500, for a one-bedroom studio apartment in Puerto Plata US$350. A three-bedroom villa in Sosúa or Cabarete would cost between US$850 and US$1500, depending on location and amenities. On the east coast, apartments in residential developments away from the beach start at about US$600 per month for a fairly basic middle-range apartment, rising into the US$1,000 plus range in the better residential developments.

Searching via the internet can always provide results which seem grossly at variance with these figures. The smart potential expat will ask why. It could be a ploy to encourage the searcher to make contact with the real estate company (as in a 'loss leader') or it could be an honest reflection of the actual rent. If the latter, it is worth studying the location: bargains may not be bargains if they are situated in areas with a poor track record for security and safety.

Many expats decide to buy property after they are certain that they wish to live in the DR and most are cash buyers. Mortgages can be obtained, but the interest rate in the DR will seem high compared with their countries of origin. One way of checking current rates is to visit the websites of banks that loan mortgages. In February 2009 rates for new mortgages were reduced by Banco Popular from 24% to 22%, with some of the Savings and Loan Associations at 20%. The interest rate for existing mortgages was as low as 11% in 2007 but of course world financial events in 2008 had some part to play in the changes. Personal loans in the DR in February 2009 came down from 36% per annum to 32% and business loans from 27% to 24%. In February 2010 mortgages dropped a further 3.5% but the DR is definitely not an inexpensive country in which to borrow money.

It is also possible that some owners are prepared to offer financing. While this is probably less expensive than a bank mortgage it can still seem high compared with country of origin experience. Naturally, both forms of financing will have requirements that guarantee repayment and borrowing money in the DR will not be immune from the problems it has recently caused in other parts of the world! For expats with assets in US, Canada or UK it is sometimes possible to obtain mortgages on a DR home from entities such as Deutsche Bank.

Food

It will come as no surprise that imported items are expensive whilst locally produced items are not. US$400-500 per month for a family of two adults who eat well and use local produce would be a reasonable outlay. This does not include alcohol. A quart (2 pints) of milk is US$1.30, a French baguette-style loaf is 70 cents, a 2lb bag of white sugar is 80 cents whilst a 2lb bag of brown sugar is 60 cents. Broadly speaking, the less processing an item requires the cheaper it will be. Rice is 62 cents a pound and spaghetti 57 cents. A 32 fluid ounce bottle of soybean cooking oil is just under US$2. White cheese is just under US$3 a pound and ham US$3.85 a pound. A dozen eggs are US$2.10, a pound of beef fillet US$4.57 and a pound of fresh red snapper US$5.70. Second grade ground beef is US$1.25 per pound.

On the east coast, food prices are higher because of the relatively remote location and the higher purchasing power of the local expatriate and Dominican population. This is changing with increased competition between the smaller supermarkets and the recent arrival of a large supermarket, Nacional, in Punta Cana Village and the imminent opening of a Super Pola at the new San Juan Shopping Center in Bávaro.

Of course many Dominicans do not spend US$400 a month on food because they are not earning sufficiently to do so. It is possible to eat at home far less expensively if the range of diet is restricted to rice, beans and the occasional chicken, but for now, costs are taken to indicate the type and range of diet an expat might require. The politics of all this will be discussed later!

There is no shortage of food in the DR and supermarkets in tourist locations are plentifully stocked. So, too, are the *colmados* or corner stores but these do not necessarily practice the art of display so you may have to hunt a bit. Or learn sufficient Spanish to be able to ask for things if you decide to live in a Dominican as opposed to a tourist area. Hunger can be a wonderful motivator!

Expats with villas or houses with gardens frequently grow much of their own fruit and vegetables. Stable year-round temperatures with minimal variation mean there are no seasons when it is not possible to grow something. Ginnie managed to grow avocado trees, bananas, mangoes, cherry tomatoes, limes and bitter oranges as well as hot peppers, melons and sweetcorn in her garden.

One of the first things the new expat notices is how the fruit and vegetables in the Dominican Republic taste like they used to back home before regulation knocked the stuffing and the taste out of most things edible. "Ooh! REAL carrots" is the gleeful cry. Not to mention 'real' bananas unfettered by European Union (or other) size, shape and weight constraints!

Unlike tourists who can fall subject to stomach complaints, this is rare among expats who cook at home. It should be remembered that tap water is not for drinking. Bottled water in five gallon containers is inexpensive and readily available and *colmados* and other entrepreneurs will deliver to homes.

Costs of eating out will vary enormously depending on location. It is possible to find inexpensive eateries, particularly those where locals go for lunch at about US$4 per head. Dinner for two with wine in a medium style restaurant in Santo Domingo or Santiago will start from US$30 and in tourist areas like Sosúa, Cabarete or Punta Cana it could easily go beyond US$100.

Other miscellaneous costs: a carton of 200 cigarettes US$26.50, employment of a full-time accountant US$714 per month, employment of a receptionist US$343 per month, employment of a chauffeur US$230 per month. A medical appointment will cost between US$7-US$15 per visit, a dental appointment for check up and cleaning US$17 per visit. Cars are expensive: a 2002 4x4 would start from US$17,630. For expats with school-aged children, fees for a Spanish language school are approximately US$1500 per year and for a bilingual school US$4000. This is detailed in the education section below. Costs of telecommunications and transportation are likewise itemised below.

Utilities

The Dominican Republic has what is probably the most expensive electricity in Latin America. As mentioned earlier, the secret is to keep usage below 700 kilowatt hours per month when the monthly expenditure will be around US$100. Use of air conditioning can easily put the kilowatt hours above the 700 mark and then the *whole* tariff doubles, not just the part over and above 700. The DR is famed (!) for its blackouts and most expats have an inverter and/or a generator to cope with this. Power outages (or blackouts) are frequent, and occasionally last for 20 hours or more, so when the power does come back on, there is often insufficient time for the inverter to regenerate before the next blackout. This is why a generator allows residents to be self-sufficient because, whilst running, it will re-power the inverter. However, with diesel currently at US$3.47 a gallon there are running costs involved, quite apart from initial outlay costs for a good quality generator. Some areas of the country (Samaná, Punta Cana and Bayahibe) are serviced by small private electricity companies whose rates are expensive, but unlike the rest of the Dominican Republic, the supply is constant.

Tanks of propane gas (LPG) are used for cooking and a 100lb tank refill costs US$59.78. Duration of the tank clearly depends on amount of usage but on average a 100lb tank in a family household lasts three months. Up until September 2008 household propane was subsidised and thus was more than US$6 cheaper. Services exist which will collect your empty propane tank and return it later in the day duly filled; for recommendations consult with neighbours, other expats or Yellow Pages. In January 2011 a 100lb. gas tank costs about US$60 to refill.

As indicated, gasoline and diesel prices are expensive, partly due to taxation. They also change weekly and will doubtless have done so a number of times between this book being drafted and being read. Nor do they always change in the same direction as world fuel markets! However, visiting the Secretary of State for Industry & Commerce website at *www.seic.gov.do* and finding the *Precios de combustibles* box should give up to date prices.

Household water costs vary depending on location: expats living in Santo Domingo and Gaspar Hernandez report water bills as US$8.50 per month; the most upscale area in Puerto Plata charges US$12.40 per month and parts of Santiago have been known to charge US$23. Water meters are now being installed in a number of areas. Local water delivery companies will deliver a tank of water if the cistern runs dry, these come in three sizes and price varies accordingly, but a ball-park figure is US$13.50 for the medium size. Residents who dig their own wells are also expected to contribute to the public water authority. Costs for rubbish collection will vary similarly from US$1.50 per month in a poor area to US$7 per month in the most upscale neighbourhood of Puerto Plata.

Health care

The public healthcare system is currently best avoided by expats. Doctors are usually capable and willing but woefully under-resourced. It is not uncommon for surgeons to finish procedures by the light of their cell phones during one of the many power outages and when the hospital has run out of funds to buy fuel for the generator. Patients are required to bring their own sutures and often blood supplies. The surgeons are not lacking in skills because many of them are the same surgeons who also practice in the private sector but in the public sector they have insufficient support to enable most expats to feel comfortable. It is worth noting that in the Dominican Republic, "*hospital*" always refers to a public facility, while a "*clínica*" usually means private.

Private healthcare is available and of a far superior standard but as in everything just because it is a private system does not automatically mean that a particular doctor or surgeon will be what is required. It is best to take a recommendation from another expat who has had the same treatment or operation. Many expats comment very favourably on the standards of medical and surgical practice in some of the modern, private facilities. All express satisfaction with the lack of waiting lists for private medicine, surgery and laboratory tests and the rapid results, which can be produced by the laboratories.

The comments above about the public health system are not to deny that advances have been made in providing the legal framework for health care in the DR. Two important laws were passed in 2001, mapping out a new direction for the national health system: the General Health Act (Law 42-01) and the Social Security Act (Law 87-01). The General Health Act separated the system's service delivery, leadership, and financing functions and created the National Health Council as the national body coordinating health matters. The act laid the groundwork for regulating public health and health-risk issues and charged the Ministry of Public Health and Social Welfare with formulating the national ten year health plans and performing essential public health functions.

Law 87-01 created the Dominican Social Security System and established the sources and mechanisms for financing the national health system's assistance. The Dominican Social Security System is funded by prepaid, mandatory contributions, based on ability to pay and employment status; it guarantees public insurance for the poor and indigent population. Law 87-01 introduced family health insurance, which is mandatory and universal and entails a basic health plan for the three established regimes: contributory, subsidized contributory, and subsidized. In 2003, the Labour Risk Administration was created to prevent and cover occupational accidents and work-related diseases. By December 2005, it had registered 30,531 companies and enrolled 1,218,737 workers.

By 2007 the national insurance scheme for healthcare was in its infancy having been put back from June 2007 to September 2007 due to lack of planning agreements. That is the polite terminology for what actually went on which in any event was not helped by the economic meltdown, which the DR suffered in 2004 as a result of the *Baninter* collapse (see Finance and Taxes section below). The national health insurance scheme is effectively still a work in progress as can be seen from the recent additions to the *Superintendencia de Salud y Riesgos* (SISALRIL) website *(www.sisalril.gov.do)*. By 2008 only 33.5% of the population was covered by family health insurance.

Private health insurance on the other hand is readily available and accepted by medical facilities and pharmacies. Some of the more state of the art facilities accept US private health insurance coverage like *HOMS* in Santiago and Clinica Abreu in Santo Domingo or Plaza de la Salud (CEDIMAT) in Santo Domingo, where the DR's first kidney transplant took place in October 2007. Other recommended hospitals are Hospiten in both Bavaro and Santo Domingo and Centro Medico Cabarete in Sosua.

Contact details for all these facilities will be found at the end of this section. Normally patients will pay with cash or credit card and claim back from their US insurer. If privately insured by a DR insurer a check should be made as to the level of the costs that will be met. Current prices for a hip replacement and five day hospital stay in one of the state of the art private facilities would be approx US$7000. A broken clavicle with a two-night hospital stay would be US$2000 and for a complicated knee replacement with a seven-night stay US$11,000. As indicated above it is absolutely crucial to go on a surgeon recommendation from someone known and trusted and preferably a patient who has had a similar operation.

This also applies to opticians and dentists, in fact to all health professionals. Prices are far less than could be expected in certain first world countries: a root canal, post and crown costs about US$530. Dental implants cost US$850 per implant plus a further US$400 for the crown. Dental tourism is beginning to make its mark on the DR where tourists combine a holiday with specific treatments. To this end there are many surgeons, doctors and dentists who speak English. There is a private hospital facility in Sosúa, specifically geared to the needs of expat retirees, which is owned and run by an English-speaking Argentinean neuro-surgeon.

One aspect of health provision in the DR that may come as a surprise to the new expat is the role which family and/or friends are expected to play in nursing recovery. There is an expectation that family members will care for the post-operative patient and most private clinics have a spare bed in the patient's room for this purpose. Nursing care by Dominican nurses may not be as constant as expats may have experienced in their countries of origin and family members are expected to make up the shortfall. This tends to be true of all post-operative situations with the exception of Intensive Care where nursing is usually more attentive. Reasons can be found in the low pay and status of nurses, limited nursing education and frequently limited ratio of numbers of nurses to patients. Either way, this is something of which the single expat in particular will need to be cognisant.

Another aspect of health provision in the DR likely to surprise the new expat is the easy availability of medications without prescription. Antibiotics and anti-inflammatory medications for example can be bought over the counter.

Dominicans on a low income can often be seen purchasing one or two tablets rather than a course of tablets and pharmacies will sell in this ill-advised manner.

There are a variety of private insurance schemes, for example, ARS Universal, La Monumental, La Colonial, Seguros Banreservas, Proseguros, and Seguros Popular. Costs for private insurance arranged individually would be around US$25 per month for one person and US$50 for family coverage. Expats frequently join group insurance schemes such as that operated through the International Residents Club (IRC). The average cost of a group scheme would be US$15 per month with a US$45 payment upfront. Most health insurance schemes only cover affiliates until the age of 70 (in some cases extendable until age 75), and the one insurer that provides cover until death, ARS Universal, has a scheme that must be bought before the age of 65.

It is crucial to check what each scheme will actually pay out when called into play. There may be limits both on daily payment for hospital and specialists' services. The aspect that most expats will want to consider is known as catastrophic coverage i.e. serious operations, which obviously are more costly. The IRC scheme for example will pay somewhere in the region of US$7100 for catastrophic coverage, and other schemes may pay up to US$10,000, but this may not meet the total costs of a complicated operation requiring an extended hospital stay. Some DR insurance policies have age limitations that the retiree expat might want to check into before giving up their coverage in their country of origin.

The other way of obtaining health (or any other form of) insurance is to use the services of a broker. Two of the largest insurance brokers are Ros & Associates and Franco-Acra & Associates. Their contact details are in the Resources section at the end of this section.

More health information about the Dominican Republic can be found in

Health in the Americas 2007 Vol. II – specific section on the DR and in Health Systems Profile of the DR: Monitoring and Analysing Health Systems Change, Pan American Health Organisation October 2007. This can be downloaded in English from the Pan American Health Organisation website:

www.paho.org/hia/archivosvol2/.../Dominican%20Republic%20 English.pdf

HEALTH CARE FACILITIES

Contact details for recommended health facilities – this is not intended to be an exhaustive list.

Santiago

Hospital Metropolitano de Santiago (HOMS),
Autopista Duarte Km. 2.8,
Tel: 829 947 2222
www.homshospital.com

Clínica Corominas, Calle Restauración 57,
Tel: 809.580.1171
Clínica Unión Medica del Norte, Av. Juan Pablo Duarte 176,
Tel: 809 226 8686
www.clinicaunionmedica.com

Santo Domingo

Clinica Abreu, Calle Beller # 42, esq. Av. Independencia, Gazcue,
Tel: 809 688 4411
www.clinicaabreu.com.do

Centro de Medicina Avanzada Dr Abel González,
Abraham Lincoln 953
Tel: 809 540 2278 Toll Free: 1 866 410 3533
www.cirugiabariatricaabelgonzalez.com

CEDIMAT (Centro de Diagnostico, Medicina Avanzada, Conferencias Medicas y Telemedicina) Plaza de la Salud, Calle Pepillo Salcedo, Esq. Alturo Logroño, Ensanche la Fe.
Tel: 809 565 9989
Fax: 809 565 7925
Call toll free in the DR: 1 200 0736
www.cedimat.com

Hospiten Santo Domingo, Alma Máter, esquina Bolívar.
Tel: 809 541 3000
www.hospiten.es

Punta Cana

Hospiten Bávaro
Carretera Higüey - Punta Cana, Bávaro. Tel: 809 686 1414
www.hospiten.es

Centro Médico Punta Cana (CMPC)
Av. España s/n (between Friusa & Plaza Bavaro)
Tel: 809 552 1506
Fax: 809 552 1974
www.rescue-puntacana.com

Centro Médico Caribe Bávaro
Plaza Brisas Bávaro
Tel: 809 552 1415
www.caribeasistencia.com

La Romana

Centro Médico Central Romana Tel: 809 532 3333

Centro de Especialidades Médicas Romana Tel: 809 550 3440

Centro Médico Coral Tel: 809 550 0097

Puerto Plata

Centro Medico Bournigal, Calle Antera Mota.
Tel: 809 586 2342 / 809 586 4140
www.bournigal-hospital.com

Sosua

Centro Medico Cabarete (CMC)
Tel: 809 571 4696
www.cabaretemedicalcenter.com

Cabarete

Serví-Med Tel: 809 571-0964 or 809 571-2903

Samaná

Centro Médico San Vicente Tel: 809 538-2535

Las Galeras

Guariquen project community health clinic,
Tel: 809 914 3055
Cel: 829 797 2636
www.guariquen.org

Dra. Khira Hiche
Plaza Lusitania.
Cel: 829 918 3233
Tel: 809 538 0111

Bonao

Centro Médico Bonao Tel: 809 525-3811

La Vega

Clínica La Concepción Tel: 809 573 0022

Cotui

Centro Médico Núñez Hernández C. x A. Tel: 809 585 2901

San Cristóbal

Centro Médico Constitución (Cemeco) Tel: 809 288 3229

Higuey

Grupo Médico Dr Reyes Tel: 809 554 2538

San Juan de La Maguana

Centro Médico San Juan Tel: 809 557 5345

Constanza

Centro de Especialidades Médicas Titi Tel: 809 539 3345

Centro Médico Dr Rodríguez Tel: 809 539 2696

Jarabacoa

Clínica de Niños y Esp. Dra. Yolanda Sánchez Tel: 809 539 2426

Clinica Inmaculada Tel: 809 574 4650

Ambulances

Movimed, Santo Domingo Tel: 809 532 0000

Pro Med, Santo Domingo Tel: 809 948 7200

For services in Santiago, Puerto Plata and La Romana
Tel: 1 200 0911 Payment is expected at the time of transportation.

Organisations

Secretary of State for Industry & Commerce website at
www.seic.gov.do

Superintendencia de Salud y Riesgos (SISALRIL) website at
www.sisalril.gov.do

Insurance

Ros & Associates in Santo Domingo on Winston Churchill at the corner of José Brea Peña
Tel: 809 567 1021 / 809 562 4556

Franco-Acra & Associates in Santo Domingo on Winston Churchill 32 Tel: 809 535 1655 and in Santiago on Av. 27 de Febrero esq. Av. Metropolitana Edif. Metropolitano I, Módulo 301, 3er. piso, Jardines Metropolitanos Tel: 809 581 5666
servicioalcliente@francoacra.com

Education

Sad, shocking even, but true: the Dominican Republic is a country where one of the lowest percentages of public funds in the Latin America and Caribbean region is spent on its education system, and in a recent United Nations survey, Dominican students scored very poorly in international tests compared to their peers in neighbouring countries. In 2006 the Dominican government allocated just 3.6% of its GDP to education (*United Nations Development Programme*); whilst this represents an improvement on the woefully inadequate records of previous years, this level of expenditure is still below the recommended rate of 4%.

The vast majority of Dominican children attend state schools and while these vary in quality, apart from the odd notable exception, the system is considered sub-standard on the whole and is not recommended for families who are able to afford a private alternative. In state schools the facilities can be downright insalubrious and the teaching standards more often than not verge on the embarrassing. The school day is short – students enter before 8am but are usually dismissed well before midday.

Lack of space means that children have to attend school in shifts known as *tandas*, morning, afternoon or evening; the latter mostly made up of mature students working towards obtaining their *bachillerato* high school qualification.

According to law, Dominican children have to attend school from the ages of five to fourteen, but there is a very high dropout rate and parents are not prosecuted for not sending children to school. In the poor rural areas especially, children are pulled out of school at an early age to contribute to the family economy by working in agriculture.

It is estimated that only ten per cent of Dominican students end up graduating from high school. Children enter first grade of primary school (*básica*) at age six and graduate after twelfth grade (also known as fourth year of *bachillerato*) at eighteen. The first set of national exams called *pruebas nacionales,* is taken at the end of eighth grade and the high school completion exams, the *bachillerato* (baccalaureate) are taken at the end of twelfth grade.

The practice of holding children back a grade for poor performance or jumping them up a grade in the opposite case means that many children are not in their correct age group.

Many children in the Dominican Republic lack birth certificates which are a pre-requisite for state school attendance after third grade. This excludes many poor Dominican children whose parents failed to register their birth because they can't afford the expense, as well as children of illegal Haitian immigrants from the education system. The *World Bank* recently put the proportion of undocumented Dominicans at five per cent of the population.

The situation is improving, albeit at a slow pace. The current government has stated its commitment to improving the population's skills and literacy levels in order to be able to compete in a globalised economy, but a great deal of time, as well as funds and political will, is needed to bring about positive and tangible changes.

At almost every socio-economic level, any Dominican who can afford it will opt to send their children to a private school. Although this will vary depending on where you live, there is usually a broad range of options to suit different economic levels. In some parts of the country this might mean the local parochial school, which although traditional, provides a more solid academic basis.

In Santo Domingo, Santiago, La Romana, Sosúa, Cabrera, Las Terrenas, San Pedro de Macorís and Juan Dolio along with the Punta Cana and Bávaro areas there are reasonable bi-lingual schools teaching in English as well as Spanish, with the exception of Las Terrenas where the bilingual schools are French-Spanish, as is the *Lycée Francaise* in Santo Domingo.

It would be difficult to compile a complete list that does justice to all the options, but five bilingual schools considered to be very good in different parts of Santo Domingo would be Carol Morgan (Mirador Sur), Dominico-Americano (La Esperilla/Zona Universitaria), St Michael (Piantini), the Community for Learning (Arroyo Hondo) and St George (Piantini). In Santiago, the schools that most expatriates opt for are the Santiago Christian School and New Horizons. La Romana has the Lincoln School, Sosua has the International School and Garden Kids (which are also accessible to students from Puerto Plata and Cabarete), Cabrera has the International Academy, Las Terrenas has one French school and a couple of Spanish schools, San Pedro de Macoris and Juan Dolio have the Villas del Mar International School, and the Punta Cana/Bávaro area has the Punta Cana International and Cap Cana Heritage Schools.

(More specific information about schools, their locations and contact details is outlined in the directory at the end of this section.)

It is worth defining the term 'bilingual', which although so freely bandied about is interpreted in totally different ways by different schools. Some teach mainly in English, with only two or three subjects being taught in Spanish to meet the requirements of the Dominican Ministry of Education. These core subjects would be Spanish Language, Civics and Values/Religion although not every school has religious instruction on its syllabus. The most obvious exceptions would be the schools that are explicitly faith-based, like the Catholic, Evangelical and Adventist establishments, but not exclusively so.

Other bilingual schools meet the full international definition for bilingual education by teaching all subjects in both languages. This is the case in New Horizons and Punta Cana International School, where there is a dual timetable and one homeroom teacher per language per grade. Typically students will be taught in one language for half the school day and in the other for the second half.

Then there are the American style schools like Carol Morgan, Dominico-Americano, St Patrick, St Joseph, St Michael and several others in Santo Domingo including the American School of Santo Domingo where the curriculum and culture is a replica of what goes on at a school in the US, including raising the Stars and Stripes alongside the Dominican tricolour, singing both national anthems, and reciting the US pledge of allegiance in the morning. Most of these schools are certified by US education boards and while they have to fulfil Dominican Education Ministry requisites as explained above, the content is US-based: the children will learn US history, social sciences, and so on.

There are a couple of schools with a British as opposed to US influence, namely St George in Santo Domingo and Lincoln in La Romana. The French schools are listed below.

Many schools in the DR bear the name *Montessori* in their titles, but this does not always mean that they are officially certified as such or even that they follow the Montessori method in their academic practice.

Pre-school

A strong positive feature about pre-school facilities in the Dominican Republic is that your children will receive an unparalleled amount of care and adoration by Dominican pre-school professionals at an affordable price. Dominicans take pre-schooling and early stimulation seriously, and work hard on teaching tots the basics.

Most parts of the country, especially the main cities have a wide range of pre-school facilities, and as with primary and secondary schooling it is best to follow personal recommendations when choosing, as well as other considerations like location, educational philosophy, facilities etc. Some of these pre-schools are attached to the primary and secondary schools, while others are separate pre-schools in their own right.

Higher education

Apart from the Autonomous University of Santo Domingo (UASD in its Spanish acronym, by which it is popularly known, and pronounced as WASS), all universities in the DR are private. The UASD has branches in several towns and cities around the country. It has a long radical tradition, hundreds of thousands of students (it is virtually free and entrance requirements are almost non-existent) and a very low graduation rate.

The best universities in the country are considered to be INTEC in Santo Domingo and PUCMM in Santiago (with a branch in Santo Domingo) as well as UNIBE in Santo Domingo. In all cases, non-Dominicans are charged much higher tuition fees, in US dollars, but the cost of a higher education in the DR is much lower than in other countries.

Spanish lessons

If you are planning to live in a country where the main language of communication is Spanish, we highly recommend that you do all that is possible to learn the language. This may be done either by taking a course in your home country, or by using a computer-based course like Rosetta Stone, BBC and others before coming to the DR.

However, these will not cover the quirks of Dominican Spanish (see separate section on Language) so it is also recommended to continue the process of learning once you are in the country by total immersion through day-to-day interaction with Dominican people – the best way to learn any language – reinforced by a structured course at a recognized institute like Dominico-Americano or Berlitz, or with a private teacher based on recommendations.

It is said that once you can read a local newspaper, you are on your way towards fluency. *Diario Libre* is probably the least daunting prospect among the DR press in that it tends to be concise and to the point, especially compared to its more long-winded broadsheet counterparts like the veteran *Listin Diario* and *Hoy*.

Some useful contacts/resources

Dominican Republic Education Ministry
www.see.gob.do

SCHOOLS

Santo Domingo

Carol Morgan School
Bi-lingual, US accredited, pre-school to *bachillerato*
Av. Sarasota esq. Nuñez de Cáceres
Mirador Sur
Tel: 809 947-1005
www.cms.edu.do

New Horizons
Fully bilingual, pre-school to *bachillerato*, US curriculum,
accredited by New England Association of Schools and Colleges
Ave. Sarasota 51
Bella Vista
Tel: 809 533 4915
www.gcnewhorizons.net

St George School
Bilingual, US-accredited, pre-school - *bachillerato*
Calle Porfirio Herrera #6
Piantini
Tel: 809 562 5262
www.stgeorge.edu.do

MC School
Calle Pedro Albizu Campos #26,
Ensanche el Millón
Tel: 809 548 6620
Fax: 809 548 6777
www.mcschool.edu.do

Ashton School
Bilingual, pre-school to high school, seeking SACS[1] accreditation
Calle Jacinto Ignacio Mañón No. 16
Paraíso
Tel: 809 562 0891
www.tas.edu.do

Colegio Dominico-Americano
Pre-school to *bachillerato*, Bilingual, US curriculum, accredited by recognised US educational body
(Instituto Cultural Domínico-Americano)
Ave. Abraham Lincoln 21
Tel: 809 535 0665
www.icda.edu.do

---

[1] Southern Association of Colleges and Schools, Orlando, Fla.

The Community for Learning
Bilingual, pre-school to *bachillerato*
Carretera La Isabela #101
La Meseta de Arroyo Hondo
Tel: 809 563-2708
www.tcforlearning.edu.do

ABC (Americas Bi-cultural Academy)
Bilingual, pre-school to *bachillerato*, traditional style
Calle Fernando Valeria, Ens. La Julia
DR Education Ministry, internationally recognised
Tel: 809 535 3371 / 535 3376 / 535 3354 / 533 0056
Fax: 809 535 3342
www.abcschool.org

St Michael's School
Primary and secondary
Bilingual, US curriculum
SACS accredited
H Incháustegui 8, Piantini
Tel: 809 616 2252
www.sms.edu.do

St Thomas
Bilingual, pre-school to bachillerato, SACS accredited
Juan Tomás Mejía Cotes # 43
Arroyo Hondo
Tel: 809 732 5869 / 809 732 5870
www.saintthomas.edu.do

St Patrick School
Bilingual, US curriculum, pre-school to *bachillerato*
Calle Jose Andres Aybar Castellanos 163
La Esperilla
Tel: 809 567 5995
www.stpatrick.edu.do

St Joseph School
Pre-school to *bachillerato*
Bilingual, US curriculum
Roberto Pastoriza 701 (Primary) Rafael F Bonelli 6 (Pre-School)
Evaristo Morales
Tel: 809 540 8992 / 732 3270
Fax: 809 540 8267
www.sjs.edu.do

Centro Pedagogico Infantil Maria Montessori
Pre-school and primary
Montessori education in Spanish with bilingual option
Calle Francisco Prats Ramirez esq Olegario Tenares
Los Restauradores
Tel: 809 530 1837 / 8
Fax: 809 530 1978
www.cpimariamontessori.com.do

American School of *Santo Domingo*
Details and contact available via their website
www.assd.edu.do

Lycée Francais de Saint Domingue (AEFE[2] accredited)
French, pre-K to *bachillerato*. Students must be French speakers, non-French speakers only accepted from pre-school level.
Rafael Damirón Esq. Jimenez Moya
Centro de los Heroes
Tel: 809 533 3338 / 535 2761
Fax: 809 535 8814
www.lfsd.edu.do

Brilliant Minds School (Bilingual)
Autopista Las Americas (San Vicente exit),
Alma Rosa II,
Santo Domingo Este.
Tel: 809 597 8800 / 809 592 5353 / 809 592 5454
www.brilliantmindsschool.com

Santiago

New Horizons
Fully bi-lingual, pre-school to *bachillerato*, Accredited by the New England Association of Schools and Colleges
Calle 15 No. 3
Los Jardines Metropolitanos
Tel: 809 247 4915
Fax: 809 241 5645
www.gcnewhorizons.net/cbnh/santiago

Santiago Christian School
Sabaneta Las Palomas
Tel: 809 570 6140
Fax: 809 570 6145
www.santiagochristianschool.org

---

[2] Agence pour l'enseignement francais à l'étranger

North Coast
Sosua

Garden Kids
Proyecto Trade Winds,
Carretera Cabarete,
El Batey
Tel: 809 571 2857
www.garden-kids.org

International School of Sosua
La Mulata 1, El Batey
Tel: 809 571 3271
Fax: 809 571 1904
www.issosua.com

Puerto Plata

Alic New World – bilingual
Tel: 809 586 5617

O & M Hostos School
Bilingual curriculum
Ave. General Imbert Barrera, No. 57-A
Tel: 809 261 2319
www.oymhostosschool.com

Torre Alta Montessori School - bilingual
Achievers International Puerto Plata
Bilingual school
Francisco J. Teunado Esquina - Elena No. 2
Tel: 809 499 0497
ais.schools.officelive.com

Cabrera

Cabrera International Academy
English, Spanish and French
Lorenzo Alvarez #57
Tel: 809 757 5772
www.aicabrera.com

Samana Peninsula

Las Terrenas
Ecole Francaise Théodore Chasseriau
Tel: 809 240 6624
esc.francesa@yahoo.fr
www.ecolefrancaiselasterrenas.com

Colegio Alianza

Colegio Nuevo Despertar

Samana City

Colegio Arcoiris - bilingual

Las Galeras - French run primary school, bilingual (French Spanish)

East Coast
Punta Cana

Punta Cana International School – bilingual,
pre-school to *bachillerato*
Punta Cana Village
Tel: 809 959 3382 / 3
Fax: 809 959 3384
www.puntacana.com/grupo-puntacana/education/puntacana-international-school

Cap Cana

Cap Cana Heritage School – bi-lingual, project based learning, pre-school to *bachillerato*
Cap Cana
Tel: 809 548 6621
Fax: 809 688 4767
www.heritageschool.edu.do

Bávaro

Colegio Jardin Verde
Spanish, English and French is obligatory
Kinder to bachillerato
Av. Estados Unidos
Tel: 809 552 1075
Fax: 809 552 1677
www.colegio-jardinverde.com

Colegio Calasanz
Centro Proyecto, Calle 128 manzana 74b
Pueblo Bávaro.
Tel: 809 455 1559
www.calasanzpbavaro.edu.do

South Coast

Juan Dolio

Villas del Mar International School
Bilingual, religious school
Tel: 809 526 3117
Fax: 809 526 1757
info@vmisschools.com

La Romana

Abraham Lincoln School – English
Central Romana Corporation, La Romana, Dominican Republic
Tel: 809 523 3333
Fax: 809 687 9740
www.centralromana.com.do/cs_colegio.php

Buena Vista School – Spanish, English and French
Avenida Flamboyán 37
Buena Vista Norte
Tel/Fax: 809 550 2735
www.colegiobuenavista.com

St John School – Spanish with English and French
Prolongacion Ave. Las Palmas
Buena Vista Norte
Tel: 809 550 4358
www.saintjohn.com.do

San Pedro

Colegio Los Pininos
Calle Enrique Rijo No. 6
Miramar
Tel: 809 529 2423
Fax: 809 529 3212

Jarabacoa

Doulos
Religious, bilingual school
Ave. Confluencia #2
Tel: 809 574 2979
Fax: 809 574 4488
www.doulosdiscovery.org

Salesian College Jarabacoa
Catholic school, Spanish
Salida Carretera Constanza
Tel: 809 574 2707
Fax 809 574 6226
www.sdbj.org

UNIVERSITIES

UASD	*www.uasd.edu.do*
PUCMM	*www.pucmm.edu.do*
INTEC	*www.intec.edu.do*
UNIBE	*www.unibe.edu.do*

LANGUAGE INSTITUTES

Santo Domingo

Dominico-Americano
Ave. Abraham Lincoln, 21
Tel: 809 535 0665
Fax: 809 533 8809
www.icda.edu.do

Entrena SA
Calle Virgilio Diaz Ordoñez No. 42,
Ensanche Julieta,
Tel: 809 567 8990
Fax: 809 566 3492
info@entrenadr.com
www.entrena.com

Berlitz
Ave. 27 de Febrero #589
Los Restauradores
Tel: 809 412 8770
Fax: 809 412 8785

Santiago
Berlitz
Av. Estrella Sadhalá #44
Plaza Madera.
Tel: 809 724 8822
Fax: 809 724 8833
www.berlitz.com/Dominican.html

Immigration and visas

The DR is foreigner friendly (unless you're a Haitian, but that is a whole different story). Most foreigners enter on a thirty day tourist visa and then apply for residency. Unless you have good Spanish and a profound understanding of Dominican bureaucracy it is better to use the services of a good lawyer to obtain residency. It is possible to operate in do-it-yourself mode but this can be a frustrating and time consuming experience with many repeat visits to the *Migración* Department in Santo Domingo. By the time you have been here three years you should have enough Spanish to renew your residency without needing the services of a lawyer. Those entering on a thirty day tourist visa who do not apply for provisional residency yet remain beyond the thirty days are subject to a sliding scale of taxes when they egress the DR depending on length of overstay; the latest taxes can be viewed at *www.migracion.gov.do*. Go to Tarifas, under Servicios, and check the list headed IMPUESTOS POR ESTADIA PARA RESIDENCIA PROVISIONAL O TARJETA DE TURISTA.

Initially application is made for provisional residency, which currently takes about five months to obtain. Provisional residency lasts for one year and then permanent residency is applied for. How permanent is permanent? Two years! Foreigners will need to visit Santo Domingo every two years to renew their residency. After living here for ten years it is possible to renew residency for longer periods: four, six, eight, and ten year periods.

Regional Migración offices are now being introduced: the one in Santiago will renew residency thus enabling a much shorter journey for north coast residents than a visit to Santo Domingo. Expats need to be mindful that in the Dominican Republic the road to hell or even Santiago is paved with good intentions. As of November 2008 a 'system glitch' obliterated all the mugshot records held in the Santo Domingo *Migración* office so despite the new regional offices being in existence, expats currently due to renew their residency have once more to make the journey to Santo Domingo for new photographs. A new *Migración* office has just been opened in Puerto Plata and it, too, will offer the service of residency renewal but – not yet. For the time being, applications may be made at the Santiago office but applicants still need to go to Santo Domingo to collect their residency cards.

Lawyer fees for provisional residency will vary depending on the lawyer – somewhere in the US$1200-

1500 range would be considered reasonable. Provisional residency will necessitate at least two visits to *Migración*, chest X-ray and medical including HIV screening. Residents with permanent residency can also apply for citizenship, which bestows the right to vote and apply for a Dominican passport. Foreigners would need to check with their own countries of origin whether dual citizenship is allowed or whether they are required to surrender their original nationality. The DR, the UK and the US all recognise dual citizenship.

Previously, it was possible to circumvent the system somewhat and end up with a perfectly valid residency, which was obtained not via the services of a legitimate lawyer but via 'someone who knew someone'. Such days are past. It is highly inadvisable to try any short cut methods now: these are illegal and could well bring penalties!

Various documents will be required such as the completion of an application form (available from *Migración* in Santo Domingo or from your lawyer), authorised medical examinations including blood test and chest X-Ray; original birth certificate (translated into Spanish by a certified Dominican legal translator, then notarised/apostilled and then, if the country of birth is not a signatory to the Hague Convention Abolishing the Requirement of Legalisation for Foreign Public Documents[3], it should be sent to the Dominican Consulate in the expat's country of origin for legalisation and then ratified by the Dominican Foreign Relations Ministry);

---

[3] www.hcch.net/index_en.php?act=conventions.status&cid=41

marriage certificate (if spouses are applying jointly); notarized letter of guarantee from a Dominican person or corporation or a permanent resident, witnessed by two people (this is usually provided by the lawyer); a separate signed declaration by the guarantor, witnessed by two Dominican citizens or residents; a good conduct certificate (obtained from country of origin or country of previous five year period of residence) and a recent good conduct certificate from the Dominican Attorney General's Office, and photographs. A good lawyer will be aware of any Governmental procedural changes to this list or its application, which can (and do) occur quite frequently.

Existing expats usually have their ear to the ground as to the reputation of lawyers so the best way of finding a reputable lawyer is to go on the recommendation of a trusted third party who used the lawyer for the same function and was satisfied with the outcome. It should be noted that there are many more qualified lawyers in the DR than there is work available. Some lawyers who speak good English and specialise in working with English speaking expats are highly dependable; others are not. If a lawyer speaks your language this does not necessarily make him or her a good lawyer. It makes them a competent linguist and there is a difference. Nor should the speaking of another language be seen as a carte blanche for the lawyer to charge exorbitant fees. Choose a lawyer with great care because bad choices can have reverberations for decades as the injured expat seeks redress, which may not be forthcoming; at least, not in the way the expat had hoped. And, as in other jurisdictions, some lawyers will be more gifted in certain areas than others: the lawyer who is good at conveyancing is not necessarily the good criminal lawyer, despite what he or she tells you.

In August 2007 a new law was signed by the President allowing for 'fast-track' permanent residency for retirees. This enables permanent residency to be obtained in forty-five days and provides for tax advantages such as a fifty per cent reduction on annual property tax plus exemption of tax for a first purchase of real estate. To qualify a minimum monthly income of US$1500 is required for retirees with a government or private pension and US$2000 in verified income for all others. Having obtained their initial residency many years ago neither of the co-authors has personal experience of whether this really is an incentive scheme or a way for the Government to gain more knowledge as to the income of new residents. As of October 2007 although the new law had been signed it had yet to be promulgated – another 'work in progress'! Finally in January 2008 the new law – Ley 171-07 – was promulgated and thus is now in effect.

The main provisions are:
a) Residence Programme by Investment, created pursuant to Decree No. 950 dated as of September 20, 2001; this allows foreign investors to obtain definite residence within 45 days;
b) Dominican Republic's Customs Law No. 14-93 dated August 26, 1993, that exempts home furnishings and personal assets from tax payments;
c) Law 168 dated May 27, 1967, on the Partial Exemption from the Motor Vehicles taxes;

Additionally, retirees and passive investors, who adopt the present Law, will have the following benefits, according to the conditions and stipulations indicated in this law:

a) Exemption of real estate property transfer tax, for the first property acquired;
b) Exemption of 50% of mortgage registration tax, when the creditors are financial institutions duly regulated by the Monetary and Financial Law;
c) Exemption of 50% of real estate property tax, when applicable;
d) Exemption from taxes levied on dividend and interest payments, accrued in the DR or abroad
e) Exemption of 50% of Capital Gains Tax, as long as the passive investor is the majority shareholder of the company that is subject to payment of this tax and that such company does not have commercial and/or industrial activities as its main activities.

Further information on the provisions of Ley 171-07 can be found on the website of lawyers Pellerano & Herrera *www.phlaw.com* where Law 171-07 (in English) can be downloaded.

In October 2008 the Senate approved a measure to reduce import taxation for Dominicans living abroad who wanted to return home. The proposed legislation offers a sliding scale of discounts for vehicle imports and is geared to attracting back to the DR those who have successfully completed a higher education qualification abroad.

At the same time as application is made for residency, application will also be made for a *cédula*. The *cédula* is an

ID card that is actually used by expats far more frequently than the residency card – it verifies identity for banking and legal transactions whereas the residency card is likely to be shown only when entering or leaving the DR to verify that purchase of a tourist visa is not necessary. New expats can be confused as to the differences between residency and possession of a *cédula*: the former denotes the holder is not an illegal alien and is issued by the Migracion department; the latter is an ID card issued by the Junta Central Electoral (*JCE – the Central Electoral Board*). The *JCE* maintains the electoral rolls and whilst foreigners are not able to vote (unless they have citizenship) they still require a *cédula* for purposes itemised above. The *cédula* for foreigners was at one time gratis but now costs about US$33 and lasts for six years at which time renewal is required. 2009 was to have seen the introduction of a biometric *cédula* for locals and foreigners alike, designed to be an aid in reducing identity theft and a requirement for banking transactions. Although this process has started, economic considerations have delayed its completion. Further information can be found on the *JCE* website: *www.jce.do* and go to *Tasas Servicios Prestados*.

Finance and taxes

Taxation in the DR is governed by Law 11-92 of May 31, 1992, commonly known as the Tax Code (*Código Tributario*) and collected by the *Dirección General de Impuestos Internos* or *DGII*. This is referred to locally as *Rentas Internas*.

All income derived from work or business activities in the DR is taxable, no matter if the person is a Dominican, a resident foreigner, or a non-resident foreigner. Income derived from work done outside of the DR by Dominicans or resident foreigners, is not taxable in the DR. Income from financial sources abroad such as stocks and bonds or certificates of deposit is technically taxable in the DR (article 269) and becomes payable three years after obtaining residency but is rarely enforced due to the difficulty of finding out exactly what investments foreign residents have abroad. Pensions and Social Security benefits are exempt from this taxation. 182 days per year of living in the DR constitutes residence.

Income tax for individuals is paid on a sliding scale: the first RD$349,326.00 (approximately US$9,500) of annual income is tax free, from RD$349,326.01 to RD$523,988.00 (approx. US$14,200) it is taxed at 15%, from RD$ 523,988.01 to RD$727,761.00 it is taxed at 20% on the difference above RD$523,988.01 and those earning RD$727,761.001 (approx. US$19,700) and upwards will pay RD$66,954 (approx US$1,800) plus 25% of the difference above RD$727,761.001. In early 2011 the tax office announced that the tax-free threshold was being raised to RD$30,195 per month, or RD$362,340 per year (just under US$10,000).

Corporations pay a flat 27% income tax on net taxable income. Capital gains are taxed as regular income but the original acquisition value will be adjusted for inflation in calculations.

Value added tax is known as *ITBIS* in the DR and is at 16%. There are exemptions for medicines, basic foodstuffs and utilities. Selective consumption tax applies to tobacco, alcohol, vehicles and guns (!) and varies item to item.

Property taxes consist of an annual luxury tax (*IPI/VSS*) on properties valued above RD$5,000,000 (US$135,000) at a rate of 1% of the balance of value above the five million peso mark and, at the point of purchase, a one off property transfer tax of 3%, plus 1.3% stamp tax plus in the near future the likelihood of a 2% Registry Tax. This is based on the market value of the property as determined by the appraisal done by the *DGII*, not on the price of purchase stated in the deed of sale, nor indeed what the property might actually be worth. For example, if a property is valued at RD$7,389,680 (about US$200,000), the owner will pay 1% on the balance above five million pesos, namely RD$24,000 (US$649) a year – not a lot when considering property taxes in other jurisdictions. Most expats are likely to be cash purchasers of property but for those who are not a 2% tax is levied on all mortgages. Property buyers who wish to lessen the impact of transfer taxes may choose to place their property in a corporation but it is advisable to take legal advice on whether this will benefit a purchaser's individual circumstances since these will vary purchaser to purchaser.

A 2% tax is also levied on any change of ownership of motor vehicles and there is a small tax on annual licence plate renewals; for older vehicles US$33 and for newer ones US$66.

The estate of any person, Dominican or foreign, whose last domicile was in the DR, is subject to Dominican inheritance taxes. Law 288-04 lowered inheritance taxes to 3% of the value of the estate, after deductions, as determined by the tax authorities. Medical and funeral expenses, as well as outstanding debts and mortgages, are some of the allowed deductions. The rate is increased to 4.5% for beneficiaries who do not reside in the DR. This is likely to apply to some retiree expats who choose to leave their property to family back in their countries of origin. Gifts are taxed at 25% with exemptions for small amounts and charitable institutions.

For a detailed description of all taxation readers of Spanish can visit the Taxation Department website *www.dgii.gov.do/Paginas/Index.aspx*

Foreigners considering setting up a business in the DR or setting up their own company would be strongly advised to consult an accountant. The DR has recently moved from being fairly lax about company taxation procedures to having an advanced case of procedural bureaucracy and understanding the minutiae and intricacies of the system is beyond the scope of this book.

Foreigners have no problem with opening a bank account in the DR subject to the usual checks and recommendations. If you enter the bank with an existing client it is even easier – who you know counts in the DR! It is recommended in any event that once you have chosen or been allocated a bank official to process the application, care is taken to remain with the same official. It has been known that different officials in the same bank have requested different documentation! Many expats also retain a bank account back in their country of origin for convenience. Retirees can receive pensions into such an account, which can then be accessed via ATMs in the DR. There have been ATM frauds such as skimming in some of the tourist areas but this is a worldwide problem. Credit cards and debit cards can be used in all tourist areas and the larger stores.

One aspect of banking in the DR that might catch the new expat unawares is the likelihood that if there are no deposits into, or withdrawals from, an account in a three month period, then the account will be deemed inactive. There is no difficulty in reactivating an inactive account, but inactive accounts will bring higher charges; after a three-month period of inactivity the charge will increase. This applies to both current and savings accounts. Ginnie discussed at length with her bank the non-logicality of applying this to interest generating accounts, where the interest payment will be automatically credited monthly thus removing the possibility of 'no deposits or withdrawals'. She was told that this does not apply and there still has to be a 'movement' (presumably an automatic credit does not count as being a 'movement').

For those who receive income written on a dollar cheque on a US bank it is possible to deposit this into a US dollar savings account in a Dominican bank. However clearance of the cheque can take forty-five days. What most expats do is to form a relationship with a local currency exchange house (*cambio*) that will change the cheque for cash immediately. It can take some time to be recognised as a person whose cheques do not bounce (!); this process will be hastened no end by going in with an existing client of the exchange house.

The DR's macro-economic environment received a shock to the system in 2003 with the collapse of Banco Intercontinental. In 2002, Banco Intercontinental (Baninter), the third largest commercial bank in the DR, started experiencing a wave of withdrawals from depositors. Later, the Central Bank of the Dominican Republic (Banco Central) intervened by extending liquidity assistance up to three times the bank's subscribed capital, double the statutory limit of one and a half times the amount. However, this was not sufficient to restore confidence and, in May 2003, Baninter filed for bankruptcy, a substantial part of its business being acquired by a large Canadian bank (Scotiabank).

It was then revealed that Baninter had been running a parallel accounting system since 1989 to channel funds, in the form of promissory notes, to off-shore entities under the control of common family interests in other words a colossal fraud by the bank's owners and administrators which was linked to political corruption and influence peddling, rife under different party political administrations. The demise of Baninter triggered a domino effect, disturbing two mid-sized banking groups, Banco Nacional de Crédito and Banco Mercantil, which were sold to other banks. The negative consequences of the Baninter bankruptcy were also felt in the insurance sector, where the three largest companies linked to the above mentioned banks also went into receivership.

The Baninter crisis and its sequels revealed serious shortcomings in accounting and financial reporting practices (loan loss provisions understated, hidden liabilities, etc.). Moreover, supervision of commercial banks by both Banco Central and the Superintendence of Banks was found to be inadequate. The impact on the Dominican economy was devastating. By January 2004 – seven months after the bank's collapse – the peso's exchange rate had fallen to 50-1 against the dollar and inflation was rampant. The economy looked like it would surrender all of the gains won during the 1990s, one of the most sustained economic surges in the history of Latin America. To make matters worse, the IMF suspended a vital loan intended to help the DR avert default on its scheduled foreign debt payment, due to President Mejía's purchase of two private energy distribution facilities that once were state-owned. The IMF eventually recanted on its threats and the loan was dispersed, but not before the peso slid even further against the dollar.

To understand the size of the impact of the Baninter collapse, economist Hector Salcedo told Hoy newspaper that the salvage operation for fraud at Mercantil, Bancredito and Baninter banks represented 18% of the DR's GDP. It is generally agreed that a twelve or fifteen year period would be required to overcome all the consequences of Baninter and that the cost to the taxpayer was in the region of US$3.2 billion.

Following Baninter, a Stand-By Arrangement with the International Monetary Fund (IMF) provided for the strengthening of the banking sector, including enhanced regulatory supervision such that there could be no repeat of this occurrence in relation to other banks. By 2008 Baninter's owners had been prosecuted and sentenced to terms of imprisonment ranging from five to ten years although there is some scepticism as to whether full sentences will be served. The political recipients of the Baninter largesse have been neither prosecuted nor sentenced. More can be read about the Baninter collapse and results in a report entitled Report on the Observance of Standards and Codes (ROSC) Dominican Republic Accounting and Auditing December 30, 2004 downloadable from the World Bank website: *www.worldbank.org/ifa/rosc_aa_dr_eng.pdf*

Since the new administration of 2004-2008-2012 the peso/dollar exchange rate has exhibited far more stable characteristics. However, since the DR currency exchange rate does not simply respond to market forces it should be noted that this stability was convenient for the Government in terms of its fuel purchases, which are dollar billed. According to the *CIA* World Factbook the economy is growing at a respectable rate; however it must be remembered that any acceptance of DR Governmental perceptions will have a certain amount of embedded spin. The Central Bank calculated the inflation rate for 2009 at 5.8%. In June 2009 *Diario Libre* reported that in just over three years, government domestic borrowing rose by US$3.08 billion. It increased from US$1.11 billion to US$4.19 billion from 2006 to 20 April 2009.

High unemployment and underemployment remain an important challenge as does marked income inequality; the poorest half of the population receives less than one-fifth of GNP, while the richest 10% enjoys nearly 40% of national income (for more on this subject see *Politics and Legal*). The Central America-Dominican Republic Free Trade Agreement (DR-CAFTA) came into force in March 2007 but as yet has not turned out to be the boon for the DR which some alleged it would be. Between May 2007 and August 2008 the DR accumulated a trade deficit of US$3.48 billion with the US. From January to August 2008, the deficit increased by US$885 million, or 85% more than during the same period in 2007 when the agreement was not in place. This trend has continued; a report by economist Luis H Vargas in May 2010, based on statistics from the US Department of Commerce, reveals that during the first quarter of 2010 the DR continued to lose its market share in the exports of DR-CAFTA countries to the US. During that quarter the deficit increased 46.6% from US$488.4 million to US$716.1 million. This was due to an increase in imports of 21.4% to US$1.53 billion from US$1.26 billion and only a slight increase in exports of 5.5%.

As of 2008, the Dominican Republic had mutual investment promotion and protection agreements in force with Argentina, Chile, Chinese Taipei (more commonly known as Taiwan), Ecuador, Finland, France, Italy, Morocco, the Netherlands, Panama, the Republic of Korea, Spain, and Switzerland and is in negotiation with 16 other countries. In order to prevent double taxation, the DR has an agreement in force with Canada and, in mid-2008, it was in the process of negotiating tax agreements with Chile, Chinese Taipei, the Czech Republic, Kuwait, the Russian Federation, Spain, and Trinidad and Tobago. It also maintains an agreement on the exchange of tax information with the United States.

Real estate

Buying real estate can be a minefield in the DR – a successful experience will depend on the quality of the potential purchaser's planning and acquiring a good lawyer. Property cannot be safely bought from the internet without ever setting foot in the country; unfortunately the gullible do and live to regret the consequences. Real estate agents in the Dominican Republic are not licensed or regulated by the government and nor are real estate websites. It is possible to find real estate websites on the internet which have clearly been set up by people who have never visited the country, let alone lived here. While these occasion much mirth among long-term residents, they sadly lead the prospective purchaser to believe that buying property in the DR is a risk-free process.

Generally speaking it is not a good idea to buy property before a permanent move to the DR. The best advice is to move, rent for at least six months, look around for an area which suits the prospective purchaser, talk to the longer term expats about any issues in the area (crime rate, for example, or local river flooding, or how often that intriguing odour wafts over from the tip or sewage works …)

Find the realtors who have a sense of integrity. Since realtors will gain a higher rate of commission by selling a property they have listed, as opposed to acting as a sub-agent and splitting the commission, there is a tendency for the purchaser not to be informed about other properties that meet the purchaser's criteria. Persistence and assertiveness on the part of the purchaser are required on this issue.

Wooden house built in the traditional Victorian gingerbread style

Quite apart from dodgy realtors there are also land titles, which are based more on optimism than legal foundation, and lawyers who technically are working for you… until you discover that they are getting an ex-gratia payment from the vendor. We could go on and on; alternatively hang out in any expat bar and the stories will hit you thick and fast. That said, the sensible real estate purchaser who has done their homework and got himself a good lawyer can make a successful purchase and many do.

Real estate purchases in the Dominican Republic do not usually follow the US pattern of a written offer tendered by the buyer to the seller, followed by the seller's written acceptance. Instead, after verbal agreement is reached by the buyer and seller on the price, a binding Promise of Sale is prepared by a lawyer or notary public and is signed by both parties. This document it is more important than the Deed of Sale, since it generally contains a complete and detailed description of the entire transaction up to the time when the purchase price has been paid in full.

It is crucial that the Promise of Sale contains a default clause. If the buyer is allowed to pay a large percentage of the price of sale without any security or direct interest over the property the buyer's remedies may be limited to suing the seller personally in the event of misuse of funds. Most developers use the buyers' funds, along with a bank loan, to finance the construction. The bank issues a mortgage on the property as collateral. If the developer runs into financial difficulties or misappropriates the funds, the bank forecloses and the buyers lose both their money and the property.

The lawyer's due diligence on the property should include a search for liens and encumbrances on the property – otherwise these will become the responsibility of the buyer. Among the documentation now required for a title search at the Land Registry is a *deslinde* – a Government approved subdivision registration that de-limits the exact location and boundaries of the plot. As well as a title search, the buyer's lawyer should arrange for an independent survey, an inspection of any plans for improvements, the existence of the correct permits, that previous employees have been paid severance, that all prior utility bills have been paid and that there are no squatters on the property. The lawyer should also discover whether the seller had arranged for any prior illegal hook-ups to utilities, otherwise the purchaser will be surprised by officials from the water company, for example, visiting to collect their monthly 'benefit'. In fact the lawyer should not allow the purchaser to inherit such a situation and should insist that it is corrected prior to sale.

The lawyer's due diligence should also include a search as to whether the land in question comes under the law concerning protected areas (*Ley sectorial de áreas protegidas, Ley 202 de 2004*). A recent (June 2010) incident in Las Terrenas concerning the Plaza Milano project has revealed that Ministry of Environment permissions have had fake signatures applied. Most of the owners are foreigners, many of whom apparently gained ownership prior to 2004, yet who were told at the time that they need not be concerned!

A squatter in the DR has the right to obtain compensation for any improvements made in good faith on the property. Land acquisition, through what is called *usucapión* (ownership through possession), can only happen when the land in question is not a registered property and if the squatters can prove they have inhabited it as theirs for an uninterrupted period of more than twenty years. However, in the case of registered properties the compensation for improvements is required. Although a Court judgement may be made against squatters that does not get them off the land! Enforced eviction of

Dominicans (if one could find someone to do it!) is not going to win a popularity contest for the new *gringo* so it is best to avoid the situation altogether.

Property law in the DR tends to favour renter over landlord so a ruling issued by the Supreme Court on December 3rd 2008 was something of a milestone. This said that property owners can evict a tenant when the tenant uses the property for a purpose other than that which was specified in the written contract and furthermore that the lease ends at the expiration of the fixed term, when this was established in writing, without the need to begin the cumbersome eviction process. Those wanting to read the ruling can do so by downloading this PDF file from the Supreme Court's website:

www.suprema.gov.do/novedades/sentencias/2008/Julio_Giraldez_Casasnovas_Vs_Antun_Hermanos%20.pdf

There are at least two companies offering title insurance in the DR – First American Title Insurance Company and Stewart Title who will indemnify the real estate buyer in case title to the property is defective. In the event of a lawsuit disputing the title, the title insurance company will defend the buyer in court and if the lawsuit is lost will pay all valid claims or losses up to the amount of the policy.

Legal advice should be sought as to whether the property should be put in the name of a company for tax reasons. As each expat is in an individually different situation the advice will vary. Retirees entering on the 'fast-track' incentive programme are entitled to a 50% reduction in capital gains tax.

The days of the under US$100,000 beachfront villa on the north coast have passed and prices of the more luxurious of the upmarket developments in the east and south can go to over US$3 million. However, go inland a little and prices drop markedly – a four-bedroom villa for US$130,000 for example. Of course, if you're really strapped for cash and fancy going native in a *barrio* then US$20,000 will buy you a block-built, two-storied house with four or five bedrooms. Building costs for the sort of home most expats would want will start at US$800 per square metre.

The option that most retiring Dominicans who have the funds use, is to buy a plot of land and build their own home exactly as they want it (vagaries of builder permitting). This is what Ginnie and her partner Grahame did and the detail is spelled out in *Quisqueya: Mad Dogs and English Couple* (Paperback).

It is possible to reduce costs markedly by becoming your own contractor and hiring the specialist labour required – doing it this way can reduce costs to US$300 per square metre. Even if you do not do this and instead employ an engineer to oversee all the work you will still need to be 'hands-on' to supervise the overseer. However, this is one way of ensuring that a developer is not selling you a shoddy property built on the cheap that will later display all manner of structural faults. Three years after Ginnie finished building her home the north coast of the DR had one of its rare serious earthquakes (minor quakes are normal). You will be pleased to hear that her home successfully withstood it, suffering nothing more than superficial plaster cracks.

More information on purchasing real estate can be found on the website *www.phlaw.com* where the February 2008 document Purchase of Real Estate in DR can be downloaded and on the website *www.dr1.com* where How To Buy Real Estate In The Dominican Republic can be found, also dated February 2008.

Safety and security

In the 1990s when the authors first moved to the Dominican Republic, it was possible to leave your front door open and no one would have entered your home. In common with the rest of the Caribbean and much of Latin America, crime and particularly that associated with the narcotics trade, is now a fact of life. Of course crime in the rest of the world has also escalated and long-term expats can easily forget this when they visit their country of origin (as Ginnie found out to her cost when she had her bag stolen in a UK shopping centre!).

The escalation of drug abuse in the DR has been very rapid and most has occurred in the past seven years. In 2007 CNN coverage of the Dominican Republic as a drug runners' haven led to increased concern over the impact of this on tourism, one of the staples of the Dominican economy.

Whilst the DR has historically been a transhipment point for drugs going from Colombia to the US for at least the last twenty years, very little remained in the country. All of that changed with the dawn of the new millennium. Latin American drug lords decided to pay off the politicians and military to 'look the other way' in kind rather than cash. As inflation spiralled upwards and the value of the peso fell by 100% as a result of the *Baninter* collapse described in the section on Finance and Taxes above, those receiving 'kind' rather than cash needed to create a market in order to liquidate their 'assets'.

Sadly, thus it was that cocaine and particularly crack entered the *barrios* of the DR. The market was created by Dominicans on Dominicans. In the space of little more than six years the Dominican Republic changed from being drug-free to being just like everywhere else. However, unlike some other places, law enforcement in the DR is both weak and corrupt. Lack of interdiction resources also weighs heavily in the equation. Then there are members of the judiciary who have handed out some findings which beggar belief; or at least lead to the conclusion that they, too, are beneficiaries of this growth industry. So, honest law enforcement personnel and prosecutors become discouraged as they see known dealers walk free.

Even more worrying are revelations of just how high up in the political hierarchy the rot ascends. In 2008 as a result of the murder of seven foreign traffickers on Dominican soil, Senator Wilton Guerrero produced evidence linking the narco-industry to the highest echelons of military and political circles. In late 2009 the spectacular escape of fugitive Puerto Rican drug lord José Figueroa Agosto, who was revealed to have lived large and unmolested in the DR for many years, opened an even more staggering can of worms with tentacles reaching to the highest echelons of the military, government and society. More detail about the DR drug industry can be found in an article on Offshore Wave (reference 2 in the reading list below) and in the latest US State Department's International Narcotics Control Strategy Report which in 2010 is presented in two separate reports, one on the drug trade and the second on money laundering (reference 5 in the reading list below).

Inevitably, crime has increased in the *barrios* as dealers and distributors fight over turf. But neither tourists nor expats tend to live in the *barrios* and visiting at night is inadvisable. Direct crime against tourists is fairly rare: guests at some of the all-inclusive resorts have suffered a few problems from addicts who need resources for their next fix, yet are residents of a country where half the population live on less than US$2 a day. In February 2007 a French Canadian lottery winner discovered that the DR is not the place for the very *nouveau riche* who cannot resist the urge to display their winnings ostentatiously (details in reference 3 at the end of this section).

The most noticeable impact of drug-related crime has been on the residents of the DR not the tourists. Expat residents are not singled out for special attention unless their behaviour is perceived as an open invitation to become a crime victim. Petty thieves seem to operate in an equal opportunity mode with Dominicans being victims far more frequently than expats simply because more Dominicans live in the DR than do expats.

The crime most likely to affect some expats is home robbery as funds are sought to fuel a habit. Some locations are more prone than others, which is another very good reason to carefully investigate the location of your intended property purchase. However, the DR is not as bad as many parts of Latin America or the Caribbean with regard to crime (the things they don't tell you about on the glossy pages advertising your second home abroad in Mexico or Jamaica) so a paranoid fortress mentally is not necessary. Sensible home protection measures and sensible reduction of setting yourself up as a target are necessary. Many homes have window protection using iron bars as a deterrent. The use of exterior lighting linked to motion sensors linked to an alarm can foil an attempted robbery before it really starts. So too can a dog or even a goose.

Kidnapping of foreigners, as yet, is not a large problem in the Dominican Republic. It did happen to a US female resident of Samaná on the north east coast in September 2007 but was resolved speedily and in an exemplary fashion with no payment of ransom or physical harm to the victim and with the captors arrested three days after the crime which should have served as a deterrent (reference 4 at the end of this section). Unfortunately, a few weeks later some of those arrested made bail in what was perceived as an all too easy fashion, which points, yet again, to flaws in the judicial system. There is a small amount of kidnapping of Dominicans; this frequently is connected to outstanding debts or drug industry issues.

It should not be forgotten that some of the expat population themselves are active participants in the drugs industry either as users or, even more lamentably, as dealers or exporters. Stiff prison sentences are usually meted out to those expats who abuse the trust of the host nation by involving themselves in the drugs business but it is a fact of life that where corruption exists it is always possible to buy one's way out of trouble. Prosecutors are currently seeking sentences of fifteen years imprisonment for foreigners caught attempting to leave their holiday destination in the DR with four or five extra kilos. In December 2008 a judge meted out a 'light' sentence of eight years to two French women because of their youth (eighteen and nineteen years of age respectively) and the fact that it was a first offence. It probably does not need to be said that our advice to new expats would be to have absolutely no involvement with drugs in any fashion whatsoever. This includes not discussing the subject with anyone you don't know and being mindful that even wearing a Bob Marley t-shirt or cannabis leaf earrings could give the police reason to detain or search. Gardeners should take note that growing certain plants could land them into trouble, not just the obvious but even ornamental plants with narcotic qualities like *bugmansia*/angel trumpets.

The numbers of expats involved in the narco-industry is small compared to those who come looking for cheap sex. Sadly, some of these are child abusers. Foreign predators are not just breaking Dominican law but many are breaking the laws of their homeland that cover offences carried out on foreign soil. There is a growing band of expat residents prepared to involve themselves in reporting such activity to international law enforcement agencies. After all, sexual predators are not difficult to spot. A pair of overweight North American or European men aged in their sixties or seventies having the time of their lives in a bar while accompanied by a couple of bored or scared thirteen year old Dominican girls (or boys) may be a telltale sign.

But not all foreigners looking for love are child molesters. The adult sex industry thrives despite the best efforts of the Dominican Government to promote the DR as a family destination. Tourists who have been here before have noted that the prostitutes are getting pushier, particularly in certain locations like Sosua on the north coast and Boca Chica in the south. Many ply a second trade as pickpockets. Some tourists and residents of these towns have found that whilst rejecting the overt massage of the service first offered, they have inadvertently become victims of a covert massage as wallets are extracted from back pockets.

The other concerning trend has been the number of alleged 'crimes of passion' involving foreigners. Whether these are drug or avarice-related is difficult to distinguish but in 2007 a number of foreign men lost their lives: In September a forty-three year-old Italian businessman resident in Esperanza was allegedly poisoned by his Dominican wife and her boyfriend; in October a twenty-nine year-old French businessman resident in Las Terrenas was murdered by the boyfriend of his girlfriend; and in November a forty-six year-old Canadian resident was clubbed to death in Costambar, Puerto Plata and his girlfriend was subsequently arrested.

In one sense it is not clear whether these men made poor choices of partner (although in another sense, it is abundantly clear) or whether the Dominicanas' boyfriend in the background was part of what the International

Narcotics Control Strategy Report, produced by the US State Department in March 2008 refers to as 'Dominican criminal organizations'. Nor is it clear whether such murders were the culmination of years of marital strife. What is clear is that pushy *putas* are not the only thing to be careful of when looking for love in the DR! Some women who make themselves available to be the girlfriends or wives of foreigners are becoming increasingly sophisticated in the scams they pull. Mostly, it is about money and the foreigner will be poorer, wiser yet still alive after the event. However, some Dominican women are now being pimped by foreigners who bring increased knowledge from their criminal pasts. If the rejected *gringo* does not have the sense to walk away and learn from his lesson, preferring to fight to reclaim that of which he was scammed, he might just find that his days are numbered.

All of the above information needs to be set within the context of what is happening in the rest of the world. The Dominican Republic is no different from other parts of the Caribbean and Latin America so there is no need to remove it from the expats' destinations list. Jamaica's wish to reintroduce hanging as a penalty is not because their crime rate has dropped! And for DR expat residents, life is not on a par with certain other Latin American countries where more of a fortress mentality is necessary. Vigilant expats will find the many advantages of life in the DR far outweigh its current disadvantages, but vigilance is necessary and it needs to become an automatic, internalised response. Then residents can get on and enjoy their lives as so many of us do; no need for a fortress mentality because self-protection is automatically considered.

It is possible to purchase home wall and/or floor safes in the DR – common sense indicates a purchase from a store that is not in the immediate vicinity of the home, and the installation of the safe either by its owner or a trusted friend. There are security companies in the DR that offer home protection services. New expats are advised to check the credentials of such companies very carefully indeed. Having a *guachiman* (Dominicanism derived from the English 'watchman') to guard your home can be a mixed blessing – companies pay their guards low wages and for this the guards are not going to put themselves at risk if confronted by armed intruders. Indeed some guards act as information conduits relaying intelligence to interested parties as to when the home has no occupants. Thus presenting oneself to a security company as a potential customer can be the equivalent of walking into the lion's den and saying 'baaaah'. That also goes for security companies set up by certain expats themselves who have, shall we say, a somewhat unorthodox methodology for drumming up business.

Never in any circumstances be fooled into thinking that just because this person is another expat they will be operating from a higher ethical position.

In the event that the expat experiences an armed robbery and shoots to deter yet unavoidably terminates the intruder, the best advice is to make sure that the body is totally within the confines of your property, that you ensure your lawyer is immediately available and you subsequently call the police. It is permissible for Dominican citizens and legal foreign residents to apply for a weapons permit but this can only be done after a *cédula* is obtained. The procedure is to buy a legal weapon at a gun dealership that remains there until the permit is obtained. Requirements are a drug test, attendance at a weapons safety class, an on-range demonstration of competence with a firearm and also a psychiatric test. Several weeks later the permit will be issued and delivered to the dealership before the weapon can be collected. Further information is available from the Ministry of Interior and Police website referenced at 6 below. Despite the high cost of weapons in the DR it is not advisable to attempt procurement of an illegal weapon; it runs the risk of being charged with the prior homicides in which that weapon was involved. In late 2010 the authorities announced a plan to 'disarm' the population in 2011 by amending Law 36 on possession of weapons; but whether this is translated into action remains to be seen.

FURTHER READING

1. Drug flights surge in Caribbean en route to US
   http://edition.cnn.com/2007/WORLD/americas/07/11/drug.flights/index.html

2. 'Crime, Drugs and Expat Security in The Dominican Republic' by Ginnie Bedggood
   www.offshorewave.com/offshorenews/crime-drugs-and-expat-security-in-the-dominican-republic-by-ginnie-bedggood.html

3. Canadian millionaire loses finger in DR robbery
   www.cbc.ca/news/canada/montreal/story/2007/02/02/mil lionaire-finger.html
4. FW retiree kidnapped in the Dominican Republic
   http://abcnews.go.com/GMA/story?id=3641680&page=1
5. International Narcotics Control Strategy Report - The Caribbean
   www.state.gov/p/inl/rls/nrcrpt/2008/vol1/html/100778.htm
   www.state.gov/documents/organization/137411.pdf
   www.state.gov/documents/organization/137429.pdf
6. Ministry of Interior and Police website
   www.seip.gob.do
7. Crime, Violence and Development: Trends, Costs and Policy Options in the Caribbean: A Joint Report by the United Nations Office on Drugs and Crime and the Latin America and the Caribbean Region of the World Bank March 2007
   http://siteresources.worldbank.org/INTHAITI/Resources/ Crimeandviolenceinthecaribbeanfullreport.pdf
8. 'Tourism and Crime in the Caribbean' by Klaus de Albuquerque and Jerome McElroy
   www.popcenter.org/problems/crimes_against_tourists/PD Fs/deAlbuquerque_McElroy_1999.pdf

Politics and legal

National powers in the Dominican Republic are divided between three independent executive, legislative, and judicial branches. The President appoints the Cabinet, executes laws passed by the Congress, and is commander in chief of the armed forces. The president and vice president run for office on the same ticket and are elected by direct vote for four year terms. Legislative power is exercised by a bicameral Congress composed of the Senate and the Chamber of Deputies.

Millions of dollars are spent on election propaganda, campaigning and vote buying of one sort or another. The political system is characterized by clientelism, which has corrupted the system throughout the years; recommended reading on this is Keefer's work, the first reference in the reading list below. An obscene visual of clientelism can be seen the day after elections as supporters line up for their perks and rewards in the shape of posts and jobs the distribution of which appears to have scant bearing on the particular talents of the appointee. This system appears to operate regardless of which political party is in the ascendancy.

The three major parties are the conservative *Partido Reformista Social Cristiano* (*PRSC*), in power 1966–78 and 1986–96; the social democratic *Partido Revolucionario Dominicano* (*PRD*), in power in 1963, 1978–86, and 2000–04; and the increasingly conservative *Partido de la Liberación Dominicana* (*PLD*), in power 1996–2000, 2004-2008 and re-elected in 2008 when incumbent Leonel Fernandez gained 53% of the vote. He defeated Miguel

Vargas Maldonado, of the *PRD*, a former minister in Mejía's government, who achieved a 40.48% share of the vote. Amiable Aristy Castro, of the *PRSC*, achieved only 4.59% of the vote despite showering the masses with salami, frozen chickens and cash thrown out of a helicopter. Other minority candidates, including former Attorney General Guillermo Moreno from the *Movimiento Independencia, Unidad y Cambio* (*MIUCA*) and *PRSC* former presidential candidate and defector Eduardo Estrella, obtained less than 1% of the vote.

Pico Duarte - the highest peak in the Caribbean, just over 3,000m

If elections in the DR sound like a spectacle, they are! Amusing for the expat on first experiencing this, but after witnessing several, what impacts is the sad exploitation of hundreds of thousands of people insufficiently educated to be able to effectively challenge the way in which they are being manipulated. And they are insufficiently educated because the current DR Government chooses to pour money into building the Santo Domingo Metro (Public Transport system) rather than adequately funding state education and health.

Municipal elections are no freer of corruption than Presidential elections – see references 2 and 3 in the reading list at the end of this section. The run up to the municipal and congressional elections of May 2010 was a particularly hard fought episode because the prize this time around was to be a six-year term as opposed to the normal four-year term, as a precursor to combined Presidential, congressional and municipal elections in 2016. What comes as a shock to many expats is not the battle between different political parties, since this is ubiquitous and universal, but the back-stabbing that occurs inside each political party as different factions and individuals jockey for pre-eminent position.

A friend of the authors has a husband who ran for municipal office in these elections; he gained the vote to be municipal candidate, defeating the incumbent, despite the latter's attempt at count rigging. What followed was a soap opera of attempted bribes, threats and worse until the rightful candidate took his case to the arbitrating body, the *Camara Contenciosa* (Disputes Chamber) of the Central Electoral Board (JCE) who duly ruled in his favour. This ruling made little difference to the incumbent who waited until the candidate was announcing his victory on local radio and at that exact same moment sent an employee to obtain the one and only inscription form from the local *Junta Municipal Electoral* and inscribed himself as candidate, in flagrant disregard for the laws of the land! And remember that this is all happening prior to the official announcement of who will be candidates. The real election campaign between different party aspirants for the same position was, at that stage, yet to come!

Against this backdrop, the corruption that foreigners come up against such as municipal and governmental functionaries expecting bribes to perform their jobs sinks into insignificance. In any event, paying for a service to be expedited (queue jumping) is acceptable to most and has even been institutionalised at the *Migración* Department where same day service for renewal of *residencia* costs about US$50 extra. Extortion is less acceptable but it is possible for expats to learn the skills and self-presentation to minimise the occurrences.

The exploitation of the under-educated masses is further enhanced by the historical significance of thirty years of dictatorship under Trujillo followed by another thirty years of presidential rule by a close Trujillo ally. Set that alongside a 'democracy' in which a President can exercise unusual discretionary authority and the putting of the word democracy into parentheses does not seem so unusual. 'Unusual discretionary authority' also spreads to the ability to issue Presidential pardons for prisoners three times a year. As of December 2008 one of the prisoners thus pardoned was a woman convicted in the multi-million Baninter scandal. In December 2009 the two French female prisoners sentenced for drug trafficking and referred to in the section on Safety and Security were also pardoned.

After the disastrous President Mejía years (see Finance and Taxes above) there was much hope in 2004 for the new President Fernandez administration, buttressed by promises of Governmental austerity. But austerity did not happen and Governmental expenditure increased (and not on education, health and infrastructure – with the exception of the Metro!). Most disappointing in view of the widely held belief that President Fernandez's administration would be different from President Mejía's.

Perhaps the electorate had forgotten the *PEME* (*Programa de Empleo Minimo Eventual*) scandal when President Fernandez left office in 2000. The Head of *PEME* was accused of paying US$60 million out of the budget for the programme to individuals in poor neighbourhoods so that they would not stage protests against President Fernandez's government. The Corruption Prevention Department alleged that *PEME* did not account for how funds were being raised or distributed, and how it was looted of over US$100 million. President Mejia chose not to prosecute President Fernandez when he took power in 2000 as a Council on Hemispheric Affairs paper clarifies (reference 4 at the end of this section). Less than a week after his inauguration in 2004, CNN's headline read 'President taps tainted officials for posts' (reference 5) – President Leonel Fernandez gave top posts to four officials charged with involvement in the disappearance of millions of dollars in public funds in the late 1990s – the selfsame *PEME* scandal. One of the four was placed in charge of the 'legacy' Metro project! So perhaps the indicators were there all along that the irrational exuberance of the Dominican electorate in voting President Fernandez into power in 2004 would inevitably lead to broken promises? Then again, what alternative did they have?

Despite the broken austerity promises President Fernandez was again returned to power in 2008. At his inauguration he announced a Constitutional Reform Bill (reference 6) that would allow him to run for office (again!) in 2016. The new Constitution was adopted in 2010. The expat can be forgiven for scratching his head in disbelief that the 'will of the people' seems prone to memory lapse or as Uruguayan political thinker Eduardo Galeano describes Latin American politics 'condemned to amnesia'. But in order to understand politics in the DR now it is necessary to set this in a historical perspective and to this end Frank Moya Pons book is required reading (reference 7). Also useful is reference 8.

It is not always easy to gain a clear picture of political achievements in the DR. Government websites are full of spin. Compare for example the Government sponsored publication Dominican Republic: A Caribbean Economic Success Story (reference 10) with the United Nations Development Programme 2008 Dominican Republic Human Development Report (reference 11). The latter makes it abundantly clear that despite increased investment into the DR, the benefits are not filtering down to the poorest. Indeed the DR province that generated the most wealth in recent years, La Altagracia, with its tourist development of Punta Cana, demonstrates dramatically low human development on the indicators used by the researchers. The most recent UNDP report of June 2010 reiterates that little has changed (reference 14).

The DR's legal system is headed by a Supreme Court of Justice which is appointed by a National Judicial Council, which consists of the President, the leaders of both houses of Congress, the President of the Supreme Court, and an opposition or non–governing–party member. One other Supreme Court Justice acts as secretary of the Council, a non–voting position. The Supreme Court has sole authority over managing of the court system and in hearing actions against the president, designated members of his Cabinet, and members of Congress when the legislature is in session. The Supreme Court hears appeals from lower courts and chooses members of lower courts. The new Constitution of 2010 has created limits on Supreme Court powers with the introduction of a Constitutional Tribunal and a judicial council.

The legal system of the DR reflects the influence of successive occupancy of the island by foreign nations. At the time of Haitian occupation the French legal system was imposed, during the US military intervention of 1916-24 the Torrens system of land registration was adopted, modelled on the Philippines and Australian Torrens system, and remains in effect today. From the 1990s onwards there were revisions to both the Criminal Procedure Code and the Penal Code designed to protect the rights of the public against arbitrary arrest and to provide services via a Public Defenders Office to those of limited resources. Access to legal services by the poor has improved markedly but certain Penal Code revisions have resulted in Fiscals having to free some arrestees who are known offenders, much to the chagrin of the arresting police officers. Further detail about the DR's legal system and how it has evolved is available in Marisol Florén-Romero's Guide to Legal Research in the Dominican Republic (reference 13).

Issues about the DR's legal system in relation to property have already been covered in the section on Real Estate. The statute book has all the legislation needed to protect property rights; the issue is not the legislation so much as its application through a judicial system the members of which are not free of the taint of corruption. The expat needs to make a judicious choice of lawyer and take recommendations from others who have employed the services of that legal firm with satisfactory results.

FURTHER READING

1. The political economy of public spending decisions in the Dominican Republic: credibility, clientelism and political institutions by Philip Keefer Report prepared for the Public Expenditure and Institutional Review, The Dominican Republic March 28, 2002
   www1.worldbank.org/publicsector/LearningProgram/anti corrupt/Keefer.pdf

2. *http://britishexpat.com/americas/dominican-republic/glitz-bling-and-merengue*

3. *http://britishexpat.com/americas/dominican-republic/can-i-count-your-vote*

4. *www.coha.org/mejia-vs-fernandez-in-sunday%e2%80%99s-dominican-republic-election-mr-almost-clean-dominican-president-all-of-a-sudden-it%e2%80%99s-a-very-tight-race*
5. President taps tainted officials for posts *www.latinamericanstudies.org/dominican-republic/taps.htm*
6. Constitutional Reform Bill *www.lapress.org/articles.asp?art=5694 www.latindispatch.com/wp-content/uploads/2010/02/Constitucion.pdf*
7. Frank Moya Pons, The Dominican Republic: A National History
8. Jana Morgan, PhD Professor, Department of Political Science, University of Tennessee -Knoxville. Rosario Espinal, Ph.D. The Political Culture of Democracy in the Dominican Republic December 2006 USAID paper
9. CIA World Factbook *https://www.cia.gov/library/publications/the-world-factbook/geos/dr.html*
10. Dominican Republic: A Caribbean Economic Success Story *www.ifcreports.com/pdf/dominicanrepublic2008.pdf*
11. United Nations Development Programme 2008 Dominican Republic Human   Development Report *www.pnud.org.do/sites/pnud.onu.org.do/files/Resumen_Ingles.pdf*

12. 'Mobilising For Change In The Dominican Republic' by Ginnie Bedggood
    www.offshorewave.com/offshorenews/mobilising-for-change-in-the-dominican-republic-by-ginnie-bedggood.html

13. Guide to Legal Research in the Dominican Republic by Marisol Florén-Romero April 2007
    www.nyulawglobal.org/globalex/Dominican_Republic.htm

14. PNUD June 2010 Política social: capacidades y derechos Volumen I: Marco teórico; La política social: capacidades y derechos; Educación; Salud. Volumen II: Empleo; Seguridad social y asistencia social; Asentamientos humanos. Volumen III: Justicia y derechos; Inmigración haitiana; Cohesión social; Hacia una política social basada en derechos. Downloadable here:
    http://odh.pnud.org.do/politica-socialcapacidades-y-derechos

Consular and Embassy assistance

Embassies for foreign nationals get mixed reviews in the Dominican Republic. Obviously there are certain protocols they have to observe; Dominican Republic Foreign Office staff and politicians are sensitive to what might be deemed 'undue interference' and those Ambassadors who have been perceived to go above and beyond the call of duty in relation to their nationals are speedily invited to operate in a more restrained fashion. Embassy websites usually clarify what an Embassy can and cannot do for its nationals.

Word quickly gets round the expat community as to the relative worth of their Embassies. Often it is the Honorary Consular staff that expats find most knowledgeable since these are likely to be long-term expat residents themselves and thus know the ropes. Embassy staff, on the other hand, can be rotated on a frequent basis and may not always grasp the subtleties of the country in which their tenure is comparatively short term.

Embassies for expats are situated in Santo Domingo; some have an Honorary Consular presence in Santiago and on the north and east coasts.

US CITIZENS

For US citizens the Embassy is situated on César Nicolás Penson esq. Leopoldo Navarro, Santo Domingo with the Consular section (American Citizen Services) on César Nicolás Penson and Máximo Gómez Avenue Tel: (809) 731 4294 Mon-Fri (7:30am to 4pm). After hours emergencies should contact Tel: (809) 221 2171 Fax: (809) 689 6142. Email address is *acssantodom@state.gov* and website is *santodomingo.usembassy.gov*

The US Consular Agency in Puerto Plata is on Villanueva Street at the corner of John F. Kennedy Ave, Abraxas Bookstore Building, 2nd. Floor Tel: (809) 586 8017, (809) 586 4204, (809) 586 8023 Fax: (809) 586 8015 Email: *acssantodom@state.gov* The Puerto Plata office is open to the public Monday through Friday, from 8:30am to 12:30pm, and from 2pm to 5pm. The website is *www.usemb.gov.do/Consular/ACS/CA_PP-e.htm*

The US embassy provides occasional mobile consular services in locations like Santiago and is in the process of opening an office in Punta Cana.

CANADIAN CITIZENS

For Canadian citizens the Embassy is at Av. Winston Churchill 1099, Torre Citigroup, Acrópolis Center, piso 18, Ensanche Piantini, Santo Domingo. Tel: (809) 262 3100 Email: *sdmgo@international.gc.ca* Mon-Thu (9am to 12pm / 1pm to 4pm) Fri (9am to 12pm). After hours emergencies should call collect: 613 996 8885 or 613 944 1310. The website is:
www.canadainternational.gc.ca/dominican_republic-republique_dominicaine/offices-bureaux/embassy-ambassade.aspx?menu_id=11&menu=L

The Canadian Consular Agency in Puerto Plata is in the same building as the US Consular Agency above: Calle Villanueva No 8, Edificio Abraxas Tel: 1 200 0012 or 809 586 5761 Fax: 809 586 5762 Email: *canada.pop@gmail.com* The Puerto Plata office is open Mon-Fri (9am to 12pm).

The Canadian Consular Agency in the Punta Cana/Bávaro area offers non-immigration consular services. For tourist and resident visas contact the Santo Domingo consular office. The Punta Cana/Bávaro office is located at the Amstar Business Centre, office No. 404, on the Veron - Bávaro Highway, Km. 2, La Altagracia. Tel: 809 455 1730 and 809 455 1734. The office is open Monday through Thursday from 9am to 12pm and from 1pm to 4pm and on Friday from 9am to noon.

BRITISH CITIZENS

For British citizens the Embassy in Santo Domingo is on 27 de Febrero No. 233 Corominas Pepín Building, 7th and 8th Floor. Tel: 809 472 7111 Fax: 809 472 7190
Email: *brit.emb.sadom@codetel.net.do*
Website: *www.ukindominicanrepublic.fco.gov.uk*
    The Puerto Plata Consular Office is in Calle Beller 51, 2nd. Floor. The Honorary Consul is Mr. Genni Mendez
Office: 829 726-0757
Email: *Genni.mendez-honcon@fconet.fco.gov.uk*
Website: *www.ukindominicanrepublic.fco.gov.uk/en/our-offices-in-dominican/other-locations-in-dominican*

GERMAN CITIZENS

For German citizens the Embassy is on Calle Gustavo Mejía Ricart No.196 (esq. Av. Abraham Lincoln), Torre Piantini (Floors16/17), Ensanche Piantini, Santo Domingo Tel: 809 542 8949 or 809 542 8950 Fax: 809 542 8955
Email: *info@santo-domingo.diplo.de*
Open Monday and Wednesday 7.30am to 4pm, Tuesday, Thursday and Friday 7.30am to 3pm. Outside of those hours the emergency number is 809 543 5650. The website is:
www.santo-domingo.diplo.de/Vertretung/santodomingo/es/02/Botschaft.html

FRENCH CITIZENS

For French citizens the Embassy is located on Calle las Damas No. 42, Colonial Zone, Santo Domingo Tel: 809 695 4300, 809 695 4310, 809 695 4330 Fax: 809 695 4311

Open Monday, Wednesday, Thursday, Friday 8.30am to 12.00, closed on Tuesdays. Outside of those hours the emergency number is 809 805 6721 The website is *www.ambafrance.org.do*

Honorary French Consuls are available in a number of locations: in Puerto Plata, Mme. Anne Goffaux Tel: 809 320 5303 Cel: 809 865 0025 Email: *agoffaux@holatours.com*

In Santiago, José Maria Hernandez, Calle Porto Rico 3, La Esmeralda Tel: 809 582-2893 Fax: 809 241 5783

In Las Terrenas M. Gérard Prystasz Tel: 809-240-6111 Fax: 809 240 6205 Email: *hotel.atlantis@codetel.net.do*

In Bavaro-Punta Cana, Hubert Touret, Touret & Cia, Cocotal Golf Club Email: *playatv@hotmail.com*

In La Romana Jean-Michel Cau Tel: 809 836-3842 Email: *jmc@viajescervantes.com*

ITALIAN CITIZENS

For Italian citizens the Embassy is on Calle Manuel Rodriguez Obijo 4, Gazcue, Santo Domingo Tel: 809 682 0830 ext. 221 (central) Fax: 809 682 8296 Open 8.30am to 11.30am and 3pm to 4pm. Email: *ambsdom.mail@esteri.it* The website is *www.ambsantodomingo.esteri.it*

Honorary Italian Vice Consuls are available in Puerto Plata, Roberto Casoni, Gran Ventana Beach Resort, Playa Dorada Tel: 809 320-2111 ext. 4300 Fax: 809 320-4017 Email: *rcasoni@vhhr.com*

In Santiago, Mauro Sgarzini, Calle 21 No.12, El Embrujo II Tel: 809 582 6914 (ext.223) and 809 727 5584 Fax: 809 724 1090 Email: *Santiago.viceconsolato@gmail.com*

In La Romana, Alberto Bernini, Edificio Monaco, Calle Tte. Amado García esq. Calle Castillo Marques Tel: 809 556 8260 Fax: 809 550 6281 Email: *icolbubu@hotmail.com*

There are also Italian Consular agents in Bavaro, Aldo Meroni, Hotel Los Corales Tel: 809 535 1010 Fax: 809 533 7095 Email: *aldomeroni@hotmail.com;* in La Romana, Enrico Citati, Edificio Monaco, Calle Tte. Amado García esq. Calle Castillo Marques Tel: 809 550 8445 Fax: 809 556 8790 Email: *makoamerican@codetel.net.do* and in Bayahibe, Giacomo Di Lauro, Club Viva Dominicus Beach Tel: 809 686 5658 Fax: 809 686 5750 and 809 221 6805 Email: *giacomo@vivaresorts.com*

DUTCH CITIZENS

For Dutch citizens the Embassy is located on Maximo Henriquez Ureña No. 50 (corner of Avenida Lincoln and Avenida Churchill), Piantini, Santo Domingo Tel: 809 262 0320 Fax: 809 565 4685 Email: *STD@minbuza.nl* The website is *www.holanda.org.do* The Embassy is open Monday to Thursday 8am to 4.30pm and Fridays 8am to 1.30pm. For out of hours emergencies the duty officer should be contacted on 809 262 0303.

There is a Dutch Vice Consul in Puerto Plata, Mr. G.E.Wijnbelt, for services to Dutch nationals residing in the provinces of Puerto Plata, Santiago, Espaillat, Valverde and Montecristi. He can be located at the General Air Services office of Puerto Plata airport Tel: 809 320 8100 Cel: 809 710 1774 Fax: 809 586 0534.

BELGIAN CITIZENS

For Belgian citizens, the Consular representative is Mr. Frederic Meurice who can be located at 207 Padre Billini, Ciudad Colonial, D.N. Santo Domingo Tel: 809 687 2244 Fax: 809 221 7369 Email: *consuladobelgica@dona-elvira.com*

JAPANESE CITIZENS

For Japanese citizens the Embassy is located on the eighth floor of Torre BHD on Av. Winston Churchill Esq. Av. 27 de Febrero, Santo Domingo. Tel: 809 567 3365 Fax: 809 566 8013 The Embassy is open Monday to Friday 8.30am to 1pm and 2pm to 5.30 pm. The website is *www.do.emb-japan.go.jp*

EXPATS OF OTHER NATIONALITIES

Check this website:
www.embassiesabroad.com/embassies-in/DominicanRepublic
Many countries have either Ambassadorial or Consular representation in the DR but for some expats their Consular coverage may come from a representative based in a neighbouring country. Australian residents of the Dominican Republic, for example, might be surprised to learn that their Consular representation is based in Trinidad and Tobago, specifically at 18 Herbert Street, St Clair, Port of Spain, Trinidad and Tobago Tel: 868 628 0695 Fax: 868 622 0659 Website:
www.trinidadandtobago.embassy.gov.au

It is advisable to research this before moving to the DR and certainly not to wait until the services of a country-of-origin representative might be needed.

Transport and driving

Public transportation in the DR is variable but long distance costs are relatively inexpensive. Metro and Caribe Tours have modern, air-conditioned buses (so cold you'll need a jacket on a long trip!), frequent schedules between major cities and towns, and are inexpensive. The current fare from Puerto Plata to Santo Domingo is around US$10 (for a four-hour journey). Further information can be accessed on *www.caribetours.com.do* and *www.metroserviciosturisticos.com*.

BUSES

The cities are served by a combination of minibuses guaguas and the more formal state OMSA service in the two main cities. OMSA buses are airconditioned and have recognisable bus stops, but the more free-spirited guaguas just stop wherever convenient. Once on board and seeking to dismount, verbal request is made of the driver. A loud noise will suffice in lieu of the Spanish language and usually fellow passengers get the message across.

The same applies to inter-urban *guaguas*, also known as *voladoras* (fliers). These are minivans normally accommodating eight passengers but the friendliness of Dominicans encourages twelve or more to board, plus baggage and sometimes chickens! The driver's assistant (*cobrador*) hangs on the outside at the open door and fares are handed to him at completion of journey. A typical half-hour journey between Puerto Plata and Sosua will cost approximately US$1.10. The same journey by private taxi would be US$27. To summon a *guagua* to pick up a passenger requires but an imperceptible finger gesture to the approaching vehicle. Those waving hands, arms or indeed both arms and head are clearly foreigners who have yet to learn the subtleties of the Dominican gesturing system.

Taxis

Shared taxis, also known as *conchos* or *carros públicos*, pick up passengers along set routes in the same way as *guaguas*. *Público* drivers may pack two passengers in the front seat and four in the back but passengers have the option of paying two fares and booking the whole front seat or paying four fares for the back seat. Journeys cost about 60 cents. Taxis in the DR do not have meters and cannot be hailed on the street; they have to be ordered by phone. Journeys within Santo Domingo in a local taxi cost about US$5. The same distance on the north coast by a taxi based at a tourist hotel would be US$15. Offical tourist taxi rates are usually displayed at hotels and airports. The most reliable taxi companies are *Tecni-Taxi* or *Apolo*. See *www.taxird.com* for a list of taxi companies in Santiago and Santo Domingo.

Motorcycles

Motoconchos or motorcycle taxis are cheap but used at one's own peril. In the more remote rural areas they may be the only public transport option. In the large cities they are a high-risk but effective way of cheating the endless traffic jams.

Rail

Over-ground railways in the Dominican countryside can be seen transporting sugarcane to sugar mills but not as a passenger service. In Santo Domingo, the controversial new Metro aims to provide inexpensive form of public transport in the capital. Following the President's inaugural ride on the Metro in February 2008 it was promised that it would be operational by April... then July... then September ... then November 2008. Free test rides were conducted prior to Christmas 2008 to iron out any remaining snags and the service went into operation at the end of January 2009. The overground and underground train links Villa Mella with the Centro de los Heroes, via Maximo Gomez, La Zurza, Gazcue and Ciudad Universitaria. The second Metro line in Santo Domingo is currently under construction and a light rail service is planned to connect the port of Haina with Santiago, which has a busy Free Zone industrial area. (See *Politics and Legal*)

Air

The DR has nine international airports, six domestic airports, and some nineteen airfields not including private airstrips used... for a variety of purposes! Domestic flights are used for in-country travel by the business community, particularly from the north coast to Santo Domingo and from the east coast to the north east by travellers of means: Punta Cana, Samaná, Santo Domingo, La Romana, and Puerto Plata. Air Century, Volair, Aerodomca and SAPair are some of the companies offering both scheduled services and private charters. Many of these routes have been subject to changes at short notice so it is advisable to double check before assuming the service is available. A one-way ticket from Punta Cana to Santo Domingo costs $149, Punta Cana to Puerto Plata $199 and La Romana to Puerto Plata $173. Information as to schedules and costs can be found at *www.colonialtours.com.do/vuelos/vuelos.asp*

Most expats will want to own their own vehicle. As with everything in the DR it is sensible to use recommendations of other satisfied customers when seeking a point of sale, to use online facilities to check the history of the vehicle, and to take a trusted mechanic with you to give the vehicle a thorough once-over (or under). As well as purchasing a vehicle and insurance it will be necessary to obtain a Dominican driving licence.

Driving licences

Watching the local population drive here in the DR, you could be forgiven for wondering whether such things as driving licences exist. They do – both legal and illegal types! However, expats will not want to know costs and procedures for fake licences, so we will concentrate on the legal variety. There are, broadly speaking, two avenues for obtaining a Dominican driving licence as a foreigner. The first is getting your foreign licence validated so that a Dominican licence is issued on that basis.

This costs approximately US$28 and requires:
1. A valid licence from a foreign country, plus two photocopies
2. Certification from the foreign country's consular or diplomatic mission in the DR stating that the foreign licence is valid
3. Authentication of the certification at the Dominican Ministry of Foreign Affairs (*Secretaria de Estado de Relaciones Exteriores* or *Cancilleria*)
4. Passport, valid for at least a year from the time of the application with residency visa or work permit or *cédula*
5. Payment of taxes and fees for medical (vision) exam and blood test at *Banco de Reservas*
6. Vision exam and blood test

Information can be found on the website:
www.dgtt.gov.do/SEOPC%20Con%20DGTT/Licencia%20Extranjera.html

While most European Embassies will validate licences the US Embassy will not, thus requiring the second avenue which is the application for a Dominican driving licence in the same way as Dominicans do and not based on a foreign licence. There are two steps to this:

1. Issuing of a provisional licence which lasts for one year
2. Issuing of full licence which lasts four years and then needs to be renewed.

A *cédula* is needed for this process. The cost of a provisional licence is US$24.50. For minors the fee is US$39.50.

For a provisional licence, as well as the *cédula*, a vision test and blood typing test are required. This has been vastly simplified recently, and now all takes place at the same location, the nearest *Dirección General de Transito Terrestre* (*DGTT*) office – previously one had to go to a clinic for the blood typing test. The *cédula* will, of course, already include a notification as to blood typing but this is verified for the driving licence so that the correct blood type appears on the licence as an aid to medics in the event of an accident requiring a transfusion. Once expats understand how many mistakes appear on official DR documentation they will realise that this checking is very much in their own interests even though it might appear to be unnecessary bureaucracy! Further information is available on the website: *www.dgtt.gov.do/SEOPC%20Con%20DGTT/Carnet%20de%20Aprendizaje.html*

Issuing of the provisional licence requires the passing of the theoretical exam – a computer-based exam in Spanish with a required pass mark of 70%. This can be retaken if failed. There is always help available if the *gringo* doesn't understand the questions; naturally a sign of appreciation (read: tip) for this help would be expected. It is expected that the applicant for a provisional licence will have some knowledge of the Highway Code in the DR even if said Highway Code is rarely applied in practice. It might take you a while to track down a copy but they are available. Surprisingly it is a fun read: for example the page indicating what the different traffic lights mean has a diagram showing: red light –Stop; green light –Go; red and green lights together –These Lights Are Not Working.

Honestly! The theoretical computer test requires you to watch videos, listen to questions and use a touch screen for a yes or no answer or to see the question again. There are twenty questions in a time allowance of twenty minutes.

The practical driving test can be taken forty-five days after the issuing of the provisional licence. Successful completion of this test will result in the issuing of a full licence valid for four years. For those who have never held a driving licence in any country, instruction is available through a driving school, although the DR would not necessarily be the country of choice in which to undertake this activity for the first time. If you do end up learning to drive in the DR, the formalities include signing up and paying for a course at an approved driving school, but you do not actually need to take the lessons with the school, but with an instructor of your choice. A full course to get the driver up to test standard costs US$180 and includes the test fees.

Four years after its initial issuance the driving licence will need to be renewed for a fee of US$24.30. Fingerprints are now taken electronically as are photographs and signature and whilst a vision test is required at renewal a blood test (unsurprisingly!) is not. The renewal process has been streamlined recently and took only twenty minutes in 2007.

One good reason to have a Dominican driving licence is to be able to claim on car insurance in the event of an accident caused either by you or someone else. Insurance companies will sell insurance to a driver without a Dominican licence but they will not necessarily pay out on a claim unless one is a legal resident. The reason for detailing the information in this section so minutely is that it is difficult to find it elsewhere, and insurance companies are unlikely to tell you unless you ask. Volunteering information that looks like it might be required could not be considered a ubiquitous Dominican trait.

Corruption in the Dominican Republic means that much fake paperwork is produced – for a price – and fake driving licences are no exception. There is a difference between an out-and-out fake licence which is not registered in the computerised system and getting a legal licence without undertaking all the necessary steps by providing 'sweeteners'. It is possible to get help answering the theoretical questions and even to avoid taking the practical driving test if it is known one is an experienced driver, yet still end up with a legal licence. What should be avoided at all costs is buying a fake licence. This can result in penalties and will almost certainly result in refusal to pay a claim by an insurance company. The extent to which fake licences are a problem can be judged by a page on the *DGTT* website which demonstrates ways of differentiating between a fake and a legal licence:
www.dgtt.gov.do/Bucone.html

Those wishing to read the DR's Transit law can do so at the *AMET* (Transport Police) website:
www.amet.gov.do/decretos_leyes/Ley_241-67.pdf
plus subsequent modifications:
www.amet.gov.do/index.php/institu/mlegal.html

Telecommunications

The Dominican Republic is considered one of the countries with the most advanced telecommunications infrastructures in Latin America with 18 companies providing service; the six major companies are Claro-Codetel, Orange, Tricom, Skymax, Trilogy-Viva and Wind. The DR offers cable internet and DSL in most parts of the country, and many ISPs provide 3G wireless internet service. There are plans to extend Wi-Fi hot spots in a number of locations. Numerous television channels are available, including Digital, Cable, Telecable, Nacional and Aster. The local cable TV channels all carry the three primary US networks, plus CNN and the BBC, and about four other English language stations. The Dominican Republic's commercial radio stations and television stations are in the process of transferring to the digital spectrum via HD Radio and HDTV. Telecable from Tricom offers a 24-hour high definition movie channel, Movie City HD.

According to the *Banco Central* the telecommunication industry contribution to the GDP grew 28 % during 2006. Growth was more significant in the mobile sector where the number of wireless subscribers in 2009 was more than six times the number of wireless subscribers in 2002. As a result, teledensity in the Dominican Republic has increased from 30.5% in 2002 to 100% in 2010 according to INDOTEL (the Dominican Institute for Telecommunications). INDOTEL is the government agency that supervises and regulates telecommunication services in the DR. It is responsible for issuing concessions, establishing standards, supervising operators, and developing national and international telecommunications policies. The DR Government has encouraged foreign investment in this industry and actively promoted the use of the DR to establish call-centre businesses.

Internet and telephone monthly rental for VIP service (24 hour connection) with flash is US$77 a month for the slowest of the three speeds available. Most expats use a computer service like Skype for their long distance calls. The telephone/internet company Codetel-Claro has a number of plans depending on individual requirements – these can be viewed at *www.codetel.com.do/solucionesvoz.aspx* Tricom also has differently priced plans depending on speed of connectivity: *www.tricom.com.do/turbo_adsl.php*

The DR is a member of the International Telecommunications Union (ITU), an agency of the United Nations in Geneva, which plays a vital role in the standardisation of telecommunications. Law 153-98 acknowledges the applications of the recommendations issued by the ITU, and establishes that all the technical norms in the Dominican Republic must be in accordance with international practices in World Zone Number 1, to which the country belongs. However, as is often the case in the DR, there can be divergence between what is written on paper and what happens in practice.

Usually a not unreasonable requirement is that connectivity means just that, that Flash speed offered is somewhere close to that purported and that in the advent of problems a relatively speedy repair service is available. Be advised that this does not always turn out to be the case! Customer service and repair time are not always on a par with those experienced in expats' countries of origin. These can vary in different locations of the DR and can be dependent on the type of individual relationship the expat has with the local office. Charming yet unrelenting persistence achieves more results than displayed anger. The two main complaints are cost (three times higher than other parts of Latin America with taxes on internet services in the DR being 28%, while the average in Latin America is 14%) and consumers not receiving what they are paying for.

The DR reached the milestone of 100% tele-density in March 2010. Cell phones are readily available in the DR – indeed everyone seems to have one. The new expat should not be surprised if the street cleaner pulls out a cell phone! As of 4 March 2010, there were 9,763,086 lines compared to a population estimated at 9,742,374 inhabitants; of these, 987,586 were landlines and 8,775,500 were cell phones. Since a third of the population are children not all of whom are old enough to operate a cell phone, it can be deduced than many users have more than one. This is especially true of the disposable variety, a crucial adjunct to the narcotics industry. Costs depend on usage but many expats use pre-payment plans of up to US$20 a month supplemented by either a landline, or a computer based voice system (known as VoIP - Voice Over Internet Protocol). Telephone calls from the DR to the US are the same price as long distance calls within the country. Those reliant on a cell phone alone can spend up to US$100 a month. Internet cafes are in all sizeable towns and tourist areas and are usually open from 8am to 10pm. As well as Codetel, Tricom, and Viva (formerly Centennial), Orange also provides services and its charges can be viewed at *www.orange.com.do*.

The DR introduced Wi-Max service in 2007 and was the first country in the Americas to do so. There is also OneMax, which provides high-speed internet and VoIP telephone services. Monthly rental depends on speed of connection: there are four plans at US$31, US$41, US$50.50 and US$85.40 per month. Further details can be viewed at *www.onemax.com.do* (click on *Planes* and then *Tarifas*).

There have been mixed reports about the accuracy of the speed of this service during its start-up in the DR. It could be that this is linked to the use of Codetel-Claro – the main telecommunications company – infrastructure and bandwidth and that the company will come into its own when it uses its own dedicated Sprint fibre. In early 2011 Codetel-Claro announced it would be dropping the Codetel name to be replaced with just Claro.

Further information can be found in a paper by Isolda Frias dated February 2007 Dominican Republic: The Telecommunication Sector downloadable from *www.buyusa.gov* A Legal Guide to Telecommunications in the DR can be found in this PDF file on the Pellerano and Herrera website: *www.phlaw.com/pubs/gleg/en/GLGTM%20-%20Telecommunications%20Guide.pdf*.

Employment

Some expatriates may arrive with a job in hand, while others may decide to move to the Dominican Republic for some other reason and only then go about seeking employment. This section is chiefly aimed at the latter.

It is not that easy to get a job here: as in many third world/developing/emerging economies around half the population is unemployed or under-employed, and the greatest challenge, even if you are qualified and experienced, is to get a job that pays a living wage. If you already have a fixed source of income and are just after an occupation to fill your time and/or supplement your income, this is not so much of an issue, but if you want to make a good living the choices are more limited. It is also true that your gringo status is not enough to qualify you for work or open doors; in fact it may even be a hindrance. Knowledge of Spanish and good local knowledge and connections are the real keys to getting a decent job in the DR.

The Dominican job market has some dramatic gaps and chasms. The same workplace may include people at the top of the scale taking home the equivalent of two or three thousand dollars a month while the office messengers and cleaners barely make two hundred. The legal minimum wage of about 160 US dollars per month is barely enough to cover a family's minimum household expenses, estimated by the Central Bank at approximately three times that amount, US$486, hence the importance of the 'informal' economic sector and remittances from relatives abroad.

A 'good' salary by local standards is anything above US$540, which is not quite enough for what most foreigners would recognise as a comfortable urban middle class lifestyle. This is more or less what an English-speaking call centre operator (see below) earns, and this is not bad if you consider that the typical employee in this sector is a young single person living in the parental home. A professional in the private sector would expect to be paid at least three times that amount. Public sector professionals like teachers and even doctors earn next to nothing.

There are several popular areas of work for foreigners in the Dominican Republic.

Language teaching can be done independently, by providing private lessons or by working at language institutes like the *Dominico-Americano* and *APEC* University (See directory for contact details). A *TEFL/TOEFL* English teaching qualification is an advantage, but any native speaker with a degree and/or teaching experience has a decent chance of landing work in this field. There are also language-teaching agencies which send private teachers to their students' homes or places of work for a fixed rate. Even on a full-time schedule, this work does not usually pay more than a subsistence wage and is only suitable as an additional source of income.

Teaching at private primary or secondary schools can be a more lucrative option for expatriates. Native English speakers with university degrees, especially if they have a teaching qualifications and classroom experience, are in great demand by private bi-lingual schools, and the pay is not bad by local standards. The school timetable means that teachers have the option of supplementing their income with private tutoring in the afternoons and evenings. The best deals are made prior to arrival in the country by applying to the top private schools, some of which recruit their staff at employment fairs in the US and Canada. Teachers contracted in this way will receive relocation costs, accommodation allowance and other benefits. If contracted locally, the salary will still be quite good by local standards but will not be accompanied by much in the way of fringe benefits apart from reduced/free tuition for the teacher's own children. A listing of private schools can be found in the Education section. Attractive locations for would-be teachers in private schools in the capital include Carol Morgan, St Michael and the Community for Learning, and outside of the capital: Punta Cana (PCIS and Cap Cana Heritage Schools), La Romana (Lincoln School) Cabrera International Academy and Sosua International School, all located in tourist/expatriate areas and which actively seek qualified teachers who are native English speakers.

Call centres servicing the US/Canadian market are a growing sector in the Dominican Republic. They are based in the country as part of the Free Trade Zone tax-exempt set-up, and the reason for their presence is the availability of English-speaking employees who can be paid much lower wages than their counterparts in the US and Canada. Companies that have set up call centres in the DR range from the mundane (directory inquiries, travel directions) to the frivolous (dial-a-horoscope), while others can be more specialized, providing services like interpreting for US health or legal sectors. Most call centre operators are young bi-lingual Dominicans (in some cases returned immigrants from the US, including deportees) and the pay is reasonable by local standards. Foreign, native-English speaking employees may also work as operators but on the whole tend to work at supervisory/management level. Most call centres are in Santo Domingo and Santiago.

At embassies, and in both the international private sector and international organisations, foreigners will be employed on a local salary and conditions if recruited locally, unlike colleagues who are recruited internationally. In some cases, not holding Dominican *residencia* may act in your favour and you will be treated as international staff in this two-tier system. No matter what, this can be an interesting work option where the expatriate can use their professional experience and language skills, working in an environment that brings them into contact with both Dominicans and fellow foreigners. Here, however, knowledge of Spanish is more likely to be a requirement than at a language school or a call centre.

The tourist sector is a natural choice for foreign residents. Here they can combine their language skills with knowledge of their clientele as well as their knowledge of the country. Tour reps for travel companies, tour guides, sales, management and administration posts are recruited locally, as with many jobs in the DR through word of mouth, or internationally via the parent company if it is not a DR-owned outfit.

Property sales or real estate is a popular sector for foreign residents, especially working with the expatriate target market in both tourist areas and the main cities.

In the professional sphere, if you are a foreign-trained lawyer, doctor or accountant you have to meet local rules/qualifications before being allowed to practice. So contact the appropriate professional organisation for details – see directory at the end of this section.

FREELANCE WORK

Once you are established in the country you can work as a freelancer in your chosen field, servicing both national and international clients. Online work may include computer programming, website design, graphic design, translation, editing and anything that can be done without personal face-to-face contact.

Although it is strongly recommended that foreign residents planning to work in the Dominican Republic should obtain a residency permit if coming to live in the country for more than one year, it is not always essential to have this in order to work. However, many employers will require it and in some cases they themselves will take it upon themselves to facilitate the process. Residency and *cédula* (ID card) are definitely needed for independent self-employed workers: this will secure an *NCF Numero de Comprobante Fiscal* and an RNC. Printed invoices are required in order to charge clients the 16% ITBIS (VAT) which then needs to be paid to the tax authorities. It is worth hiring an accountant to advise and help with this.

Once your Spanish skills improve and your local connections and knowledge of the DR and its workings increase, so will the employment opportunities.

RESOURCES

Dominican Medical Association
www.cmd.org.do

Architects and Engineers Association
www.codia.org.do

Dentists Association
Asociación Odontológica Dominicana
Avenida Privada Esquina Miguel Monclús 169,
Santo Domingo
Tel: 809 543 0880
Fax: 809 531 0104
arn@codetel.net.do

Lawyers Association
Colegio de Abogados de la República Dominicana
Casa del Abogado,
Calle Isabel la Católica No.151
Santo Domingo
Tel: 809 682 4122
colegiodeabogados@msn.com

Accountants Association
www.icpard.org

APEC University
www.unapec.edu.do

Instituto Dominico-Americano
www.icda.edu.do

Translators' Association
ATIRD - *Asociación de Traductores e Intérpretes de la República Dominicana*
Ave. Winston Churchill esq. Roberto Pastoriza
Plaza de las Américas, Suite #309
Piantini, Santo Domingo
Tel: (829) 904 5983
www.atird.com

Expat employers

The intention of this section is not to provide a manual as to how to set up a company in the Dominican Republic, but rather to highlight some of the differences between procedures and expectations of employers in the DR as compared with the expats' country of origin. At the very least, this section should serve as a warning not to go into business here until the new expat really knows the turf. 'Knowing the turf' isn't just about grasping complex legal procedures, and recent changes in company law (both implemented and pending). A reliable lawyer with a good reputation is an essential adjunct to company formation, and a reliable accountant is an essential adjunct to understanding company taxation, working one's way through the plethora of required documents, and how to pay said taxation. Perhaps more than this 'knowing the turf' pre-supposes an understanding of the culture of the

DR, what workers expect of employers, and how Dominicans view foreign competition. It is for this reason that our advice would be that the new expat should not set up a trading company until they have lived in the DR for about a year and have under their belts an understanding of 'how things are done'.

Not all expats will wish to set up a company but the vast majority will find themselves employing a maid or cleaning lady, the nomenclature depending on the expats' country of origin. So perhaps it is appropriate to start with the authors' combined wisdom in this area gleaned over some thirty years. Expats should not expect the maid or gardener to speak English, so there will be a requirement for the expat employer to be able to communicate at least the basics of what the job entails. It will be necessary to spell this out clearly and to check that you have been understood. Since asking "do you understand me?" will always elicit the response "yes", given that people tell you what they think you want to hear, it will be necessary to check via a series of detailed questions such as, "And what do you do after you've done that first task?" The questions will vary depending upon the content of the communication you wish to check, but always make sure that you do not include the answer in the question!

Telling you what you want to hear does not mean that the cleaning lady or gardener is being patronising, antagonistic, unduly subservient or placating. It is simply that interpersonal relationships are held to be important in the DR so every attempt will be made not to upset you particularly when you are the person paying the wages. Of course it usually works the other way and most expats would rather receive an accurate answer than one designed not to upset them!

New expats can often be heard bemoaning the stupidity of their domestic staff. Such unwarranted stereotyping is no truer of the DR than it would be of anywhere else. What it tends to indicate is the expats' lack of knowledge about the employee's lifestyle. At this point it would be a good idea to skip forward to the Language section in the HOW chapter and to read the In The Home example of Ginnie and Marisol, the cleaning lady. Marisol did all that was requested of her, boiled up some water for the washing up because Ginnie had a non-functioning water heater. What she did not do was to pour the hot water into the sink over the dirty dishes, because Ginnie didn't ask her to. Ginnie assumed (wrongly) that this would be common sense. It might have been had Marisol's prior life experience included living in a home with a water heater and automatically using hot water for washing up. But Marisol, in common with most workers employed as maids or gardeners, had never lived in a home which had a water heater and so she did what would have been normal for her at home – washed up in cold water with an over-abundance of dishwashing liquid. Such behaviour is not indicative of stupidity (except perhaps on the part of Ginnie who had lived here long enough to know about the scarcity of water heaters in the homes of those with low incomes!) but merely indicates a difference in lifestyles and the need for the expat employer not to make assumptions.

Being a successful employer of domestic staff will require more hands-on supervision in the early stages than the expat might expect in their country of origin. Domestic tasks are carried out differently here, sometimes with a good reason but not always. Frequently they are carried out exuberantly and with a certain amount of excess – pretty much a metaphor for the whole of life in the DR. For some domestic staff, electricity in the home was not necessarily something they grew up with. Generous torrents of water could thus be poured onto concrete floors with reckless abandon as part of the cleaning and mopping process. The relatively new invention of electric cable linking to all important employer computers, TVs and suchlike acts as an impediment to this reckless abandon – at least it should. Here again, the expat employer should explain and re-explain the non-mixability of water and electricity, or at least make sure suitable precautions are taken. Excess can also be witnessed in the amount of detergent and/or bleach added to washing machines; many expats take a while to cotton on why their shirts end up disintegrating after four washings! The answer is to either supervise closely or to do that part of the job yourself.

There is a further reason why hands-on supervision is necessary and this has nothing to do with the successful completion of the task as much as the expectation that 'the boss will be the boss'. The Dominican Republic is a blatantly socially stratified country, one of the most classist that Ginnie and Ilana have ever dwelled in (and between them they have lived in a few). People thus tend to 'know their place' both socially and in the work setting. Whilst the twenty-first century is seeing inroads into this outdated concept particularly among the young and lower middle-class inhabitants, it is still prevalent among older and working class Dominicans. Thus the expat lady of the house who treats her cleaning lady as a personal woman friend will end up either confusing the worker or being perceived as weak and open to be taken advantage of.

This can be a difficult area for new expats, particularly the enlightened ones who are determined at all costs not to fall into the 'I know better than you do' trap. There is indeed a tension between not coming over as the colonialist, imperialist oppressor and treating the worker as a quasi-serf, yet ensuring sufficient distance to garner respect. The Dominican domestic worker will not be expecting egalitarianism on the part of their employer because this is not the way in which Dominican employers of domestic staff behave. In fact, the way some Dominican employers of domestic staff behave can strike the new expat as unduly harsh.

We have already noted in the section on Safety and Security that tourist locations of the DR, in common with tourist locations worldwide, can attract the less reputable of local inhabitants. Many expats live in tourist locations and thus will be seeking locally based domestic staff. It is absolutely crucial to rely on recommendations from others whom you know and trust (in exactly the same way as you would for lawyers, accountants, doctors and dentists). Clearly the first requirement for staff entering the home regularly will be honesty and integrity. Neither Ilana or Ginnie ever experienced any difficulties in this area but then both are in the habit of spelling out expectations clearly and precisely. Of course domestic employees know that theft of cash or jewellery is not permitted and warrants dismissal at least (provided there are witnesses to prove it) but the more normal confusions arise over less clear cut issues. Sometimes a request to 'borrow' an item is actually a request for a gift, particularly if the home has more than one of the items concerned. Ginnie's maid requested the loan of a travel iron twelve years ago and it is still out on loan. Perfectly acceptable to Ginnie who never does any ironing in any event and who recognised the request for what it was at the time.

Frequently, there will be requests to 'sub' in advance from wages due in the future; this is normal practice if the worker wants to buy a large ticket item and rarely a problem provided the employee already has a reasonable time period with the expat concerned and thus a reasonable expectation of continuing in employment. It is also normal practice to provide lunch for daytime domestic staff, although they might well cook it themselves, or certainly a snack and drink for part-time workers. If certain items in the refrigerator are off-limits then this should be made clear.

Most misunderstandings that occur do so because the employer has failed to fully clarify what their expectations are. It is possible to communicate expectations clearly and without 'attitude'. Likewise it is possible for the expat to train themselves not to make assumptions that what is normal for them is not a universally shared phenomenon. In the DR cleaning staff appear to see dirt and dust at eye level and below but not above, so if you want the tops of cupboards or high shelves cleaned regularly then this expectation needs to be made explicit.

Similarly, in the garden there is a tendency for gardeners to machete weeds above the surface of the earth but not below, so if you want the roots taken out then say so. Many concepts are not culturally neutral; pruning to a British citizen, for example, means not just thinning out the bush but shaping it and reducing its height. Not so to a Dominican gardener! Nor should the new expat assume that a jobbing gardener will arrive with anything more than a machete – they might have an armoury of tools, but on the other hand, they might not. The expat might also choose to use implements and machines which were part and parcel of their life in their country of origin. If deciding to introduce these to staff in the DR it is best not to assume that, for example, the intricacies of a dish-washing machine or a rotovator are familiar territory. In fact Ginnie was one of the first people to install a dish-washing machine in her kitchen in Puerto Plata some ten years ago and subsequently word went round and neighbours arrived for a demonstration. The master builder thought the machine was the niftiest thing he had ever seen and would regularly describe it to employers for whom he worked after finishing her kitchen; inevitably they asked to see it and so the master builder would make frequent visits with his new clients for demonstrations!

Those expats thinking of setting up their own company would be well advised to seek advice from other expats who have done the same, particularly with regard to the recommendation of a reliable lawyer. Whilst it was technically possible to visit the new website *www.creatuempresa.gob.do* and do your own company formation, it would not be recommended for anyone unfamiliar with Dominican bureaucracy or who is not fluent in Spanish. At the time of editing the site is not accessible so queries should be addressed to *ONAPI, Oficina Nacional de la Propiedad Industrial* (National Office of Industrial Property) *onapi.gob.do*

The rest of this section will provide an overview of the process of company formation; this is not intended as a 'how to' manual, but it might be useful to provide a prompt list so that expats can supervise how their lawyer is progressing!

There are, broadly, eight steps to be taken.

1. First, the company name has to be checked to avoid duplication and the fee paid, then arrangements are made for the publication of the name in the monthly publication of the National Office of Industrial Property *(ONAPI)* and the publication fee paid.
2. After about ten days the company name announcement is published in a national circulation newspaper – this happens on the fifteenth or thirtieth of each month. The National Office of Industrial Property also publishes the list of requested business/corporate names and their petitioners twice a month. After that publication, third parties may lodge protests within forty-five

days. Assuming that there are no protests, a Certificate of Registry is provided.
3. The third step (which can be undertaken simultaneously with step two) is to have notarised a sworn declaration of subscription of shares.
4. Step four is the payment of incorporation tax, usually 1% of authorised capital, at the *Dirección General de Impuestos Internos* or whichever banks are authorised to receive.
5. Step five is the registration of the company and the obtaining of the identification number, the *RNC, Registro Nacional del Contribuyente.*

On 19th June 2009 parts of the Law on Business Associations and Individual Proprietorships with Limited Liability, Law No 479-08, came into effect. The deadline for businesses with assets of over RD$30 million to bring themselves into compliance with the new law was subsequently extended a further eighteen months; on 9 June, 2010, President Fernández implemented Law No 73-10 which extended the deadline for existing corporations to comply with the new company law until December 11, 2010. This Law constituted a move from an outdated and deregulated company law system to a modern and more regulated one and repeals and replaces title III of the Dominican Code of Commerce. It is intended to regulate company processes that previously lacked regulation and to strengthen the protection of interested parties and stakeholders. In this vein, the new law introduces two new vehicles for doing business: the *Sociedad de Responsabilidad*

Limitada (*SRL*) which is similar to US limited liability companies (*LLC*s) and the *Empresa Individual de Responsabilidad Limitada* (*EIRL*), individual proprietorships with limited liability (*IPLL*s), which allow individual business owners to keep their personal property from the reach of their business creditors by placing their business assets in a limited liability entity. For the formation of *SRL*s and *EIRL*s the paid-up capital has to be deposited in a bank until the company is registered. After this is done, the company can use the funds for its business operations. The Law also regulates the most significant corporate processes (mergers, spin-offs, increase and decrease in capital, purchase and redemption by a company of its own shares, dissolution and liquidation) and sets forth corporate governance rules and provisions intending to achieve greater transparency.

Under the new system incorporation documents have to be filed at the Mercantile Registry and the fees paid in relation to authorised capital; the Mercantile Registry then issues a Certificate normally within three working days and subsequently the RNC is applied for as above. The Mercantile Registry Certificate is renewable every two years at the Mercantile Registry of the Chamber of Commerce in the area where the company head office is located.

6. The next step is to file for the National Taxpayers Registry at the Internal Revenue Service (DGII) and apply for fiscal receipts. According to Decree 254–06, companies that render services or whose operations require the transfer of goods must issue

receipts with a fiscal number, the NCF (*numero de comprobante fiscal*). Even where the application for the National Taxpayers Registry is made online through the Internal Revenue Service's webpage, actual documents still need to be filed at the Internal Revenue Service.
7. The next step is to register local employees with the Department of Labour; forms DGT-3, DGT-4, and the employer's registration form *RNL* (*registro nacional laboral*) must be completed within the first week of employment. This procedure can only be completed after the taxpayer's identification number has been obtained.
8. Finally, step eight is to register employees at the main social security office, *CNSS* (*Consejo Nacional de Seguridad Social*). A certain percentage will be paid into a pension fund, a health plan and a labour risk plan; both the employer and the employee contribute.

As was said at the outset of this chapter, a reliable lawyer and a reliable accountant are a must for the expat who intends setting up a company. A lawyer who is really worth his salt and who has worked with expats before, might also take the time to explain Labour Law in the DR, mainly governed by Law 16-92, particularly where some of its provisions might be sharply at variance with labour law in the expat's country of origin. There are certain business practices which are regarded as normal here which might not be the case elsewhere: professional protectionism, indeed protecting 'the turf' at all levels and in particular how *'gringo* competition' might be handled can be illuminating. Perhaps the most obvious example is how Law 19-92, the Labour Code, has strong protections for workers and that are rigidly applied.

Contracts can be verbal or written; employers should not think that just because there is no written contract, then there is no contract. Normal working hours are considered to be eight hours a day and forty-four hours a week with at least thirty-six hours of uninterrupted time away from work. When hiring staff it should be remembered that, generally speaking 80% of the company's workforce must be Dominican nationals.

As might be expected, there is a considerable amount of paperwork that the employer is required to record: employee, wage and schedule listings, vacations, overtime and the corresponding official inspection visit records. However these are also for the benefit of the employer because they can be used in the event of litigation.

Minimum wage limits exist and are dependent on the size of the company and the sector in which it operates: currently for businesses worth more than RD$4 million the minimum monthly wage is RD$7,360.00 (US$200); for those companies worth more than RD$2 million (US$52,000) but less than RD$4 million (US$108,000) the minimum monthly wage is RD$5,060.00 (US$136) and for those less than RD$2million (US$52,000) the minimum is RD$4,485.00 monthly (US$120). These minimums do not apply to certain industries such as tourism. The minimum salary for a hotel worker is

RD$5,575.00 (US$150) per month. Law 16-92 also covers overtime payments - every hour above the forty-four hours weekly limit is to be paid at 135% of the normal hourly wage; every hour in excess of sixty-eight hours a week is to be paid at 200% of the normal hourly wage. Night hours are paid at an additional 15%.

Most expat employers have not encountered the 'thirteenth month' salary before arrival in the Dominican Republic. Every employee in the Dominican Republic receives, on or before December 20th, a so-called 'Christmas salary' equal to one-twelfth of the total regular salary earned during the year. To calculate the Christmas salary, only the regular salary received is taken into account, excluding tips, overtime and benefits received from profit sharing. The Labour Code establishes a maximum Christmas Salary of five times the minimum wage but many employers waive this limitation and pay the full monthly amount.

DR Labour law also covers items such as profit sharing, time off and termination. Employees have rights in relation to paid maternity leave, paid leave of absence on the death of a close relative, marriage, or partner giving birth, and of course annual vacations, and public holidays.

The issue that seems to cause expat employers most difficulty is that of termination of the employee and it would not be wise to attempt this without seeking legal advice. Any party to an employment contract has the right to terminate it unilaterally without the need to specify a cause. The terminating party must give seven, fourteen, or twenty-eight days advance notice of this decision to the other party depending on whether the agreement has been in force for more than three, six, or twelve months respectively. A late notice or no notice at all will entail a penalty of one day's salary for every day of non-compliance. Employers who exercise their right to terminate their employees without cause must make severance payments to the terminated employee. These will depend on length of time in employment, for example three to six months employment will be awarded five days salary, six months to a year will gain ten days salary and longer than one year, fifteen days salary.

Where the employer is seeking to terminate 'for cause' this requires evidence of the commission by the employee of one or several of the listed grounds for termination (thus the paperwork and records referred to above). It also requires that the employer give notice of the termination and the grounds on which it is based to the Department of Labour within forty-eight hours of the dismissal. Failure to prove cause or to render the notice within the stated forty-eight hours will make the employer liable for payment of severance to the employee. The right of the employer to base the dismissal on a specific cause for termination expires fifteen days after the employee has committed the act alleged as grounds for termination.

Firing a pregnant employee is strictly forbidden during the pregnancy or up to three months after the birth. The pregnant employee has the right to paid maternity leave during the six weeks that precede the birth date and the six weeks that follow it. The employee has also the right to three rest periods of twenty minutes each per workday to breast-feed her child.

Domestic staff are not covered by many of the provisions of the *Labour Code*. However, if the location of their domestic work is registered as a company then they would be considered as covered by labour law, even if the location is a home. Likewise domestic staff who work in condominiums are not considered as domestics. All domestic staff are entitled to two weeks paid vacation a year after their first year and they also have the right to the 'thirteenth month' Christmas bonus. There is no entitlement in law to liquidation pay for domestic staff who are laid off but sometimes it is better for the employer to part on reasonable terms than under circumstances which invite potential future consequences.

Expats intending to set up businesses where they will be employing staff are advised to thoroughly acquaint themselves with the provisions of the DR's labour law. Those with insufficient Spanish should discuss the provisions with their bi-lingual lawyer well in advance of embarking on this venture. Failure to do so can produce unexpected consequences and expensive reparations! In a similar vein, the application of DR company taxation has become a lot more punctilious recently and the services of a good accountant are essential to protect the employer from infracting an obscure sub-section of a requirement which he didn't know existed.

Readers will be relieved to know that the next section is on Leisure Pursuits!

FURTHER READING

Law 16-92
www.dnicostarica.org/wordpress/wp-content/uploads/pdf/Plataforma%20Subregional/Rep%20Dom/CodigodeTrabajo.pdf

Income Tax
www.dgii.gov.do/dgii/impuestos/Paginas/ImpuestoSobrelaRenta.aspx

NCF
www.dgii.gov.do/NCF/Paginas/default.aspx

Leadership/followership similarities between people in a developed and a developing country: the case of Dominicans in NYC and Dominicans on the island by Max Montesino. Journal of Leadership & Organizational Studies, Summer, 2003
www.entrepreneur.com/tradejournals/article/106559615_1.html

Leisure pursuits

Having understood the length of time it takes in the DR to achieve the normal tasks associated with daily life, readers might be forgiven for emitting a hollow laugh on seeing a section entitled 'Leisure Pursuits' and wondering whether they will have sufficient time for any leisure. That combined with having read and inwardly digested the potential minefield of real estate purchasing, the growing narco-industry and resultant crime, and the power and water shortages, the picture could be emerging of life as an obstacle course rather than life pursuing interests that can be followed without a care in the world.

Kitesurfing hot spots include Cabarete, Salinas and Punta Cana

A host of recreational pursuits is available for both residents and tourists. In a country bordered by sea on three sides, water sports such as windsurfing, boogie-boarding, kite-boarding, surfing and sailing are to be expected. The Dominican Republic is known as the kite-boarding capital of the world among those who travel the water sports circuit, and the World Cup is held annually in Cabarete on the north coast of the DR. Windsurfers also make an annual pilgrimage to Cabarete for the annual World Cup Windsurfing Competition held every June. Salinas near Baní in the southwest is an alternative windsurfing and kite-boarding area more accessible to residents of the capital, and it is also possible to enjoy these pursuits in the south and east coast areas. For more details see the Ministry of Tourism's website:

www.godominicanrepublic.com/activities/2-water_sports? activity_id=15-kite_boarding_wind_surfing_and_surfing

Inland white-water rafting is also available; most of the kayaking and white-water rafting trips are done on the turbulent Yaque del Norte River, near the mountain resort of Jarabacoa. This activity should not be attempted after heavy rainfall when a turbulent river becomes an almost impossible river!

Fishermen recognize the Dominican Republic as one of the best hideouts for dozens of species of prized fish. It is the home of several international billfish tournaments each year, including ESPN's Billfish Xtreme Tournament at Punta Cana Resort & Club. More information can be found at *www.flyfishing-punta-cana.com* and *www.mikesmarina.info*

Whale watching is available from January to March in Samaná Bay on the north east coast; thousands of humpback whales of the North Atlantic population return to mate and breed. Canadian Kim Beddall is the expat marine biologist whose company organises tours at *www.whalesamana.com*

The DR's underwater world offers exceptional reef diving and snorkelling, incredibly clear waters, and a variety of colourful marine life. In fact, the country is often listed as one of the top diving locations in the Caribbean. Expats so inclined can explore centuries-old shipwrecks on the country's north coast. Most dive schools will ask for your *PADI* card or number before allowing you to dive, otherwise scuba diving certification is available at suitably qualified schools. A list of these together with contact information can be found at: *www.godominicanrepublic.com/activities/2-water_sports?activity_id=16-diving_and_snorkeling*

Land-based sports activities are plentiful: baseball is the national pastime, closely followed by basketball. Expats thinking of joining the locals would need to be fit! Other land-based activities popular with Dominicans are dominoes and cock-fighting – the latter might be a little violent for some expats and the noise level in the cock-fighting arena will take a while to adjust to. This is not the noise of the birds but the exuberant onlookers who bet on the outcomes. Expats seem to have more interest in the calmer pursuits of horseback riding and golf, although the tranquillity of the former is heavily dependent on the steed chosen!

Golfing is one of the most popular expat pursuits

The DR has more golf courses than any other country in the Caribbean and new ones open every year. Golf can be played throughout the year and because most rain showers are of brief duration, even these do not interrupt the games of the majority of players. Some of the DR's courses have been designed by golf legends such as Pete Dye, PB Dye, Jack Nicklaus, Arnold Palmer, Robert Trent Jones, Gary Player, Tom Fazio and Nick Faldo. Many of the courses incorporate spectacular views to distract from the game.

On the east coast perhaps the best known and highest rated course is *Punta Espada Golf Club*, Cap Cana which has hosted the PGA's Champions Tour every March since 2008. Click on the *View Punta Espada Hole by Hole* button here: *www.capcana.com/site/index.php/en/punta-espada-golf-course*

La Cana Golf Club, Punta Cana Resort has a similarly high reputation but fees are less expensive. A Course Diagram can be downloaded in PDF format from this site: *www.puntacana.com/assets/File/Map-LaCana-Golf.pdf*

Also in Punta Cana, the Tom Fazio designed Corales course opened in 2010 and PB Dye's Hacienda is set for opening in 2011.

Punta Blanca Golf Course was designed by Nick Price who won the British Open in 1994. Further information is available at *www.punta-blanca.com* Click on *Golf Course* and then each of the flagged numbers for photographs of each tee. This course also offers a free meal at the nineteenth hole (Clubhouse!) after the game so that resident players, locals and tourists can socialise.

A downloadable list in PDF format of all east coast golf courses with contact details is available at: *www.godominicanrepublic.com/system/activities/attachments/17/original/GolfDigestDRInsertGuide.pdf*

On the south coast of the Dominican Republic La Romana Country Club has a course with twenty-seven holes. This is a private club so players would need to be invited by a member. Casa de Campo has a number of public courses such as Teeth of the Dog, Dye Fore and The Links *www.casadecampo.com.do*

In La Romana look for La Estancia Golf Resort at *www.laestancia.do*

Further west is Guavaberry Golf & Country Club near Juan Dolio. A description of each hole can be found at the virtual course tour link on this website:
www.guavaberrygolf.com/course/tour/hole1.html

A list of all south and south east coast golf courses with contact information can be found on this website: *www.godominicanrepublic.com/system/activities/attachments/17/original/GolfDigestDRInsertGuide.pdf*

On the north coast of the DR are the courses of Playa Dorada and Playa Grande. You can take a video virtual tour of Playa Dorada here *www.playadoradagolf.com/default.aspx* or read about the course at *www.playadoradagolf.com/golfcourse.html* Playa Grande is considered a far superior course but there has been talk of this becoming a private venue.

Photographs of Playa Grande can be found at *www.playagrande.com*

In the central region of the DR are the courses of Las Aromas, known as Santiago Golf Club, and Jarabacoa also noted in the Golf Digest linked above. Expats who intend playing golf regularly would be advised to obtain a Fedogolf membership as this reduces costs considerably. Information can be found at *www.golfdominicano.com*

It would be remiss of the co-authors, both of British extraction, not to mention the possibilities for playing cricket in the Dominican Republic. These tend to be limited and vary over time with the enthusiasm displayed by, in the main, British, Indian, Pakistani and Sri Lankan expats. *Quisqueya: Mad Dogs and English Couple* by Ginnie outlined the efforts of the handful of British expats on the north coast back in 1994 drawing on the background of interest in this sport imported to the DR by migrant workers from the British West Indies in the late nineteenth and early twentieth centuries. The DR has produced its own cricketers, most notably Enriquillo (Harry) Ureña.

More recently as a result of efforts by a former British Ambassador, Andy Ashcroft, continued by his successor Ambassador Ian Worthington, OBE, the Dominican Cricket Federation was set up in March 2006. Expat residents of Santo Domingo will find cricket played at UASD (*Universidad Autonoma de Santo Domingo*) on weekend afternoons. The Federation's website has not been updated recently but could turn out to be a future resource *www.dominicancricket.com*

Expats often feel that Dominicans were born in the saddle; indeed in some of the more remote locations of the DR four-legged transport is the only way of getting around, although two-wheeled transport is rapidly replacing this. Opportunities abound for horse riding in the DR since this is one of the activities provided in the tourist areas. Other land-based activities include bicycling, quad-biking, hiking on nature trails and for the more adventurous, hill-trekking in the national parks.

The DR has some twenty-four national parks that cover about 10% of the island's entire area. These national parks are put up mainly to help in the preservation of the countryside and in the protection of wildlife. Almost all of the national parks and other protected areas have tourist facilities and most often conduct guided tours. These places are the top choices for seeing tropical plants, trees, and the wildlife of the Dominican Republic up close. They are also the preferred location for another leisure pursuit – wildlife photography – although landscape and portrait photographers will also find countless opportunities everywhere they go. The Dominican Republic and her people are highly photogenic and are usually happy to have their photo taken, but it is advisable to ask permission before doing so.

For those who prefer subterranean delights the DR has some renowned caves to be explored, many of which contain *Taíno* paintings thousands of years old. La Cueva de las Maravillas (Cave of Wonders) is at Cumayasa off the road between San Pedro and La Romana. Near San Cristobal, not far from Santo Domingo, are the caves of El Pomier renowned for their pictographs and petroglyphs. In Mirador del Este Park, Santo Domingo, Los Tres Ojos sports stalactites and stalagmites. In Hato Mayor in the east of the DR Cuevas Fun-Fun is probably the longest cave in the Caribbean with over seven kilometres of tunnels, underground rivers and spectacular rock formations. In the Los Haitises National Park, the San Gabriel cave also has stalactites and stalagmites. In the north of the DR the El Choco National Park outside Cabarete is home to the Callejón de la Loma caves.

If all of this sounds a trifle energetic there are a variety of more cerebral leisure pursuits such as museums, theatres, concerts and art galleries in Santiago and Santo Domingo especially. These are itemised in the chapter on Culture below and it is also worth checking the Ministry of Culture's website for further information *www.cultura.gob.do*

Expats wanting to socialise with others can join the many formal and informal groupings for example in Santo Domingo the International Women's Club *www.iwc-santodomingo.org* The north coast of the DR has an International Residents Club but it also has other groupings, not all of which are organised by expats about whom there are no question marks. As in everything else in the DR new expats should seek advice from a trusted friend. Yes, even about clubs set up by and for expats!

Sports and pastimes

Dominicans share a passion for dominoes with many of their Caribbean neighbours. It is played on barrio street corners and in the mansions of the wealthy. It is played enthusiastically and aggressively, often but not always for money.

Cockfighting, though perceived as a poor rural pursuit, also spans the social divide with high stakes gambling in urban as well as rural *'galleras'* – cockfighting pits. Most small rural settlements will have their own *gallera*, shaped like a small stadium and often very basic and wooden.

Baseball is the number one national pastime, passion and obsession. It is one of the areas in which Dominicans have made a massive contribution, exporting dozens of top players in the US. One effect of this is that becoming a Major League baseball star is every poor – and not so poor – Dominican boy's dream, often at the expense of a more realistic education. Still, the undeniable success of Sammy Sosa, Pedro Martínez and David Ortíz encourages thousands of Dominican youngsters to train hard in the hope of being spotted by a 'scout' and offered a contract. The DR has its own baseball league and leading teams include *Las Aguilas Cibaeñas, Los Tigres del Licey* and several others.

As well as baseball players Dominicans have produced world-class hurdlers (Felix Sánchez), table tennis champions, boxers and have excelled in the martial arts. Other favourites include basketball and to a lesser extent, soccer, but practically any sport can be enjoyed in the country: golf, tennis, water sports, volleyball, surfing, windsurfing and kite-surfing to name just a few.

Animal companions

The quality of life for some expats is vastly enhanced by bringing their animal companions with them to enjoy their new lifestyle. Bringing pets to the DR is not a huge hurdle – correct documentation is required showing proof of vaccination and a health certificate valid for a certain period immediately before and including time of travel.

On arrival at the port or airport an airport veterinarian will examine both paperwork and animal. Some English speaking DR veterinarians or veterinary technicians offer a meet and greet service at airports to ease arrival issues. Those arriving on the north coast can obtain more information from Judy Liggio at the *Asociación de Amigos por los Animales de Sosúa www.aaasosua.com*

In Santo Domingo, Dr Jose Raul Nova operates Servican which offers kennels and dog training *servican.com.do* For veterinarian services Hospital Veterinario Arroyo Hondo, Calle Euclides Morillo No. 76, Arroyo Hondo, Santo Domingo, Tel: 809 328 2776 and 809 616 1204. The most well known veterinarian on the north coast is the legendary Dr Bob (Dr Robert Amelingmeier B.S/D.

V.M.) who can be located off the main Sosúa-Cabarete road near the Coastal Gas Station Tel: 809 571 2286 and 809 430 5503. When not in his veterinarian's surgery Dr Bob can be found running Dominican Crossroads – a voluntary organisation which will also appear in the next section on Voluntary Work. And if you thought you had something in common, he is also an expat.

Of course there are many potential animal companions already in the DR who are currently homeless and very appealing! Expats can find themselves being 'adopted' all too readily; local dogs tend to be highly intelligent (they have to be to survive!) and make excellent security assistants.

Voluntary work

Part of the culture shock of adjusting to life in the DR for the new expat is seeing stark and obscene poverty up close and personal; perhaps for the first time in their lives. Reactions will vary, as they do to any traumatic situation, but it is likely that underpinning these reactions will be a profound sense of guilt. This can be experienced either consciously or unconsciously - even those expats who live a privileged yet blinkered existence, seemingly unaware of the miserable conditions of life for some Dominicans which lurk just down the road, are reacting to guilt by denial. Others might attempt to build a wall around their emotions by blaming the poor for their poverty and subsequently labelling them as lazy or shiftless. Either way, there is a strong possibility that the guilt experienced by the expat in not being poor, can lead to feeling overwhelmed by the size of the problem and a paralysis from acting to overcome it.

The only effective way to deal with this is to employ the same methods as in dealing with any other trauma: recognise it, allow yourself to feel the pain and then move on and find ways, however small, of contributing to your new homeland. Of course we expats cannot help all the poor we come across in the DR, nor can we live our lives hand wringing and paralysed through guilt. In expat heartlands like the north coast many expats seem to spend the better portion of their days propping up the bar of expat watering-holes whilst bemoaning the dreadful conditions many Dominicans have to endure. Better to find a way of making one's own special contribution, however insignificant that might appear to us. Better to slightly toughen one's hide in order not to harden one's heart. It could be that the global financial crisis will prove to be something of a leveller as expats the world over have to tighten their belts somewhat. At least we have a belt to tighten. And from two authors who know – it does get easier the longer you live here.

The DR is defined as a middle-income country, with an annual income per capita of around US$5,000 (*IMF*, 2008 puts it at US$5,132), a ninth of that of the UK (US$45,681). While there is a small but visible wealthy minority in the country and a sizeable middle class, most of the Dominican Republic's citizens live, if not officially under the poverty line as defined by the United Nations (living on less than US$1 per day), in what most people would describe as poverty. Even those earning the minimum wage (less than US$200 per month) are engaged in a daily struggle for survival, and remittances from relatives who emigrated to wealthier countries are what make the difference between survival and collapse, on a national as well an individual level. Many people live on less than the minimum wage, as the 'informal sector' makes up a large section of the economy.

The problem is not so much about lack of resources than their poor management and distribution, and as a result the DR has one of the worst income distribution rates in the world. Former president Joaquín Balaguer is reported to have said: "This is a rich country, (but it is) poorly administered." In a sort of vicious circle, the lack of funding for the education system (see section on education) and government corruption misappropriation of funds have prevented the country and its people from fulfilling their true potential.

Aware of the fact that they are living in a country where most people live in poverty, some expatriates may decide to contribute in some way, perhaps by donating a small amount of time on a regular basis to some local institution or cause, or helping a friend, acquaintance or member of their family.

Many international development organisations and the main large international multilateral entities like the United Nations, the World Bank and others also have a presence in the Dominican Republic. As a rule, the large international organisations do not take volunteers but there may be exceptions so it is worth contacting them, especially if you have a specific skill they can use. Some United

Nations agencies and others may consider taking volunteers/interns.

There are also structured schemes like US Peace Corps and the UK's Progressio (formerly called ICD – International Cooperation for Development) volunteer placements, and it may be an idea for people considering a move to the country to make this their way in – a sure-fire way of learning the language, mingling with the locals and making life-long friends who are not all expats. Ilana came to the country as an ICD (now Progressio) 'cooperante' (skill-sharer) over ten years ago and has never looked back. Some of her closest friends date back to this time, including Dominican neighbours from the small inland town where the project was based, to fellow ex-cooperantes who 'went native'.

There are also smaller outfits that will host a volunteer or make good use of your services on a non-residential basis. Of course, as well as motivation and good intentions, you should also be able to offer a specific skill or service that is needed by the organisation you wish to help. Just being foreign and enthusiastic is not enough! And as ever, at least basic conversational Spanish is essential.

Depending on your skills and interests, there is a good range of organisations to choose from. Street children, AIDS orphans, people with disabilities, women's organisations, environmental campaigns, rehabilitation for addicts and animal welfare all come to mind.

Volunteer work opportunities on the north coast

The development of tourism on the north coast of the DR in the 1970s and 1980s led to some of those tourists returning to the north coast as expat residents. Faced with the unequal access to opportunities and resources ubiquitous in the DR, some of these expat residents decided to contribute by working as volunteers to ameliorate the vast array of need, which faced them. A small mountain biking and adventure tourism company called Iguana Mama decided to devote its interest and a percentage of its income to the educational needs of Dominican children from families with limited economic resources. When Tricia Thorndike Suriel sold the Iguana Mama company in 2002 she then devoted herself to the full time continuation of this work by setting up the Dream Project (Dominican Republic Education and Mentoring Project). This organisation receives support from new generations of tourists and expats and it accepts teaching volunteers who can make a sustained time commitment.

Dominican Crossroads was founded by two expats Dr Bob and Jana Amelingmeier – Dr Bob is the north coast veterinarian mentioned earlier. Dominican Crossroads is a Christian-based organisation, which has a number of outreach programmes with some of the poorest, mainly Haitian, residents of the sugar cane *bateyes*; these include medical, welfare and food provision. Volunteers are accepted for a range of ministries; those with medical skills are particularly valuable. Groups of young visiting volunteers elect to live in the Mission House in the heart of the Haitian village in order to further develop their own project for outreach but volunteers of all ages are welcome.

Integración Juvenil (*IJ*) is focused on helping deprived and neglected children and their families in Puerto Plata. It offers a homeschool for downtown street children, barrio outreach work and at the other end of town the IJ farm which houses another school, a medical and dental clinic and a halfway house.

The Meeting Place in Puerto Plata is an English bookshop, theatre and cultural centre aiming to preserve and promote Puerto Plata's rich history for future generations of Dominican children. It is also designed as a meeting point for locals, foreign residents and tourists in order to break down barriers to fruitful interchange. Profits from the sales of English books are devoted to stocking the local library with Spanish books.

Mustard Seed Communities is a Catholic organisation focussed on the needs of children with physical disabilities many of whom also have learning disabilities. On the north coast of the DR it runs *Hogar Immanuel*, a residential facility.

Island Impact Ministries is a non-denominational Christian organisation that provides health care for the under-resourced at their clinic in La Maranatha, Sosua. They are currently working to set up a facility in La Cienaga for general medical, dental and eye care.

Some expats might be interested in using a lifetime of business skill acquisition in their countries of origin to assist organisations like Kiva who make interest free loans to micro-entrepreneurial business coalitions. The objective is to address the exclusion of the very poor from the banking sector where they would not normally qualify for loans to assist in micro business development. Kiva partners with local organisations, and in the DR one of these is Esperanza International.

Those interested in working with the substance dependent should contact *Hogar Crea* which has facilities throughout the DR and on the north coast, a residential facility in Puerto Plata. Charity golf tournaments organised by expats have also raised funds for this much under-resourced organisation. Given the public attitude towards narco-trafficking it is perhaps not surprising that this organisation is under-resourced at the local level, although addicts will always need treatment at such times as they are willing to engage in it.

Voluntary work can also be carried out in more informal ways: in a developing country it is easy to spot need. Then all one has to do is figure out how to do something about it, either by teaching English to a local child or teenager, for example, or sponsoring a child's education, including checking on how skills are being developed, or assisting individual indigent adults, or volunteering in rural clinics. The possibilities are endless!

Some expats might be more interested in helping animals. The *Asociación de Amigos por los Animales de Sosúa* for example, provides surgical neutering and rehabilitation to animals in need. It offers services for free roaming street dogs/cats and for families without resources with pets, for spaying/neutering, vaccination for rabies and treatment for parasites; it also traps, sterilises and then releases free roaming dogs and cats.

Many Dominican and international companies based in the country have a charitable arm, and embassies also support development projects.

A list of these organisations with brief details and contact information is included at the end of this section.

Getting involved in local community activities: cultural issues

One way an expat is almost certain to get involved is by joining their local residents' association, which are practically ubiquitous in the DR. Almost every neighbourhood, apartment building or residential project will have one, usually known as a *'Junta de Vecinos'* and this spans the social spectrum. Much of the neighbourhood organisation's activities will be centred round the administration of the residential area, but could also extend to joint social, charitable and campaigning activities.

If you do end up involved in a local campaign, or working with local people, here are a few tips:

- Try and take a back seat, and to adopt an enabling rather than a leadership role. In these situations, local people will often expect the foreigner to take the lead, and while sharing valuable experience and knowledge will yield results, it is important to ensure that the local people see themselves as the lead actors in the process

and not just passive followers. Otherwise any progress made will cease once the expat leaves.
- Ensure that the project you embark on is something the potential beneficiaries consider a priority.
- Try and see them as stakeholders rather than beneficiaries, as actors rather than recipients. This will influence the way they see themselves and their role.
- Ensure that you are empowering the people you are trying to help by sharing your skills, rather than just doing things for them.
- Meetings will involve an interesting combination of ceremonial formalities and friendly chaos, people will be late, and will expect refreshments to be laid on, and travel expenses reimbursed.
- Things will take longer than you expect – development is a long process, but there should be a point when the initiative can continue without your help or involvement.
- Often helping can involve more than just giving stuff – if a community needs something tangible like repairs to a school or clinic, one option may be to do the work yourselves – always making sure that the beneficiaries are involved in the work so that they feel ownership and responsibility for it – but it may be more effective to help the community members lobby the relevant authorities to get the job done.

A lot will depend on the type of group you are working with – levels of ability, confidence and skill will vary according to age, gender, educational level, rural/urban, degree of poverty and exclusion experienced by the beneficiaries.

Dominicans in general tend to mistrust charitable organisations, and the strong family and community ties mean that they will opt to help someone in their personal network rather than donating to an organisation. This is true as a rule but there are some exceptions, especially at times of emergency – when there is a national tragedy like the devastating floods caused by Tropical Storms Noel and Olga in late 2007, or the Jimaní mudslides in 2004, people will rush forward with donations that are channelled through religious organisations and private companies – many supermarkets served as massive collection points in the aftermath of the 2007 storms. This has also happened in the case of foreign disasters, most recently the unprecedented outpouring of solidarity and support shown by the Dominican people in response to the January 2010 earthquake in Haiti.

In general though, visitors and/or expatriate residents should not feel bad about feeling wary about local charities. In many countries in all parts of the world, corruption and poor administration can be a real problem, and again, people must use their judgement while sounding out potential recipients. Enlisting the help of a trusted local friend or associate is advisable. But it is not just local charities that fall victim to corruption or a certain lack of scruples. Expats should exercise due diligence in their investigations of charitable efforts set up by fellow foreigners or, indeed, by visiting missionaries. Regrettably there have been cases of expats scamming others' goodwill and there have also been those allegedly operating under a 'Christian' banner whose behaviour is decidedly ungodlike! Then there are outfits where the provision of a meal or the building of a school can appear to be dependent on the willing receipt of a bible. Most of these organisations will make the mistake of viewing the locals in need as recipients rather than as equal partners in a community effort (see above).

Once settled in the country, residents will encounter people from all walks of life, and may decide to help poorer acquaintances in some way, by helping with school supplies, school fees, tutoring, and so on. This is not to be confused with random requests for loans or handouts, which although at the expat's discretion are not beneficial to helping people become self-sufficient or emerge from poverty.

For example in the case of beggars, be aware that in many instances there are 'pimps' living off beggars by forcing them to beg and taking the proceeds. This is most systematic and exploitative in the case of the young Haitian women who beg at traffic intersections with babies and small children in Santiago and Santo Domingo. They are transported illegally from Haiti and put 'to work'. It is not known how much of the proceeds they are allowed to keep.

Depending on the situation, you may prefer to buy food for a beggar instead of giving money. If you want to help the children you see begging, consider donating to a registered charity like *Don Bosco* or *Niños del Camino* instead of giving to an individual. You will be spared the inevitable pleading from other children and your money will be put to more effective use.

The hazards of handouts

In tourist areas especially, giving random items to children is tempting as it undoubtedly makes for quick rapport and is pleasurable for both the giver and the recipient. However, it may not always be the best way to go about things, for several reasons:

- First of all, children will get the idea that foreigners = freebies and are likely to mob every visitor that crosses their path. Enlightened tour guides often discourage this for the very reason that all tourist groups will get harassed if all the children on their route become accustomed to receiving gifts. In some cases it leads to an increase in petty crime against tourists who don't oblige. Unenlightened tour guides, on the other hand, might encourage tourists to propel sweets at local children from the backs of their safari trucks as if a visit to the campo was a visit to the zoo. Such ignorance has ended in tragedy as children rush forward unaware of the dangers of a moving vehicle.
- It happens at random so children living in areas frequented by tourists benefit in a disproportionate way.
- It creates dependency and encourages begging. Unless the child has provided a reasonable service for the giver, like showing them the way somewhere, a reward is not necessary.
- Giving sweets and money is definitely not a good idea. Sweets are bad for the children's health, and money can have a corrupting effect on the children, in that they

are in danger of progressing to exchanging other sorts of 'charms' for money as they grow older.
- Handing out educational items like pens and exercise books – this may seem more worthy but many of the arguments above apply. However, if you make this sort of gift having got to know the child and their family, it is often the most appreciated gift you can give.
- Food – certainly in the case of children begging while you are eating at a restaurant it would not be amiss to order the child a slice of pizza or a sandwich if you prefer not to give money. Always remember that this may not go down well with the owners of the establishment who do not want beggars harassing their clients.

Some charities and international organisations in the DR

This is not meant to be a comprehensive list but a range of examples.

UNITED NATIONS AGENCIES

UNICEF
Ave. Anacaona 9,
United Nations House, 3rd floor
Mirador Sur
Santo Domingo
Tel: 809 473 7373
www.unicef.org/republicadominicana/english

INSTRAW
United Nations International Research and Training Institute for the Advancement of Women
Cesar Nicolas Penson 102-A
Santo Domingo
Tel: 809 685-2111 ext. 241
www.un-instraw.org

INTERNATIONAL ORGANISATIONS THAT PLACE VOLUNTEERS IN THE DR

Progressio (formerly known as ICD – International Cooperation for Development)
Unit 3 Canonbury Yard
190a New North Road
London N1 7BJ, UK
Tel: +44 (0)20 7354 0883
www.progressio.org.uk

Peace Corps
Ave. Bolivar
Gazcue
Santo Domingo
Tel: 809 685 4102
www.peacecorps.gov

SOME INTERNATIONAL ORGANISATIONS WITH A PRESENCE IN THE DR

Intermón (Oxfam Spain) - *www.intermonoxfam.org*
Plan International - *www.plan-international.org*
World Vision - *www.worldvision.org*

Catholic Relief Services - *www.crs.org*

Save the Children (through local counterpart FUDECO) - *www.savethechildrendominicana.org*

GTZ - *www.gtz.de/de/index.htm*

Jesuit Refugee Service - Haitian migrants and refugees - *www.jrs.net*

DOMINICAN ORGANISATIONS

ProFamilia - Family planning, health services
Calle Socorro Sánchez 160, Gazcue,
Apartado Postal 1053
Santo Domingo
Tel: 809 689 0141
www.profamilia.org.do

Casa Rosada – home for AIDS orphans and children with HIV/AIDS
Hogar-Escuela-Hospital
Av. Prol. Venezuela,
C/Isabel Aguiar 'Loly'
Los Tres Brazos
Santo Domingo Este
www.zenbizness.com/CASA

Muchachos Don Bosco – Project providing training and help for young people, especially street kids
Tel: 809 536 7171
www.muchachosdonbosco.com

Niños del Camino – street kids project that uses volunteers
Ave. Jiménez Moya no.37, El Manquito
Santo Domingo

Tel: 809 508 2630
www.shinealight.org/spanish/NinosCamino.html

Colectiva Mujer y Salud – feminist organisation working on health and women's issues
Calle Socorro Sánchez # 64, Gazcue,
Santo Domingo
Tel: 809 682 3128
www.colectivamujerysalud.org

Vida Azul – environmental campaigning organisation
Calle Mustafa Kemal Ataturk No 10 Local No 1,
Naco, Santo Domingo,
Tel: 809 566 7780
www.vidaazul.org

Hogar Crea – rehabilitation for addicts
www.hogarcrea.net

PADELA – animal welfare charity
Isabel la Catolica No. 5,
Zona Colonial, Santo Domingo,
Tel/Fax: 809 685-0999
www.padelard.org
www.padelard.org/en
Fundemar – animal welfare organisation
Idelisa Bonnelly de Calventi
Tel: (809) 547 3677
Email: *ibonnelly@codetel.net.do*

North coast based organisations
The Dream Project, Cabarete
Plaza de Patio

Cabarete, Puerto Plata
Tel: 809 571 0497
www.dominicandream.org

Crossroads
Tel: (809) 571-2286 or (809) 430-5505
www.dominicancrossroads.com

Integracion Juvenil
Calle Duarte, No. 61, Puerto Plata
Mailing Address: Integración Juvenil, Apartado Postal 182, Puerto Plata, Dominican Republic
Tel: 809 586 2020
Fax: 809 586 2638
www.puertoplataguide.com/ij_en.html
www.popreport.com/ij/programs.html

The Meeting Place
Calle Juan Bosch #60
Puerto Plata
www.meetingplace-dr.com

Hogar Immanuel, Mustard Seed Foundation,
Cangrejo, Puerto Plata
www.mustardseed.com
Island Impact Ministries, Sosua
www.islandimpact.net/about_us.html

Asociación de Amigos por los Animales de Sosúa
Mailing address
EPS D4145,
P.O. Box 02-5648,
Miami, FL, 33102 USA

Tel: 809 571 1167
www.aaasosua.com

East coast based organisations
The Punta Cana Ecological Foundation
www.puntacana.org

Environmental Programmes
PUNTACANA Ecological Foundation
Tel: 809 959 9221

Community Activities
PUNTACANA Foundation
Tel: 809 959 2714

Samaná based organisations
Fundación Mahatma Gandhi
Calle Salome Urena 8
Las Terrenas, Samana
Tel: 809 240 6596 / 809 386 3086 / 809 496 0245
www.fundacionmahatmagandhi.com

Guariquén - Ecological and Community Tourism Organisation
Arroyo el Cabo 13,
Las Galeras, Samaná
Tel: 809 914-3055
Fax: 829 797-2636
www.guariquen.org

CEBSE Conservation Group
Av. La Marina, Tiro al Blanco
Centro Para La Naturaleza
Samaná

Tel: 809 538-2042
www.samana.org.do/cebse.htm

South east based organisations
NPH Orphanage
Carretera Ramón Santana
Frente al Batey Nuevo
San Pedro de Macorís
Tel: 829 962 9931
www.nphdr.org

Shopping

Food shopping presents no problems in the Dominican Republic – Dominicans eat too! There will be some items that appear both alien and with extra-terrestrial powers; *tayota* for example is a pear-shaped vegetable with the potential for removing skin from the palm of your hand when peeling (yes, we have flesh-eating vegetables). If this doesn't serve as a deterrent, you may like to know that *tayota* is actually called christophene or christophine in English, and is also known as *chayote* in the US, from its name in Mexico and Central America. It is eaten boiled and tastes like a bland courgette.

All towns have small or medium-sized supermarkets and even the tiniest hamlet will have a *colmado* or corner store. The larger supermarket chains are concentrated mainly in the capital and to a lesser extent in the second largest city *Santiago*: the main names are Supermercados Nacional, Super Pola (part of La Sirena department store), La Cadena, Bravo, Carrefour and Jumbo. La Sirena also has branches in San Francisco de Macorís and Puerto Plata, and Jumbo is in Santiago, La Romana and San Pedro de Macorís.

Colmados can be found in most places, from small rural towns to upmarket urban neighbourhoods

Fresh fruit and vegetables abound as do meat and fish. Some of the cuts of meat may differ from the expat's country of origin; trial and error is the only way to approach this. Insistence on a cut similar to 'back home' might be an unnecessary expenditure of energy. Fruit is often best bought from street vendors although these may be inclined to charge *gringo* prices: this will diminish if you establish yourself as a regular customer.

Toiletries and household cleaning items are also in good supply.

Larger household items such as furniture and electrical appliances are best bought at some of the chain stores found mainly in Santiago and Santo Domingo but also opening every year in other provincial locations. The DR's electrical supply is 110 volts, alternating at 60 cycles per second (similar to that in the United States). Many expats from the US decide to bring electrical items with them in a container because prices in the DR are generally more expensive, but expats from the United Kingdom and some parts of Europe will not be able to use their appliances based on 240 volts unless they build a home in the DR which runs two cycles of 110v to provide 220v outlets or use a voltage converter. The latter come in two types: light weight resistor-network converters that support high-wattage electrical appliances like hair dryers and irons. However, they can only be used for short periods of time and are not ideal for digital devices. Transformers will have a much lower maximum Watt rating, usually 50 or 100. Transformers can often be used continuously and provide better electricity for low wattage appliances like battery chargers, radios, laptop computers, cameras, mp3 players and camcorders. However, they are heavy because they contain large iron rods and lots of copper wire. Plugs in the DR generally have two flat pins or sometimes two flat pins and one rounded pin. Electric drills and saws from the UK run at a lower speed, so it is advisable to bring one that can be charged up or buy one in the DR.

When shopping for household appliances apart from the obvious advice to shop around it is always worth asking for a discount for cash. Such discounts are not always proffered unless you ask. Buying many appliances at one store should entitle the purchaser to considerable discounts. Just as negotiation is the name of the game here for tourists buying items to take home, it equally applies to those who live here purchasing durable (we hope) items. Always check that the required number of components is in the box – it is fairly common practice in the DR to 'borrow' a lead or some such because the first box did not have one. Better to check in the shop than to get home and curse.

Rattan furniture is ubiquitous in the DR, not just for patios but for interiors also. In the northern region, one can either purchase from some of the larger furniture stores in Santiago or Santo Domingo or go straight to the manufacturers and distributors like Mimbre y Rattan of Navarrete or the rattan shops in Gaspar Hernandez. Mahogany and ironwork furniture is also sold throughout the DR and of course every home has a rocking chair or set thereof. The new expat might be surprised at the straight-backed chairs that abound and which are somewhat uncomfortable and the habit many locals have of leaving the plastic covering on the cushions to protect against dust. There is a large market for contemporary style furniture but this tends to be on the pricier side. It remains to be seen whether the advent of *IKEA*, which opened a store in Santo Domingo in February 2010 will change this.

For expats who cannot be bothered to buy their own furniture there are even interior design companies who will furnish your home for you such as *www.puntacanafurniture.com* in Punta Cana.

Listed below is a non-exhaustive directory of some of the larger stores.

SUPERMARKETS

El Nacional – branches in Santo Domingo and Santiago, also in La Romana (*Casa de Campo*) and Punta Cana *www.centrocuestanacional.com/tiendas.asp*

Super Pola – branches in Santo Domingo and Santiago, San Francisco de Macorís, Puerto Plata and Bávaro *www.superpola.com*

Bravo – branches in Santo Domingo *www.superbravo.com.do*

La Cadena – branches in Santo Domingo *www.supermercadoslacadena.com*

Jumbo – branches in Santo Domingo, Santiago, La Romana, San Pedro de Macorís *www.jumbo.com.do*

Carrefour – Santo Domingo *www.carrefour.com*

Price Smart – branches in Santo Domingo and Santiago *www.pricesmart.com*

Once you leave the main cities, the predominant tourist/expat areas have limited supermarket options, but this is slowly improving and the smaller independent outlets have in many cases adapted to serve their international clientele. The North Coast has Playero in Sosua and Tropical in Puerto Plata, and now the new La Sirena on Puerto Plata's Malecón seafront avenue. Residents of Samaná have to travel to the city of San Francisco de Macorís for the nearest good-sized supermarket – also La Sirena/Super Pola. Las Terrenas has Supermercado Lindo *www.lasterrenascontacts.com/AlimentationEn.htm*

In the east, Higuey has two large supermarkets, Iberia and Zaglul, La Romana has a *Jumbo*, and Punta Cana has

Nacional, Super Pola (due early 2011) as well as several small minimarkets in Verón and Bávaro.

SPECIALIST FOOD STORES

Orgánica – health foods, mainly imported, organic
Plaza Cataluña,
Ave. Gustavo Mejía Ricart,
Piantini, Santo Domingo

Mercado Ecológico – Organic fruit and vegetables and some health foods
Calle Ana Josefa Puello No. 33
Mirador Sur, Santo Domingo
Tel: 829 435 8190
mercado_ecologico@yahoo.com

L'Epiciere de l'Orient – Mediterranean,
Middle Eastern and Asian foods
Plaza Paseo de la Churchill
Ave. Winston Churchill esq. Calle Roberto Pastoriza
Santo Domingo

Various Chinese Supermarkets in Chinatown (Ave. Duarte esq. México) and on Ave. Rómulo Betancourt, Santo Domingo

Asiatico
Ave. 27 de febrero esq. La Privada
Santo Domingo

ELECTRICAL AND HOUSEHOLD GOODS

Santiago

Plaza Lama
Calle El Sol Esq. Sánchez,
Tel: 809 276 5262
www.plazalama.com

La Sirena
Ave. Bartolomé Colon
Tel: 809 247 4447
www.tiendalasirena.com

Ochoa, Ochoa Hogar
Plaza International
Tel: 809 724 0888
www.ochoa.com.do/index.php

Price Smart
Ave. Estrella Sahdalá No.21,
Tel: 809 336 1999
www.pricesmart.com/Local/Membership/Club-Details.aspx?warehouseid=6802

Haché
Ave. Salvador E. Sadhalá
Tel: 809 971 1111
www.hache.com.do

Santo Domingo

Multicentro La Sirena
www.tiendalasirena.com
Ave. Winston Churchill Esq. Ave. Gustavo Mejía Ricart

Tel: 809 472 4444
and Av. Charles de Gaulle,
Nr. Esq. Carretera Mella,
Santo Domingo Este
Tel: 809 593 2000

Plaza Lama La Megatienda
Ave. 27 de Febrero Esq. Ave. Winston Churchill
Tel: 809 274 5262
www.plazalama.com

Distribuidora Corripio
Ave. John F Kennedy near Esq. Nuñez de Caceres
Tel: 809 227 3000
www.corripiocm.com

Americana Departamentos (Ferreteria Americana)
Ave. John F Kennedy near Esq. Ave. Abraham Lincoln
Tel: 809 549 7777
www.americana.com.do

Almacenes Unidos
Ave. John F Kennedy near Esq. Ave. Winston Churchill
Tel: 809 472 6911

Casa Cuesta/Ferreteria Cuesta – several branches around the city:
Calle El Conde, Zona Colonial, Ave. 27 Febrero esq Ave.
Lincoln, Bella Vista Mall, Ave. Sarasota
www.centrocuestanacional.com

Price Smart
Ave. Charles Summer
Tel: 809 334 3333
www.pricesmart.com

Molina
Ave. Tiradentes,
Centro Comercial Naco II,
Local 2-d
Tel: 809 368 3131
www.molina.com.do

Kitchen Center
Gustavo Mejia Ricart No. 114,
Plaza Cataluña
Tel: 809 540 4119
www.kitchencenter.com.do

FURNITURE

Santiago

Haché
Ave. Salvador E. Sadhalá
Tel: 809 971 1111
www.hache.com.do

Ochoa, Ochoa Hogar
Las Colinas Mall
Tel: 809 724 0888
www.ochoa.com.do
Muebles Méndez
Carr Luperón Km 7 1/2
809 736-7444

Casa Mobel
Autopista Duarte Km 1
Tel: 809 581 9455 / 809 971 9344
www.casamobel.com

Artesanía Rattán CxA
Ave. R Vidal 3
809 971-6440
Muebles Angel Mimbre Y Ratán
J J Dominguez 2
Tel: 809 570 8466

Castibú
Gurabo
Tel: (809) 581 6874 / (809) 241 4467
www.tiendademuebles-rusticos-castibu.art-online-rd.com

Santo Domingo

La Sirena, Cuesta Hogar and Ferreteria Americana - see above.

Ilumel
Ave. Abraham Lincoln # 908-912,
Tel: 809 732 7337
www.ilumel.com

Batavia
Rafael Augusto Sanchez 37
Piantini
Tel: 809 683 4428
www.batavia.com.do

Conforama
Ave. 27 de febrero between Aves. Lincoln and Churchill and MegaCentro, Santo Domingo East (Zona Oriental)

Castibú
Roberto Pastoriza, 204
Tel: 809 381 4545 / 809 736 7825
www.tiendademuebles-rusticos-castibu.art-online-rd.com

Artesania Rattan CporA
Ave. Romulo Betancourt 1516
Ed. San Carlos
Tel: 809 533 0590

Hogareña Home Furniture
Prol G M Ricart 1
Tel: 809 548 6662

La Novia de Villa
Roberto Pastoriza 406 and
Paseo de Los Locutores 11
Tel: 809 566 0914 / 809 566 9853
www.lanoviadevilla.com

Gonzalez Muebles
Tel: 809 732 0025
www.gonzalezmuebles.com.do

Muebles Haché
Ave. John F Kennedy near esq. Ave. Lope de Vega
Tel: 809 566 1111
www.hache.com.do

IKEA
Ave. John F. Kennedy, esq.
Calle Bienvenido García Gautier
El Pino
www.ikeasantodomingo.com

North coast

Sosua/Cabarete
PatioWorx, Carretera Sosua-Cabarete 1/2 KM

Tel: 809 571 4547
patioworx@codetel.net.do

Puerto Plata

Distribuidora Gonzalez (2 stores)
Calle Beller 78,
Tel: 809 586-6945
and Calle Separacion
Tel: 809 586 3993

Punta Cana

Ilumel - Punta Cana Shopping Mall
Tel: 809 732-7337
www.ilumel.com

Unicane
UNICANE BAVARO, S.A.
Ave. Estados Unidos
Tel: 809 468 4833 / 809 984 3200
www.unicanebavaro.com

Casa Holanda
Carretera Veron-Punta Cana
Tel: 809 455 1065

SHOPPING MALLS

Santo Domingo

Acropolis – Ave. Winston Churchill – one of the glitziest and largest, with international names including Zara, Mango, Nine West, Tommy Hilfiger and Fridays, as well as a food hall and multi-screen cinema.

Bella Vista – Ave. Sarasota – one of the best, home to a large branch of Supermercado Nacional, all the main banks, as well as shoe shops, fashion boutiques, food hall, interior decoration, Cuesta Hogar and a multi-screen cinema.

Blue Mall – Ave. Churchill: luxury brands like Cartier and Louis Vuitton are represented at this brand new mega-mall.

Diamond Mall – Ave Los Proceres north of Ave John F Kennedy: boutiques, shoe shops, children's clothing, golf supplies, food hall and multi-screen cinema.

Mega Centro – Zona Oriental – the biggest in the country, it includes a branch of Jumbo Supermarket, Ferreteria Americana, Conforama and much more.

Plaza Central – although since overtaken by the newer, glitzier malls, this was once the biggest and best. Still very popular, it includes a wide range of stores.

Santiago

Santiago has Plaza Internacional with many local and international chains, a Gold's Gym and a multi-screen cinema. The east coast has Palma Real Shopping Village in Bávaro with several international franchises like Hard Rock Café, Tony Roma's, Guess, Diesel, Mail Boxes Etc, a cinema and Banco Popular and Banco de Reservas.

Bookshops

Thesaurus
Branches in Santo Domingo and Santiago. Small selection of books in English.
Santo Domingo:

Ave. Abraham Lincoln esq. Sarasota
Tel: 809 508 1114
Thesaurus Santiago
Centro Plaza Internacional, Ave. Juan Pablo Duarte, esq. Ponce
Tel: 809 581 1818
www.thesaurus.com.do

Libreria Cuesta
Ave. 27 de febrero esq. Lincoln
Santo Domingo
www.cuestalibros.com

New Horizons Bookshop
Ave. Sarasota 51, Bella Vista
Santo Domingo
Tel: 809 533 4915
www.gcnewhorizons.net/onlineshop/Default.aspx

Helen Kellogg Library
Ave. Independencia, casi esq. Danae, Gazcue
Santo Domingo
Behind the Church of the Epiphany
A well-stocked, well-run lending library that also sells a selection of donated second-hand books.

The Meeting Place
Calle Juan Bosch 60
Puerto Plata
www.meetingplace-dr.com

Paper Moon Books
Galerias Puntacana
Punta Cana Village

TOY SHOPS

El Mundo del Juguete
Tel: 809 227 3000
www.corripiocm.com/retail/elmundodeljuguete
Branches:
Santo Domingo:
Ave. J. F. Kennedy 47
Ave. J. F. Kennedy casi esq. Av. Núñez de Cáceres
Plaza Naco, Ave. Tiradentes
Santiago
Calle El Sol esq. Duarte
La Novia de Villa
Lope de Vega esq. Roberto Pastoriza.
Tel: 809 566 5111
www.lanoviadevilla.com

Juguetón
Santo Domingo branches in Plaza Naco, Plaza Central, Zona Oriental and more. One branch in Santiago on Ave. Duarte
www.jugueton.com.do

Imaginarium
Santo Domingo branch in Plaza Acropolis
www.imaginarium.com.do
Most department stores like *La Sirena* have toy sections.

Online shopping

Favourite brands and items that are not available in the DR may be ordered online. The only snag is that although the Dominican Republic has a postal system it is on a par with such illustrious institutions as the Paraguayan Navy in that if it does exist, it does not carry out the functions its name implies. Its sole purpose in life is not to relay correspondence to, from and within the DR, but to provide employment for the party faithful. I would urge visitors to the capital to go to the main post office at *La Feria*, which is fully equipped and staffed, but handles minimal volumes of mail and virtually no members of the public. It is a strange, surreal experience.

Dominicans have got round the unreliability of the service by creating private substitutes, hence the armies of motorcycle *mensajeros* (messengers) zipping around at all times.

For international correspondence, the private mailbox services provide the solution. They give you a US address with a P O Box number and street address in Miami, and a courier service to the DR. The rental fees are low – around US$10 annually, but you pay per item according to weight and dimension. If the item is ordered from a US-based retailer you will only pay national postage charges.

PRIVATE MAIL BOX COMPANIES

Santo Domingo

P O Box International
Calle Girl Scouts # 4, Naco
Tel: 809 381 2627
info@pobidom.com
www.pobidom.com

Jet Pack
Roberto Pastoriza No. 216,

Ensanche Piantini
Tel: 809 563 2727
www.jetpack.com.do
servicio@jetpack.com.do

Business Mail
Business Mail & Cargo, S A
Ave. Roberto Pastoriza 1
809 683 1919
www.bmcargo.com

EPS
Ortega & Gasset esq. Fantino Falco 40, Naco
809 227 1448
www.eps-int.com

Mail Boxes Etc
Ave. Tiradentes 10, Naco
Tel: 809 412 2330
www.mbe.com.do

Santiago

Business Mail
Calle 7 No 22
Jardines Metropolitanos
Tel: 809 241 0625
www.bmcargo.com

EPS
Calle Hostos 3
809 581-1912
and Ave. 27 de Febrero
Tel: 809 724 2900

www.eps-int.com
servicio@eps-int.com

Mail Boxes Etc.
Ave. Bartolomé Colón esq. Ave. Texas
Santiago
Tel: 809 336 2330
www.mbe.com.do

North Coast

Banker Trust
Pedro Clisante No. 25, Sosua
Tel: 809 571-4622
www.Banker-Trust.com

EPS Business Services
12 Pedro Clisante, Sosua
Tel: 809 571 3451
www.eps-int.com

Business Mail
Turisol Plaza, Puerto Plata
809 970 0942
www.bmcargo.com

North east coast

Mail Boxes Etc.
Ave. Duarte 39, Plaza Claudio,
Las Terrenas, Samaná
Tel: 809 240 6347
www.mbe.com.do

East coast
Mail Boxes Etc
Palma Real Shopping Village
Bávaro
Tel: 809 552 6399

Mail Boxes Etc.
Punta Cana Village
809 959 0666
www.mbe.com.do

Weather

Unlike the unpredictable nature of much of life in the DR, the weather is one of the more consistent features. On the coast, temperatures range from 25°C to 34°C (77°F-93°F) so although locals and long-term expats will refer to 'winter' and 'summer' the new expat will have a different understanding of these terms. The temperature on the south coast tends to be warmer by about one or two degrees Celsius compared to the north and north east coasts. It can get very chilly - by Caribbean standards - in the highlands – although what the local media describes as "snow" in the Cordillera Central mountain range invariably turns out to be frost. In highland cities like Jarabacoa and Constanza the average temperature ranges from 18°C to 28°C (66°F-84°F).

There are slight variations between the summer and winter months. The so-called 'cool' or winter season, runs from November to April. The humidity is relatively low during these months and it tends to cool down in the evenings much more than in the summer months. The coastal/beach regions generally experience highs of around 28°C (83°F) during the day and lows of about 20°C (68°F) in the evening. The summer season in the Dominican Republic runs from May to October. Average daily highs for the coastal/beach regions rise to around 31°C (87°F) during the day, dropping down to about 22°C (72°F) at night. It is the higher humidity during this period that can make it feel much hotter during this season.

Regardless of season, the coolest area of the country is the Central Cordillera mountain region, around Jarabacoa and Constanza, where the average highs can hover around 16°C (61°F). The desert regions in the southwest of the country experience the highest average temperatures, at times soaring to the high 30s Celsius.

A question frequently asked by the new expat is 'when is the rainy season?' The northern areas of the Dominican Republic tend to see the greatest amount of rainfall and do so predominantly between October and April. The southern areas of the Dominican Republic experience their greatest rainfall between May and November. Torrential downpour-like conditions can certainly occur in all areas of the Dominican Republic, mostly occuring in short bursts. Other than major storms that may move through a particular region, most showers are short-lived and have the sun shining brightly within half an hour. Rainfall varies from 43 centimetres (17 inches) annually in the western areas to 208 centimetres (82 inches) in the northeast. When the authors first moved to the DR there were more

clearly definable periods that could be described as 'the rainy season' but with recent climatic changes this is no longer a relevant concept. Raw data on rainfall and temperature going back to the early twentieth century can be found at:
gcmd.gsfc.nasa.gov/records/GCMD_NCL00249_250_251_256_259.html

Although this is not the place for a treatise on the existence or otherwise of global warming it is perfectly clear that there have been climatic changes in the DR in the past ten years. Those interested could consult *Global Climate Change and the Dominican Republic* by Michael C. MacCracken of the Climate Institute, Washington DC written in June 2006:
www.climate.org/topics/climate-change/climate-change-dominican-republic.html

According to MacCracken 'the rise in the CO_2 concentration itself will tend to acidify the oceans, creating a problem for all tropical regions because it will become more difficult for ocean organisms to generate shells and coral. Global climate change will affect the world economy, the production and purchasing capabilities of trading partners, the extent and spread of vector-borne and infectious diseases, and the vitality of natural resources that the Dominican Republic shares with the world (eg, migrating birds and whales). In addition, global climate change will affect the large-scale circulations of the atmosphere and oceans (so the strength and phasing of the intertropical convergence zone), the characteristics of hurricanes, and the rate of melting of mountain glaciers and polar ice sheets, which, along with warming of the oceans, will accelerate the rate of rise of global sea level to roughly 0.3 to 0.5 metres per century, or higher if the Greenland Ice Sheet starts to rapidly deteriorate.'

Of these perhaps the most worth noting is the possible change to the strength and phasing of the intertropical convergence zone. The DR is in the hurricane belt; the concern is that the relatively few hurricanes currently experienced here could escalate in both frequency and intensity. In 2009 NASA produced its report for 2008 identifying that year as one of the worst in recent memory.
www.nasa.gov/mission_pages/hurricanes/archives/2008/2008_ra infall.html

2009, on the other hand, was an uneventful year for hurricanes in the DR. The Global Foundation for Democracy and Development also addressed this issue in the 2007 National Forum on Climate Change: *Evidence of Global Warming in the Dominican Republic*
www.globalfoundationdd.org/seminars/climatechangesII2007/cpo _news07.asp

Concomitant with this and of significance to the DR are the rising sea levels and the scarcity of water availability. Another paper worth reading is *Climate Change: Driven by the Ocean not Human Activity* by William M. Gray, Professor Emeritus, Dept of Atmospheric Science, Colorado State University March 2009:
typhoon.atmos.colostate.edu/Includes/Documents/Publications/gra y2009.pdf

The DR is subject to both tropical storms and hurricanes: a tropical storm is identified as such when its winds reach a strength of 39-73 mph (63-118 kph), hurricanes are major storms with winds over 73 mph or 118 kph and are categorised according to the Saffir-Simpson Hurricane Scale. A Category One Hurricane has winds of 74-95 mph (64-82 knots or 119-153 km/hr) and generally results in no significant damage to building structures but there can be damage primarily to unanchored mobile homes, shrubbery, and trees. A Category Two Hurricane has winds of 96-110 mph (83-95 knots or 154-177 km/hr) and will cause some roofing material, door, and window damage of buildings plus considerable damage to shrubbery and trees with some trees blown down. There can also be considerable damage to mobile homes, poorly constructed signs, and piers. Category Three means winds 111-130 mph (96-113 knots or 178-209 km/hr) with some structural damage to small residences and utility buildings with a minor amount of curtain wall failures plus damage to shrubbery and trees with foliage blown off trees and large trees blown down. Category Four signifies winds of 131-155 mph (114-135 knots or 210-249 km/hr) with more extensive curtain wall failures and some complete roof structure failures on small residences. Shrubs, trees, and all signs are blown down and there is complete destruction of mobile homes. A Category Five means winds greater than 155 mph (135 knots or 249 km/hr). Complete roof failure on many residences and industrial buildings and some complete building failures with small utility buildings blown over or away.

Fortunately, the DR has not been hit by hurricanes all that often; in the last forty-five years there have been ten hurricanes or approximately one every four and a half years. Two of these landed at Category One (Eloise in 1975 and Jeanne in 2004), one at Category Two (Edith 1963), three at Category Three (Gilbert 1988, Hortense 1996 and Georges 1998), three at Category Four (Inez 1966, Beulah 1967, and Emily 1987) and one at Category Five (David 1979). Of perhaps more interest to potential expats is the landing site: three hit the south coast, Santo Domingo and La Romana, four hit the south-west, Barahona and Bani, one hit the east coast, Punta Cana and two hit the north-east coast, Samaná.

Hurricane David in 1979 swept through the DR with winds of up to 150 mph removing roofs from buildings, downing many structures and resulting in some 2000 fatalities; it was the most serious hurricane for the DR since San Zenon of 1930, which had killed some 8000 citizens. As with many hurricanes, the fatalities were mostly the result of flooding rather than wind damage. In 1979 whole villages were swept away by raging floodwaters and mudslides. Far fewer fatalities in the DR were reported as a result of Hurricanes Emily (1987), Gilbert (1988) and Hortense (1996) but reported fatalities do not tell the whole story. The reported fatalities in the DR from Hurricane Georges in 1998 were somewhere in the region of 400. However, this was a hurricane that altered course at the last moment; it had been predicted to hit the north coast but instead veered to the south catching Santo Domingo off guard and largely unprepared. Local knowledge put the death toll in the thousands since incidents like the breaking of the wall of the dam at San

Juan de la Maguana sent a wall of water to the school below which was being used as a refuge for the town's children and families. This was in the shanty neighbourhood of Mesopotamia, built as it name suggests between two rivers, and which was washed away, with a death toll estimated in the hundreds. After the floods subsided, the area was repopulated.

As well as the human death toll, the rainfall associated with hurricanes and resultant flooding decimates both livestock and agriculture. And sometimes can alter the plant ecosystem in perpetuity. A study carried out in the Los Haitises National Park examined the effects of previous agricultural land use on the damage and recovery of plant communities affected by Hurricane Georges (see *Effects of Land Use History on Hurricane Damage and Recovery in a Neotropical Forest* by M.Uriarte et al in Plant Ecology Vol. 174: 2004)
www.eeb.cornell.edu/flecker/pdf/Uriarte%20et%20al%202004_Plant%20Ecology.pdf

In the DR it is often rain damage that is more pernicious than wind damage and water damage and flooding can occur as much during a tropical storm as during a hurricane. Residents therefore need to be prepared ahead of hurricane season which runs June to November annually, although historically most hurricanes which have hit the DR, or close to it, have been in September.

It would be ill-advised to think that the state is in much of a position to help expats as a result of storm damage; Governmental resources are too thinly stretched to meet the needs of the poor whose homes are frequently in those locations most prone to flooding, so expats stand no chance! The best advice is to have preparations well advanced and to take care of oneself and one's neighbours. Street power will be shut off ahead of a storm so stocking up with fuel for a generator can be done in advance as can the buying of supplies of drinking water and food that will not spoil if refrigeration is not possible. All moveable objects in one's own garden should be removed plus a check of neighbouring gardens to ensure their debris does not crash into your windows, windows boarded, vehicles securely parked and if they have to be out in the street, then cross taping of windscreens can be carried out a few hours before the hurricane is due to pass to ensure minimal damage from broken glass.

It is possible that if this is the expat's first experience of a hurricane that there will be more anxiety from family members than is warranted. Ginnie had stayed awake monitoring a message board overnight when Hurricane Jeanne was due to pass through on the north coast in 2004, it stalled out to the east for hours, so that she eventually went to bed and slept through the whole thing when it did pass. However, that was as a Tropical Storm that her house was well able to withstand.

Decisions about evacuation should be made well in advance of this and partly based on how safe the home is and what the projected strength of the hurricane will be when it reaches you. As yet neither Ginnie nor Ilana have lived through a really strong hurricane bearing down on their respective abodes. If they knew a category four or five was barrelling in their directions it would be fairly safe to assume you would not locate them at home! Expats will make their own decisions about tolerance levels; the DR emergency authorities do evacuate those in vulnerable areas (near river banks, the mouths of rivers prone to storm surge) but most expats do not choose to live in vulnerable areas, so their decisions are theirs.

Sometimes the DR authorities make unwise decisions to rapidly empty dams. In October 2007 the slow moving Tropical Storm Noel saturated the DR with rain for days and days; then in early December Tropical Storm Olga dumped even more rain on soil already saturated and a disaster occurred for many residents of the DR's second largest city, Santiago. This was not a disaster caused by Mother Nature but by the men or women who made the decision to open the *Tavera Dam* at full bore in the middle of the night and send 1.6 million gallons per second into the Yaque River without a prior full scale evacuation of those living in the areas which would be flooded. Not only were the residents not evacuated but many claim they received no warning whatsoever. Those who did said they were told about fifteen minutes before the torrent of water rushed through, destroying everything in its path. More on this can be found in an article by one of the co-authors: *Natural Disaster, Human Incompetence Or Criminal Negligence? The Tavera Dam Tragedy In The Dominican Republic*, appearing on *OffshoreWave.com*:
www.offshorewave.com/offshorenews/natural-disaster-human-incompetence-or-criminal-negligence-the-tavera-dam-tragedy-in-the-dominican-republic-by-ginnie-bedggood.html

Expats will have their own favourite radio or TV stations to consult at these times since up-to-date information is important. Online weather forums are also an important source of information. The DR's Meteorological Service can be found at *www.onamet.gov.do*

There are many English language online sites, which provide hurricane and tropical storm information. Some of the most popular are:
www.wunderground.com/tropical
www.stormcarib.com
www.storm2k.org

As if potential expats have not read enough already about natural hazards in the DR we could not end this section without a mention of earthquakes. Earthquakes typically occur near faults in the Earth's crust where rock formations, driven by the movements of the tectonic plates that make up the Earth's surface, grind slowly past each other or collide, building up stress. At some point, stress overcomes friction and the rocks slip suddenly, releasing seismic energy in the form of an earthquake, which decreases the stress in one area but raises it elsewhere along the fault line. The DR sits on top of crustal blocks that are sandwiched between the North American and Caribbean plates. The island of Hispaniola faces a double risk: an earthquake from the Septentrional fault on the island itself as the plates move past each other, and an earthquake deep in the earth in the subduction zone on which the island sits.

The north coast of the DR is therefore conveniently situated between two fault lines: the Puerto Rico Trench, roughly parallel to and about 75 miles off the northern coast of Puerto Rico, is about 900 kilometres (560 miles) long and 100 kilometres (60 miles) wide. At the deepest point in the Atlantic Ocean, the trench is some 8,340 metres (27,362 feet) below the sea surface. The Hispaniola Trench parallels the north coast of the Dominican Republic and Haiti, and is 550 kilometres (344 miles) long and only 4,500 metres (14,764 feet) deep. The Septentrional fault zone cuts through the highly populated region of the Cibao Valley including Santiago.

Some dozen major earthquakes of magnitude 7.0 or greater have occurred in the Caribbean near Puerto Rico, the US Virgin Islands and the island of Hispaniola, shared by Haiti and the Dominican Republic, in the past 500 years, and several have generated tsunamis. Until the Port-au-Prince, Haiti earthquake of January 2010 the most recent major earthquake, a magnitude 8.1 in 1946, resulted in a tsunami that killed a reported 100 people at Matanzas, near Nagua. Although the waves were only about 2.5 metres (8 ft) high at this location, they moved inland several kilometres, causing such severe damage that the town was abandoned. In 2003 Ginnie experienced a 6.2 earthquake in Puerto Plata. It might not count as 'major' for the record books but it was plenty large enough for the first time experience of an earthquake. The January 2010 Haiti earthquake was also felt noticeably on the DR's north coast; while small quakes occur all the time in the DR, major ones are fairly infrequent.

Unlike a hurricane which, generally speaking, is a forewarned event, an earthquake will come as a surprise and if it is a first experience, the first ten seconds or so are likely to be spent working out what 'it' is. The 2003 earthquake initially sounded like a train thundering across the roof, the noise preceding the movement of the house. Attempts to get out of bed to rush outside were unsuccessful; it was as if an unseen force was holding the writer down on the bed. There is much debate as to whether it is safer to stay inside or attempt to get outside during the shaking of an earthquake; advice can be found at www.fema.gov/hazard/earthquake/eq_during.shtm

Earthquake alarms are designed to provide instant warning of seismic activity by detecting the 'P' wave (compression wave) of an earthquake, which travels faster than the more destructive 'S' wave (shear wave). It is also worth observing some animal companions. During the weeks of aftershocks following the 2003 earthquake, Ginnie discovered that she had her own early warning system in the shape of one of her two dogs. Once the dog had learned that we all went outside into the garden at the first signs of a quake, she would come running to advise what she sensed and she regularly beat the alarm system by thirty seconds. The other dog was less helpful, calmly chomping through her food regardless of the fact that the earth was moving.

The results of the 2003 earthquake in the north of the DR were some 121 buildings damaged in Santiago, of which forty-two were private dwellings. The tally also includes forty-four public schools, four hospitals, four government offices, and twenty-four shops. In Puerto Plata, 103 buildings were affected: forty-seven dwellings, six public schools, one hospital, ten government offices, thirty-four shops and five miscellaneous structures.

Shoddily built state schools seemed to suffer most so it is fortunate that the 'quake occurred in the early hours of the morning and not during the school day. Fatalities were minimal, three people died and two of those were the result of heart attack.

Clearly seismic activity has ramifications for home building standards for expats and locals alike. It is also worth being prepared to the extent of knowing what action to take in the event of a major earthquake, and which parts of the home offer greatest protection, for example the load bearing walls or columns.

FURTHER READING

1. *Earthquake Shakes 'Big Bend' Region of North America-Caribbean Boundary Zone* by P Mann, E.Calais, and V.Huerfano Eos, Vol. 85, No 8, 24 February 2004
   coastalhazards.uprm.edu/references/Mann_Calais_Huerfano.pdf
2. *Reconnaissance study of Late Quaternary faulting along Cerro Goden fault zone, western Puerto Rico* by Paul Mann et al. Geological Society of America Special Paper 385 2005.
   meije.univ-savoie.fr/jhipp/MannHippolyteCerroGoden.pdf
3. *High Risk Of Major Tsunami in Northern Caribbean: Over 35 Million Could Be Affected* – article in Science Daily, March 28th. 2005
   www.sciencedaily.com/releases/2005/03/050325143726.htm
4. *New System For Early Earthquake Warning* – article in Science Daily, November 10th. 2005
   www.sciencedaily.com/releases/2005/11/051110083748.htm

5. *Seismology of Haiti Earthquake* – Jackson School of Geosciences, Feb. 2010
   www.jsg.utexas.edu/news/rels/011310.html
6. *Enriquillo-Plantain Garden Strike-Slip Fault Zone: A Major Seismic Hazard Affecting Dominican Republic, Haiti and Jamaica* Paul Mann et al. March 2008

Environmental issues

Hispaniola is is the only Caribbean island with desert landscape as well as tropical highland forests, wetlands, mangroves and lowland dry forests. Despite intensive tourism development a reasonable portion of its 1,500-odd kilometres of coastline remains unspoilt. Although on paper at least, Dominican environmental law is progressive and thorough, the problems lie with interpretation, implementation and enforcement. Public education and awareness of environmental issues is improving.

The interior of the island is dotted with natural treasures like Socoa waterfall in Bayaguana province

At the micro-level, one aspect that many foreigners comment upon is the result of apparent deficiencies in citizen education when it comes to individual responsibility for the environment. After a public holiday, any beach, park or riverside picnic area can be a depressing sight, strewn with litter dominated by plastic bags, drinks bottles, used nappies and polystyrene cups, plates and containers. At the macro-level, the triumph of private interests over the law, often aided by corrupt officials, does much to undermine the good intentions of the environmental authorities. The apparent public indifference to environmental preservation could be said to enable the authorities' lax approach, and conversely, lack of respect on the part of government and business interests does not exactly serve as a great example to individual citizens.

As in many other countries, the situation in the Dominican Republic has improved over the last few years and a combination of increased awareness and Environment Ministers with a true commitment to their role have contributed to this.

Wildlife

The south western part of the country especially is a birdwatchers' paradise, yet at the same time some birds like the Hispaniolan parrot are categorised as endangered species. Despite its protected status, some people trap this emerald green parrot and openly offer it for sale along the country's highways. Other common birds include the woodpecker (*carpintero*), mockingbird (*ruiseñor*), egret (*garza*), hummingbird (*colibrí*), tody (*barrancolí*) and palm chat (*cigua palmera*, the national bird), pelican, flamingo and heron.

Separation of the Caribbean islands from the American mainland millions of years ago during the Jurassic period has meant that there are no monkeys, mountain lions, anteaters or armadillos as one finds in Central and South America.

There are only a couple of wild land mammals on Hispaniola – the *hurón* (ferret), the *hutía* and the solenodon. Of these three, the second and third are indigenous and the ferret was probably introduced by the Europeans. The solenodon is a rare shrew-like creature that lives in the Central Cordillera and also features on the endangered list. The *hutía*, which is also quite rare, resembles a large rodent. Both animals have recently come to worldwide attention - including BBC coverage - as part of a project called The Last Survivors, funded by the UK Government's Darwin Initiative. The project aims to promote the solenodon and *hutía*'s conservation through a monitoring programme and increased awareness: *www.thelastsurvivors.org*

Reptiles are more abundant and include a variety of vibrantly coloured lizards, including the galliwasp, described as half-lizard, half-snake, non-poisonous snakes, iguanas, frogs, toads and crocodiles. As a tropical country, it also has its share of creepy-crawlies, the most impressive being the '*cacata*', a tarantula-like spider that has a painful although not poisonous sting. Offshore the main attractions are the humpback whales that arrive in Samaná Bay and Silver Bank off the north coast between January and March every year, dolphins, sea turtles and the manatee or sea cow, another protected species.

Forest cover

The DR has a good track record on deforestation, especially compared to its neighbour, Haiti. According to the United Nations Environment Programme[4], 19% of the country is forested, compared to 12% in Cuba, 5% in Puerto Rico and just 2% in Haiti. It is believed that a measure introduced under former president Balaguer to provide poor rural residents with gas cooking stoves and subsidise propane led to a dramatic reduction in deforestation as *campesinos* stopped burning wood for charcoal, a practice that persists in Haiti out of sheer necessity. In the context of this legislation, expats should be aware that cutting down a tree on one's own property may well require a permit from the forestry authorities (*Forestal*).

Plants

One of the most striking spectacles in the Dominican Republic is the bold dash of colour provided by trees in blossom like the *flamboyán* (flame tree) and the *amapola* blossom, a tree presumably named after the poppy fields of Spain by the first conquerors. Bougainvillea (*trinitaria*), hibiscus (*cayena*) and birds of paradise (*ave de paraiso*) also abound. The national tree is the Royal Palm (*Palma Real*), one of several varieties of palm common to the island, the most abundant being the coconut palm. Surprisingly for a Caribbean island, cacti also feature in the landscape of the

---

[4] www.unep-wcmc.org/forest/data/cdrom2/carchts.htm#Chart2

semi arid areas of the north west and south west, and pines can be found in many places, especially the highlands. Gardening lovers from cooler climes will relish the chance to cultivate tropical flower like orchids and bromeliads, and tropical fruits - both familiar and unfamiliar.

National parks

Another area where the DR has excelled is the National Parks, also a Balaguer creation, which cover an impressive 12% of the national territory (some sources say 15%).

SOUTH EAST COAST

The National Park of the East includes the idyllic Isla Saona. Access to the park is from the towns of Bayahibe and Boca de Yuma.

Cueva de las Maravillas National Park is on the highway between San Pedro de Macorís and La Romana. The main attractions are the *Taíno* petroglyphs and impressive rock formations like stalactites and stalagmites. It has been well fitted out to receive visitors with walkways, lighting and trained guides.

NORTH EASTERN REGION

Los Haitises National Park on the south shore of Samaná Bay is accessible by boat from Sabana de la Mar, Sánchez or Samaná. Mangrove channels and caves with *Taino* petroglyphs.

NORTH COAST

El Choco National Park with caves near Cabarete. Isabel De Torres National Park in Puerto Plata, accessible by cable car.

South west

The Jaragua National Park is accessible from Cabo Rojo near Pedernales. Includes the magnificent Bahía de las Aguilas.

Isla Cabritos National Park in Lake Enriquillo for iguanas and crocodiles.

Sierra De Bahoruco National Park is a highland pine forest and the site of the Hoyo El Pelempito canyon.

CENTRAL MOUNTAIN RANGE

These remote highland areas do not resemble what one recognises as Caribbean landscape. Highland cloud forest dominated by pines and high-altitude plains with *pajón* grass. Temperatures go down to freezing at night, and although it doesn't snow, frost and ice are not uncommon.

Armando Bermúdez National Park in the Central Cordillera. Includes the highest peaks in the Caribbean (Pico Duarte and La Pelona, both just over 3,000m).

José del Carmen Ramírez National Park near San Juan de la Maguana.

Valle Nuevo or Perez Rancier National Park near Constanza.

NORTH WEST

Monte Cristi National Park near the Haitian border includes the Moro, a 300m flat-topped mountain or mesa overlooking a beach and the Cayos Siete Hermanos.

At the same time there is certainly some room for improvement. On the whole the parks themselves are well managed, but there are some neglected areas, and their protected status is under constant threat from private interests including would-be developers and impoverished campesinos. As a result, the Ministries of Environment and Tourism are often at loggerheads, with the former trying to prevent the latter from overriding the law in order to allow tourism development, logging, farming and sand extraction from riverbeds in protected areas. In 2009 the government approved plans to build a cement factory on the perimeter of the Los Haitises National Park. The protests that this generated led to the appointment of a UN commission that ruled against the decision, which was duly reversed.

Eco-Tourism

In the broadest sense, the term eco-tourism can refer to any travel that focuses on natural features, and can thus include hiking, diving, cycling trips as well as jeep safaris and motorbike or quad excursions which do not come under everyone's definition of 'eco'. In recent years, the Dominican Republic has begun to discover that there is money to be made from so-called eco-tourism. The traditional tourist model is being enhanced by excursions beyond the All-Inclusive resorts to rivers, waterfalls, mountains, nature reserves and caves, among others. The idea is that this will eventually lead to a greater proportion of tourists coming to the DR primarily for its broader natural attractions, not just as an added-extra to lazing on the beach.

Other key issues are population pressure, especially in urban areas but this is also a major problem in areas prone to natural disasters like river basins, low-lying plains, riverbanks and hillsides. Water table issues, salination, untreated sewage and industrial discharge and water pollution are also areas of concern. There is a lack of effective urban planning – although every Dominican town has its *parque central* there are not enough urban green spaces for recreation in most cities. Santo Domingo has the large Parque Mirador del Sur, the Botanical Gardens, the Zoo, the Mirador del Este and Norte parks, but many neighbourhoods do not have even a small recreational space.

Polystyrene is the most visible element in the litter mountain. Hundreds of thousands of cups, plates and trays are used for packed lunches and drinks every single day, and many of these end up clogging rivers and streams, streets and open spaces.

Although the DR is a scuba diving and snorkelling destination, many of the offshore reefs are not in the best of nick. Reef degradation is caused by water pollution and increase in the temperature of the sea, as well as by fishing and direct contact by humans with reefs.

Riverbeds are under threat by sand and gravel extraction for the construction industry. This is technically against the law, but powerful business interests tend to override the legalities and continue with this destructive practice.

Recycling in the DR is a mixed bag. Traditionally a lot of stuff was recycled out of necessity and bottles and cardboard especially are still collected by street traders (*botelleros*). In recent years there has been a huge boom in scrap metal of all types for export to China, prompting a massive wave of theft of public and privately owned metal installations like fences, gates, manhole covers, electrical wiring (for the copper) and more. In the Punta Cana area the Puntacana Group runs a recycling programme for household waste, where plastic is processed into school desks and chairs and organic waste is processed into fertiliser using the worm composting (vermiculture) method. Waste generated by the Punta Cana International Airport, the PuntaCana Hotel and surrounding residential areas is segregated and collected for this purpose.

Air pollution from motor vehicles and the accompanying noise pollution and traffic congestion is a problem in all cities and towns. While the wealthier members of society opt for large gas-guzzling SUVs and luxury vehicles, those at the other end of the social scale use small motorbikes as their transport of choice.

Waste management – not all areas have waste collections, especially in the countryside and a lot of households and businesses dump or burn their rubbish. Where rubbish is collected, it usually ends up in vast dumps or landfill sites.

DIRECTORY OF ORGANISATIONS AND ECO-TOURISM COMPANIES

Vida Azul – environmental campaigning organisation
Calle Mustafa Kemal Ataturk No 10 Local No 1,
Naco, Santo Domingo,
Tel: 809 566 7780
www.vidaazul.org

Reef Check DR
Prol. Fantino Falco #5,
Piantini
Santo Domingo
Tel: 809 227 4409
www.reefcheckdr.org

Tody Tours (bird watching in the SW DR)
Kate Wallace
Calle Jose Gabriel Garcia 105, Zona Colonial
Santo Domingo, Dominican Republic
Tel: 809 686 0882
www.todytours.com

Victoria Marine (whale watching in the Bay of Samaná)
Tel: 809 538 2494
www.whalesamana.com

Tours Trips Treks & Travel
Customized Educational, Adventure & Service Programs
Tel: 809 867-8884
www.4tdomrep.com

Who?

The Expat As…

Expatriates come in all shapes and sizes, ages and stages in life. There is no one typical DR expat, although some stereotypes do exist, as we will see below. In all cases, expatriates will need to make a conscious decision about how they might mould the composition of their circle of friends. In the areas with large expatriate communities it is almost inevitable that newcomers will get caught up in an expat bubble unless they make a concerted effort to go beyond this.

Moving to a new environment is always a challenge, even when this change takes place in the familiar setting of your own country, language and culture. Moving to a new country where there are few common points of reference is naturally much more daunting. It is understandable that many newcomers, particularly those who have not yet learned Spanish and/or have never previously lived abroad, will feel the need to gravitate towards fellow expats and compatriots.

Experience shows that having only expatriate friends can be an unsatisfying experience: for the obvious reasons of missing out on what the Dominicans have to offer, but also because of the stark fact that expats tend to come and go. It can be distressing when you have cultivated a close friendship with someone only to be left bereft when circumstances take them to the next posting or back to the homeland.

In non-tourist areas, especially provincial towns it will be the other way round. The expatriate will make a lot of Dominican friends, but will crave the company of fellow foreigners from time to time. In the larger cities it will be easy to build up a more varied circle of friends, consisting of Dominicans and expatriates.

Whatever your circumstances, being able to communicate in Spanish is crucial to living life in the DR to the full. Even if your Dominican friends speak English, this will not necessarily be the case for the rest of their family.

The single male

A single male foreigner coming to live in the DR will often be assumed to have chosen the country for less than wholesome reasons, especially if he is an older man.

There are single expats who come here for retirement, work or business-related reasons too, although there is no denying that a community of males does exist whose main pursuit is to date local younger women, especially in some tourist/expat enclaves on the north and south coasts, and to a lesser extent in the capital.

A single male foreigner who wishes to avoid being lumped into that category will have to take care to mix in very different circles, especially if he wants to be accepted and respected by mainstream, respectable Dominicans. The best way to go about this is to cultivate friends through work, business, sports or hobbies.

The single female

It is not much different for women. Yes, many women of all ages may choose the DR as a place to live for work reasons, as a retirement destination, or even for their health, but a great deal of foreign women are here for their DR man and this assumption will also be made about many who are not, especially in tourist areas where male predators known as *sankies* (short for *sanky-panky*, said to derive from the English *hanky-panky*) ply their trade. Although some women visitors on the DR's more touristy beaches will sunbathe topless, it should be pointed out that Dominicans do not look favourably upon this. In what may seem out of character for such a sensuous and flamboyant culture, Dominican women can be surprisingly demure when it comes to swimwear, often bathing with clothes over their swimsuits.

In some cases where a relationship with a Dominican man has played a part in a woman's decision to move to the DR, the love affair with the country survives the relationship and the expatriate woman stays on, often remaining friends with many of the people in her former partner's extended family and circle of friends.

The DR still being an overwhelmingly male-dominated society, single, divorced or widowed women will have a harder time of it than men. Be aware that a lot of Dominican men will see the unattached *gringa* as easy prey so it is a status that has to be handled with skill. Befriending women and families and not getting into situations open to misinterpretation are key here.

The expatriate couple

An expat couple might take a while to cultivate a circle that includes Dominican friends. One of the hazards for married or cohabiting couples that decide to move to the DR because of a job, or to set up a business, is the risk of losing one partner to a Dominican admirer. Partnerships built on weak foundations have a habit of floundering when the couple move to the DR – if one's *gringo* spouse is perceived as insufficiently supportive, there will be a ready availability of attention from a local man or woman. The true motivation for such attention might not always be apparent to a new expat in a heightened state of emotional neediness.

There are stresses associated with the relocation and adjustment process, which can result in regression to less than mature behaviour such as blaming the partner for one's own uncertainties. If the couple are not equally motivated and committed to making the relocation work, this will rapidly become obvious, so it is sensible to discuss these issues in depth with one's partner before the move takes place. The key factor is teamwork: there will be days when it feels like 'us against the world' and if 'us' isn't a team then it will feel like 'me against him/her against the world'. The ability of each member of the team to laugh at themselves will go a long way to ensure that the team can also laugh at itself.

Again, work, business, sports and hobbies that bring the couple into contact with Dominicans are a good starting point for meeting friends. For the couple with children, the school environment and parent-teacher activities can also provide avenues for making Dominican friends.

Bi-national couples

Then there are the men and women who are married to a local. Their experience is very different from the foreign couples or singles as they have a direct route into everyday Dominican family life, for better or for worse. The advantages are many – you have a ready-made support network and social life, although for a non-Latin foreigner the intensity of Dominican family life may at times feel a tad smothering.

The foreign partner often has to balance accepting the way things are done in Dominican families without completely losing his or her identity in the process. It helps to have friends – Dominicans as well as expats – outside the family circle. Dominican friends will be able to provide informed but impartial advice about Dominican family politics.

A foreigner married to a Dominican will often come up against situations where their partner's cultural conditioning leads to very different reactions to small setbacks or crisis situations. When faced with a serious injustice a Dominican will often accept the situation with seasoned resignation, or remain passive in the hope that the problem will sort itself out. In contrast, foreigners will have to restrain themselves from marching in with all guns blazing, threatening legal action, media exposure and public shaming. These actions might work in the expat's country of origin but the only recourse in the DR might be some tactical string pulling, or just accepting the situation.

Mixed couples where one is a returning Dominican

Because of the high rate of Dominican immigration to countries like the US and Canada, children and grandchildren of immigrants grow up outside the DR. There are instances where a couple consisting of a second or third generation immigrant and a non-Dominican spouse decide to settle in the DR.

They will have the benefit of a support network but will have to deal with culture shock – not just the *gringo* who has never lived in the DR, but the Dominican partner who is confronted by the reality that despite their heritage they are primarily North American in culture, mindset and attitudes, and not as Dominican as they might think.

Couples with children

Couples with children will need to take into consideration factors like schools, recreation and safety when choosing where to live. The best international-type schools can be found in Santo Domingo, and to a lesser extent in Punta Cana, Santiago, Sosua and La Romana.

Dominicans are very child-oriented and this will ease the family's integration into Dominican society as children, who are typically quicker at picking up a new language, make friends with Dominican classmates, and bring their parents into contact as a result.

On an everyday basis, children are a great ice-breaker for interaction between foreigners and Dominicans, but foreign parents used to more rigid boundaries where adult-children interaction is concerned had better be prepared for lectures on childcare, offers of sweets without consulting parents first, and affectionate gestures.

A converse effect of this situation is that foreign children who grow up in the DR may well be taken aback when returning to their native country when they find that they are no longer the centre of attention, but are totally ignored or even resented in public places.

Single parents

Single parents are by no means a rarity in the DR, so there is no stigma involved. In fact, it is common to ask a woman if her children are 'all from the same father' without intending offence.

Non-Dominican single parents who move to the DR and live amongst Dominicans will appreciate the amount of support they get from other members of their community, combined with the fact that good childcare is much more affordable than in North America and Europe, whether employing a nanny or sending a small child to day care.

All parents who decide to employ a Dominican nanny to look after their children are likely to encounter a difference in beliefs and standards when it comes to child rearing. The 'machista' culture means that many Dominicans, especially the older generation and people with more traditional values, are inclined towards leniency when it comes to boys compared to girls. A nanny may not automatically share a foreign parent's opinion on what a child should or shouldn't eat, watch on TV, and so on, so it is a good idea to establish ground rules in all these areas in advance and monitor the situation closely.

Registering a child born in the DR to foreign parents

A couple where one or both parents are foreign must obtain a Dominican birth certificate for their newborn baby before applying for a consular birth registration.

If the father is Dominican the registration procedure is the same as for any Dominican child. The baby has to be declared at the Civil Registry during the first sixty days after birth (ninety days in rural areas). Once this deadline has expired, there is a more complicated procedure for late registration (*Declaración tardía*).

If the mother or both parents are foreign the birth is registered in a book for children of foreign mothers at the civil registry: *www.JCE.gov.do* FAQ section.

For British parents, note that at least one parent has to be British-born in order to register a child's birth at the

British consulate. Check the embassy website for precise requisites depending on your circumstances and for current fees: *ukindominicanrepublic.fco.gov.uk/en/*

Canadian parents must apply for a Certificate of Canadian Citizenship for a child born outside Canada by contacting the nearest consulate or the embassy in Santo Domingo: *www.voyage.gc.ca/faq/birth_naissance-eng.asp*

The child's Dominican birth certificate needs to be translated and submitted with the application and certified copies of parents' proof of citizenship (Canadian birth certificate or citizenship card).

US citizens have to make a Consular Report of Birth Abroad (CROBA). Again, a Dominican birth certificate is required along with a list of documents as set out on this site: *santodomingo.usembassy.gov/crba_main-e.html*

Expat parents of other nationalities should check with their respective country's consular representation in the Dominican Republic.

Retired people

The concerns of the retired expat, apart from those in common with younger and working expats, tend to centre around the areas of: how will I spend my time; will I be healthy enough to have time to spend; and what happens when I die as an expat in the DR? For the first year of living in the DR it is likely that the retired expat will be kept more than occupied adjusting to their new home and learning its culture, language and customs. Earlier sections of this book have covered the use of leisure and health facilities.

Generally speaking, retired expats will be in the older age category, chronologically at least. It is refreshing to note that family structure in the DR accords elderly relatives a position of respect that values their life experience. There are changes with the advent of the move of numbers of the population from the countryside to the towns, leaving more Dominican elderly living some distance from the family but generally speaking, it is expected that elderly family members live with sons and daughters or at the very least receive frequent visits and certainly on public holidays. Thus the elderly expat will be pleasantly surprised that their opinion is sought and not dismissed as the meanderings of the senile (provided they can communicate in Spanish, of course). Likewise for the elderly and partially infirm, there are many helping hands to see one across the road, and on and off the bus; this habit has lessened in many expats' countries of origin, so do not mistake a helper for a pickpocket!

Dying in the DR

If the expat has advance notice of impending death, it can often be more convenient for relatives if this takes place in the hospital. This usually precludes any police intervention. A death in the home could involve the nearest relative being taken to the police station for questioning to rule out any involvement; this is not always desirable at a time of maximum grief.

Foreign nationals who die in the DR must be autopsied by law (this is not a DR law but International Law to which the DR is a signatory and has ratified). The autopsy will usually be performed at the Institute of Forensic Pathology in either Santo Domingo or Santiago, and a preliminary autopsy report will be issued almost immediately stating the cause of death. If toxicology tests are required this can take a few days or weeks depending on the tests. Death certificates and copies of the final autopsy report are obtainable from the *Procuraduria General*.

Dying without family can produce problems since a power of attorney will be needed in order for the body to be released for burial. For expats dying without next of kin in the DR this means a family member in the country of origin will need to contact an efficient lawyer to arrange power of attorney, payment of fees and provision of necessary paperwork. Disposal of the body is usually carried out by the Blandino Funeral Services who will do all the necessary (including getting copies of the documents) to bury, cremate or repatriate the remains:

www.funerariablandino.com.do/sucursales.htm

US insurers usually accept the certificates issued by the local authorities as proof of death. In specific cases insurers will request an investigation to confirm the circumstances, cause of the death, verify documentation and records, and in very extreme cases to verify the identity of the cadaver, if buried in the DR.

For British citizens further information is available on the How To Register A Death page of the UK Embassy website: *ukindominicanrepublic.fco.gov.uk/en/help-for-british-nationals/living-in-dominican-republic/how-register-death*

Relatives in the UK of a family member deceased in the

DR should consult: *www.fco.gov.uk/en/travelling-and-living-overseas/things-go-wrong/death-abroad* and the Foreign and Commonwealth Office booklet Death Overseas *www.fco.gov.uk/resources/en/pdf/2855621/death-overseas*

US citizens should consult Death of a US Citizen in the DR on the US Embassy website: *santodomingo.usembassy.gov/death_of_citizen-e.html*

The US Embassy will issue a *Consular Report of Death Abroad*, which is an official document that can be used to settle all legal matters relating to the deceased's estate and insurance. The completed Report of Death is official and acceptable in any US jurisdiction. US citizens should also consult Death Notification on the US State Department website: *www.travel.state.gov/law/info/death/death_712.html*

Canadian citizens should consult the Foreign Affairs and International Trade website, Death Abroad FAQs *www.voyage.gc.ca/faq/death_deces-eng.asp*
www.canoe.ca/Travel/Tools/ForeignAffairs/abroad_problems_death.html

Next of kin may need a local death certificate (authenticated and translated if necessary by officials at the Canadian Embassy) in order to register the death with the Vital Statistics Office of the Canadian province or territory where the deceased last resided.

Overseas students at DR universities

Another breed of expatriate comes in the shape of foreign students who choose to study in the DR. The main incentive is the relatively lower cost of tuition fees especially compared to universities in the US, and in the case of children or grandchildren of Dominican émigrés who choose to study in the DR it is a way of rediscovering their roots.

A returnee of this type will often experience an unexpected variety of culture shock in a country they thought they knew well. Living in the DR, struggling with public transport and everyday bureaucracy is a different kettle of fish to coming to the DR on holiday and spending it with grandparents, aunts and uncles.

Lesbian/Gay

Like most societies on earth, the Dominican Republic is conservative and homophobic to an extent. Gay residents are likely to encounter negative attitudes expressed in a casual way – like the way the words *pájaro* and *maricón* (both roughly equivalent to 'queer' in English) are bandied about as insults.

The age of consent for both sexes, whether straight or gay, is eighteen, although in practice many teenage girls marry or set up home with older men at a younger age without any apparent legal repercussions. There is a general law on violations of public decorum (article 330) that is more likely to be used against gay people, as in the case of Santo Domingo's Parque Duarte, where many young people, both gay and straight, congregate at night. It has been the focus of clampdowns by the police and anti-gay diatribes by the Cardinal. Compared to certain other Caribbean islands the Dominican Republic is reasonably open and tolerant. Gay cruises call in at the ports, there are openly gay people on television and local Lesbian and Gay campaigners have held annual Gay Pride marches for a number of years.

In practice, Dominicans can be tolerant and accepting of gay family members, and there is a certain amount of openly gay culture in the two main cities and the tourist areas in the shape of bars and nightclubs.

There are also support groups and gay, lesbian and transsexual rights campaigning organizations like *Amigos Siempre Amigos* (*ASA*).

As far as physical displays of affection between same-sex couples goes, it's worth remembering that in the DR all public displays of affection are frowned upon, whatever your sexuality.

USEFUL CONTACTS

Lesbian
Colectivo lésbico Las tres gatas,
http://3gatas.blogspot.com

Gay
ASA (Amigos siempre amigos),
Calle Galván #11,
Gazcue, Santo Domingo.
Tel: 809 689 8695 / 809 689 8529 / 809 685 6768
Contact Leonardo Sánchez
REVASA (at the same office as ASA), contact Deivis Ventura

Trans
TRANSSA, Contact: Cristian King (Marlenne Bennedeck),
 Cel: 1 829 922 6979 / 1 829 921 8141
www.transsadominicana1.blogspot.com

Disabled

An expatriate with a disability will note the lack of facilities in countries like the DR compared to their home countries in terms of accessibility and mobility. Erratic pavements and inaccessible buildings are par for the course. The main exception is that most large supermarkets and shopping centres have reserved disabled parking spaces but as in all countries, they are often taken up by drivers whose only handicap is of a moral nature.

At the same time, the DR's family oriented social structure makes for a supportive community where your neighbours will look out for you. Hiring a carer or an assistant is also much more affordable.

Freedom seekers

Many expatriates in the Dominican Republic relish the fact that 'there are no rules' or at least not many that are enforced. They have turned their backs on the overregulated nanny states of Europe and North America and all the political correctness that accompanies these for a more libertarian lifestyle where the individual is king and the state is weak. In the DR there is much more freedom to ride a motorbike without a helmet and drive around swigging a cold beer although it would not be recommended practice for new, or indeed any expats.

Ironically these freedom lovers are often the first to complain when they are in a situation where they fall victim to the non-existent policing, emergency or health services.

As one expat put it, the best thing about living in the DR is the freedom to pretty much do as you please, but the worst thing is that everyone else is also able to do pretty much as they please!

Dominican joie de vivre

How?

Cultural Context

History

Why would a potential expat need to understand the history of the country which they intend to make home?

There will most likely be two reactions to that question: "good question" and "must be rhetorical". Readers with the second reaction will consider it normal preparation to read up on the history of the DR. Those with the former reaction are probably more interested in reading real estate websites. But Ginnie recalled having a 'light bulb moment' after some four years of living in Puerto Plata when she read *The Dominican Republic: A National History* by Frank Moya Pons. It truly helped with understanding the complexities of her adopted motherland; so too did Julia Alvarez's novel based on true events *In the Time of the Butterflies* and Junot Díaz's *The Brief Wondrous Life of Oscar Wao*. If you read nothing else, consider these three books as required potential expat reading matter. If you are interested in the effect of foreign influences on the DR, *The Washington Connection and Third World Fascism* by Noam Chomsky and Edward S.

Herman has an interesting third chapter entitled *The Dominican Republic: US Model for Third World Development*. Those wishing to learn more about the DR's troubled relationship with Haiti should read *When the Cocks Fight* by Michele Wucker (non-fiction) and Edwige Danticat's *The Farming of Bones* (a fictionalised account of the 1937 massacres). *The Feast of the Goat* by Mario Vargas Llosa is well worth reading as is the historical account of Trujillo's assassination by Bernard Diederich.

Santo Domingo Cathedral – the first to be built on the American continent

For some expats, particularly those who are not historians, perhaps the dates and 'facts' of the history of the Dominican Republic have less significance than the emerging themes and overarching concepts, which are resonating today. However, behind the many-layered canvas on which is painted the DR and the colourful psyche of its people today, are themes such as exploitation, colonisation, slavery, foreign occupation, dictatorship, resistance, patriotism, and the repetition of mistakes.

Despite what some history books might tell you, it didn't all start in 1492! 5000 years before Christopher Columbus arrived, *Taíno* Indians settled the land; these were believed to be a mix of two indigenous groups, one from Central America (probably Yucatan and/or Belize) and the other from South America, *Arawak* Indians from Amazonia who passed through the Orinoco Valley in Venezuela.

The *Taínos* inhabited the island of Hispaniola and lived in groups headed by chieftains (*caciques*) known as *cazicazgos*. They were peace-loving and hospitable, which made exploiting their gold easy enough for the Spanish. To this day the expression *espejitos por oro* - "little mirrors for gold", an allusion to this first encounter, is used to describe any deal with foreigners perceived as unfair or exploitative. When Columbus returned to Spain to tell them of his discovery, the sailors he left behind mistreated the local population.

Caonabo, a *Taíno* chief, killed the settlers after several months of this abuse and on Columbus's return he paid the price, as did his widow Anacaona who was duped into organising a feast for the next governor, Nicolas Ovando, where she gathered all the tribal chieftains who were subsequently slaughtered by Spanish soldiers. Thereinafter resistance took the form of escaping from the clutches of the brutal Spanish rule and running to the mountains or other less hospitable parts of the island where sporadic attacks on the invaders lasted for years led by *cacique* Enriquillo. He was an expert in guerrilla tactics and achieved heroic status by forcing the Spaniards to request a peace treaty that granted the *Taíno*s freedom from the *encomienda* system that had enslaved them. The *Taíno* population was indeed decimated through forced labour and by the illnesses that the Spaniards imported but it was not wiped out as is evidenced by recent DNA studies. Eventual depletion of Hispaniola's gold stocks provided some relief from Spanish rule as the Spanish, intent on amassing even greater riches for the Crown, moved on to Mexico and later, Peru.

In the late 16th and early 17th century Hispaniola attracted the attention of buccaneers of all nationalities. Once the French took control of the Spanish-vacated north-western part of Hispaniola, they began a campaign to limit piracy. In fact, the French offered the pirates women, who had been imprisoned for prostitution or thievery. It was in this way that the French began to occupy what they called Saint-Domingue in 1697. Saint-Domingue was the western third of the island, later to become Haiti. Slaves from Africa were imported to the island by both the Spanish and the French. The slaves produced sugar for the foreign powers and the island became a prosperous colony. A resistance movement, partially inspired by the French Revolution, was led by Toussaint L'Ouverture in 1791. This remarkable slave rebellion eventually led to independence for Haiti, which became the world's first black republic in 1804.

Sugar production is still an important economic activity

The slave struggle for freedom was intertwined with French aspirations to control the whole of Hispaniola and Spanish determination that they should not. Napoleon sent a disastrous mission to quell the slave revolt and failed and thus Haiti was born. However, the Spaniards on the eastern side of the island re-introduced slavery. Fearful of another attack by the Spanish, in 1822, Haiti's president Jean-Pierre Boyer invaded and took over the eastern portion of Hispaniola. Slavery was abolished again and Santo Domingo became part of the Republic of Haiti.

Dominicans refer to the next twenty-two years as 'The Haitian Occupation'. It has been suggested that any current resentment of Haitians in the DR stems from nineteenth century resentment by the former Spanish ruling class of that occupation. This is something of an irony when one considers that the former Spanish ruling class were white and the vast percentage of current Dominicans are not! During this period of Haitian rule, an underground resistance group, *La Trinitaria*, emerged under the leadership of Juan Pablo Duarte. Duarte, Ramón Matías Mella and Francisco del Rosario Sánchez are today known as the founding fathers of the Dominican Republic – their fight for independence from Haiti ended on February 27, 1844, a date that is commemorated by Dominicans every year as Independence Day.

As an independent nation, the Dominican Republic began a turbulent period characterised by dictatorships and corruption, even reverting to colonial status in 1861 as a result of a pact signed with Spain by General Pedro Santana. Resistance surfaced again in the two-year War of Restoration, which produced heroes like General Gregorio Luperón and was successfully won in 1863. In 1882 the rule of General Ulysses Heureux started out with some popularity and led to some stability.

However, his increasingly despotic behaviour led to violent repression of his opponents and his handling of the economy led to economic crisis, currency devaluations (fast forward to 2004) and massive debt to foreign powers, specifically France and other European countries (fast forward to just about any year you care to mention). Following Heureux's assassination in 1899, several individuals came to power, only to be rapidly overthrown by their political opponents, and the country's internal situation continuously degenerated into chaos. Not an auspicious start to Duarte's lofty ideals!

Foreign powers again entered the foray. US President Theodore Roosevelt sought to prevent European intervention, largely to protect the US's interest in the Panama Canal. He proclaimed his famous Roosevelt Corollary to the Monroe Doctrine, whereby the United States had the right to intervene to stabilize the economic affairs of small states in the Caribbean and Central America if they were unable to pay their international debts. In 1905 Roosevelt obtained the DR's agreement for US administration of DR Customs, then the chief source of income for the Dominican government. A 1906 agreement provided for the arrangement to last fifty years. The US agreed to use part of the Customs proceeds to reduce the immense foreign debt of the Dominican Republic, and assumed responsibility for said debt.

It was at about this time that US interests developed in the sugar industry, with many US citizens buying plantations in the DR. Such commercial expats did not want to see their investment go down the tubes as political instability continued to plague the DR, and so in 1916 US president Woodrow Wilson ordered in the Marines. The ensuing US occupation, though it lasted only eight years, set the tone for a turbulent century. The occupation was deeply resented by many Dominicans as evidenced by ministers' refusal to serve in the puppet government; nor did many Dominicans approve of the US disbanding the DR army. The upside of the occupation was the elimination of political violence and improvements in the DR's infrastructure and educational system; the downside a remodelling of the legal structure into one that benefitted

American investors at the expense of Dominican businessmen, allowing them to take control of greater sectors of the economy and remove customs and import barriers for any American products being brought into the DR (fast forward to DR-CAFTA).

With their exit, the US left behind a passion for baseball and a trained Dominican army to replace the one that had been disbanded. The idea was that the DR army would establish law, order and public security, all of which had, admittedly, been lacking.

Rafael Leonidas Trujillo, who took power upon the departure of the US forces, was a brutal character. A former telegraph clerk who had risen to head the Dominican army during the US occupation, he ruled his country with an iron fist for over thirty years. Trujillo systematically acquired much of the country's wealth, in the form of banks, the sugar industry and major businesses, for himself. For anyone who dared question his rule, repression, torture and 'disappearance' awaited. Thousands of people went into exile during those years. For those who lived through this period, Trujillo and his legacy remain very much alive. Many Dominican citizens, in response to their limited power, display a 'learned helplessness' when faced with Dominican bureaucracy. One of the more positive contributions expats can make is to encourage the challenging of obdurate and endemic Dominican bureaucratic small-mindedness towards its own people.

Of course there were gains during the dictatorship – progress in healthcare, education, and transportation, with the building of hospitals and clinics, schools, roads and harbours. Trujillo also carried out an important housing construction programme and instituted a pension plan. He finally negotiated an undisputed border with Haiti in 1935, and in 1941 achieved the early end of the 1906 agreement with the US whereby they controlled customs payments. He also made the DR debt-free in 1947 – no small achievement. Alongside this he instituted the Parsley Massacre of 1937 whereby the army killed an estimated 17,000 to 35,000 Haitians living in the DR over a five-day period. That, too, has reverberations in the present day as have, albeit for a different reason, Trujillo's assassination of the Mirabal sisters (*Las Mariposas,* or 'The Butterflies', as per Julia Alvarez's book referred to above) whose deaths went on to become the outward manifestation of the covert but active Dominican resistance to Trujillo's regime.

Trujillo's lengthy stay in power was partly enabled by the support he had from the US government, the Dominican elite and the Roman Catholic Church. Although Trujillo claimed to support the US stand against communism, he went on to take control of major, foreign-owned industries (principally those owned by US corporations in the DR), such as the sugar industry. The US finally broke with Trujillo in 1960 after Trujillo's agents attempted to assassinate Venezuelan president Rómulo Betancourt. Trujillo himself was assassinated on May 30, 1961 in Santo Domingo.

Trujillo's rule was initially followed by that of his associate, adviser and erstwhile puppet president Dr Joaquín Balaguer, but the first democratically held elections saw the return of Juan Bosch of the Dominican

Revolutionary Party and a leftist programme. This irked the US, who had become paranoid about the possible spread of communism after Fidel Castro's successful revolution in Cuba. Seven months later the Dominican army, supported by the CIA, instigated a coup d'état and ousted Bosch from the presidency.

The Dominican Republic, now under military rule, went through a period of rebellion and resistance. On April 24, 1965, a dissident army faction took action to re-establish constitutional order. Thus began a civil war led by Colonel Francisco Alberto Caamaño Deñó and the *Constitucionalistas*, who were successful in seizing the capital city. In response, US president Johnson ordered an invasion, arguing that U.S. citizens in the DR were in danger. Of course, many contend that this invasion was based on fears that the *Constitucionalistas* would follow in the footsteps of Cuba. For footage of these events, see YouTube. Search for 'Colonel Francisco Alberto Caamano Deno', 'patriota dominicano' and 'USA Invasion of Dominican Republic 1965'. Also well worth watching is René Fortunato's award-winning documentary film series *Bosch: Presidente en la frontera imperial* (2009) (in Spanish with English subtitles).

After a few months of fighting, the *Constitucionalistas*, outnumbered and outgunned by the foreign forces, accepted the inevitable. In 1966, elections, supervised by US forces and generally agreed to have been rigged, resulted in Joaquín Balaguer gaining the presidency. Caamaño did not give up, however. He fled to Cuba where he started a guerrilla group that liaised with supporters in the DR. In 1973, after several years of keeping a low profile, Caamaño led the landing of a small group of rebels at *Playa Caracoles* in the south-western province of Azua, with the purpose of starting a peasant revolution to overthrow President Balaguer. Balaguer's government was repressive and highly centralised during this period, reminding many of the Trujillo regime in which Balaguer had been one of the dictator's right-hand men. After a few weeks of guerrilla war against Balaguer's regular army and not having received the much hoped-for peasant support, Caamaño was wounded and captured by Dominican government forces, and then summarily executed. Some twenty years passed before Caamaño was officially honoured by the Dominican government as a hero for his attempts to restore rightful government to his country; today, a Metro station is named after him!

Such events are well within the living memory of many Dominicans. Where Ginnie lived in Puerto Plata there is an active branch of the *Fundación Francisco Alberto Caamaño* and once she had acquired sufficient Spanish to understand, she listened enthralled to the stories of a resistance survivor – as well as his somewhat blistering condemnation of present day politics in the DR!

More recent history might have been politically less turbulent but in no way less corrupt. During the 1970s, 1980s and the start of the 1990s, Joaquín Balaguer was in power more often than he was not. His tenure was praised for an ambitious infrastructure program, which included construction of housing, theatres, museums, aqueducts, roads, highways, and the massive, and hugely controversial

Columbus Lighthouse completed in 1992. Balaguer oversaw the country's transition from that of a monocrop economy to one dominated by remittances from family members abroad, the tourism industry and industrial free trade zones. Many Dominicans migrated to the US as the gap between rich and poor began to widen further.

Balaguer attempted to fix the 1994 elections, though finally conceded to a two-year, rather than four-year, term. In 1996, current president Leonel Fernández won the elections with his Dominican Liberation Party. Fernandez had in fact been placed second in the first round to José Francisco Peña Gómez of the PRD. The only reason he won the second round was because of an alliance between Balaguer's PRSC party and the PLD, so the hand of Balaguer was not exactly absent from President Fernandez's administration.

President Fernandez's first administration marked a time of increased prosperity for the DR and his own visionary plan for its future development. Unfortunately this did not encompass ploughing much needed resources into fundamental social reform – things like public education and health and the dissatisfaction of the poorer classes combined with a wave of sympathy and some might say collective guilt following the death of Peña Gómez led to the PLD defeat in 2000 and the election of President Hipólito Mejía of the PRD. Again, be careful what you wish for! The section on politics above has noted the economic meltdown of the Mejia administration and the Baninter scandal.

Admittedly the situation was not helped by surging oil prices and a slumping international economy post-9/11. Fernández was re-elected in the presidential election held on 16th May 2004 – he gained an absolute majority and the second highest percentage ever in Dominican history (57%) – and again in 2008. The new Dominican Constitution of 2010, while prohibiting consecutive re-election, does not provide term limits so the current president is free to run again in 2016. There are many who think that, after the congressional elections of 2010 handed the president's party dominance of the Senate (thirty-one out of thirty-two seats), it would not be too difficult to ensure yet another rerun for president in 2012.

The 2008 United Nations Development Report on the Dominican Republic entitled *Human Development: A Matter of Power* pointed out that the current model for economic growth in the DR both creates wealth and generates poverty. Nowhere is this demonstrated more starkly than in the two main tourist provinces of Puerto Plata on the north coast and La Altagracia on the east coast. The report states that 'living conditions in tourist provinces are below the national average'. The UNDP Report concludes: 'There is no reason to believe that political institutions and power structures will change spontaneously. There will be no human development if people fail to organise, to become empowered, to mobilise and to restructure power relationships because human development is a matter of power.' Where we are at now is very much the beginning of this process. If you, the potential expat, want to take an active part in contributing to this process come on down and join the collaborative effort to ensure the lessons of history are not, once again, lost. Prove finally to Junot Díaz that just as expats brought the *fukú* or curse with them back in the fifteenth century, they can also be active in exorcising it.

Yes, we're serious. What greater contribution could an expat make?

People

RELIGION, BELIEF AND RITUAL

The official religion of the DR is Catholism. However, not all are baptised or confirmed, and many are not officially married in the eyes of the church. Although it is rare to find a Dominican who would admit to being a non-believer (and they will not look kindly on someone who declares this), churchgoing and religious practice are limited to the upper social echelons and the particularly devout. There is also a growing influence of evangelical Protestant churches, whose appeal to converts (from Catholicism) stems from the emphasis on abstinence, moderation and modesty, perhaps a response to the prevalence of drinking and sexual promiscuity and their subsequent social effects. Earlier Protestants in the DR include the African-Americans who settled in Samaná and the *Cocolos* from the English-speaking Caribbean islands who migrated to the south east of the country. There are also tiny Muslim, Jewish and Buddhist communities with places of worship in the capital, and in the case of the Jewish community, also in Sosúa on the north coast.

In the rural areas especially, religion, ritual and belief are fused with ancient influences, both African and dating back to pre-Columbian times. When African slaves were first brought over to the New World, their Spanish masters and priests obliged them to convert to Catholicism. The slaves merely disguised African deities as Catholic saints, in a similar way to Brazilian *Candomblé* and Cuban *Santería*. These folk religious beliefs, known as *religiosidad popular* in the Dominican Republic, survive to the present day, combining Catholicism with elements of African worship.

Architectural treasures include this Victorian gingerbread church in Sánchez

Not all Dominicans believe that these influences came directly from Africa. Some see them as a more recent import by immigrants from neighbouring Haiti. This can be a sensitive issue: some Dominicans choose to distance themselves from their African origins, while others are more eager to embrace them. Although the Catholic Church in the DR is highly critical of *religiosidad popular*, labelling it as 'pagan' or even 'satanic', the traditions endure.

While they may not admit to this openly, Dominicans across the social spectrum believe in a form of *vodou* and visit *brujos* (witchdoctors) in search of remedies for physical and emotional ailments from *botánicas* (mystical herbalist shops).

Still, exploring this fascinating topic in more detail is not within the scope of this book and readers will have to judge for themselves by doing their own research into the subject and attending events like the annual *Gagá* in Yamasá. On St Anthony's Day (*El Día de San Antonio*), which falls in late June, people from surrounding rural areas come together to worship and celebrate by chanting, drumming and praying. The occasion comes to a thrilling climax with the arrival of the *Gagá* – a large group of musicians and dancers, drumming and cracking whips – that invades the area in a colourful and chaotic spectacle. The event is open to the public and is held less than an hour's drive from the capital.

Other traditional folkloric groups like the *Guloyas* of San Pedro de Macorís, whose dance and mime performances originate in St Kitts in the English-speaking Caribbean and *Los Congos de Villa Mella*, have both been declared UNESCO Masterpieces of the Oral and Intangible Heritage of Humanity. The *Congos* – full name The Brotherhood of the Holy Spirit of the Congos of Villa Mella – is a three-hundred-year-old tradition of worshipping both the Holy Spirit of Christian tradition and the West African god of the dead *Kalunga*.

Other fascinating syncretic celebrations are held in Baní, Guerra, Monte Plata and many other parts of the country.

SUPERSTITIONS

Dominican superstitions include a widely held fear that opening the fridge after ironing holds the risk of suffering a *pasmo* or spasm and that the night air (the deadly *sereno*) will make you sick. A woman should under no circumstances put her handbag on the floor because it will cause her to lose all her money – although in many cases this may prove to be a practical piece of advice rather than a superstition. Many newborn babies are given a jet or *azabache* bracelet as protection against the evil eye.

Dominican folklore is peopled by mythical beings like the *ciguapa*, a woman whose feet point backwards and who is said to roam the countryside at night for her victims. The *cuco* is a type of bogeyman invoked by Dominican parents to make their children behave.

Customs

Christmas (*Navidad*), Easter (*Semana Santa*) and Lent are observed and although church leaders frequently remind the faithful that Lent is supposed to be preceded by Carnival, celebrations continue through the month of February and sometimes into early March.

CARNIVAL – *CARNAVAL*

While there has been an increase in commercialization over the past few years, Carnival in the Dominican Republic is still very much a traditional, homegrown celebration. Most cities have their own brand of carnival tradition with emblematic characters or costumes. The La Vega carnival is generally considered the best in the country. It's worth venturing to smaller, remote cities and towns like Montecristi, Cotuí and Cabral, where age-old traditions persist.

Carnival takes place all over the country throughout February and a national procession in Santo Domingo is held at the end of the month or at the beginning of March, where the best *comparsas* (troupes) selected from each city parade along the city's seafront boulevard, the *Malecón*.

Carnival characters include *mácaros, diablos cojuelos, cachuas, toros* or *papeluses* – just some of the names for the horned devils in terror-inducing sharp-toothed masks and flamboyant costumes. *Robalagallina,* portrayed by a garish female impersonator, is always a favorite with the crowds, along with drag queens.

Most carnival processions will feature a satirical take on a topical situation, with troupes disguised as a particular politician or public figure.

Many carnival-goers engage in the practice of whacking fellow participants and spectators on the backsides with water-filled pig bladders or gourds – so watch your rear!

CHRISTMAS – *NAVIDAD*

Christmas Eve or *Noche Buena* is the main focus of the festive season, marked by a huge family meal of *puerco asado* (roast pork), *moro de guandules con coco* (rice with pigeon peas and coconut) and *ensalada rusa* (potato salad). Christmas drinks are *ponche* (egg nog) and *sidra* (sparkling apple wine). Christmas Day is a public holiday, but not much goes on as most people spend it recovering from the excesses of the previous night. In the north of the country the 25th is when children receive their Christmas gifts from *El Niño Jesús* (the Baby Jesus). But most Dominicans observe the tradition of Three Kings Day – *el día de los Tres Reyes Magos*, inherited from the Spaniards, which means that many children don't receive their presents until January 6th. A traditional procession through Santo Domingo's Colonial Zone takes place on the night of January 5th. Many of these traditions, including the charming *charamicos* – life-size animals, trees and angels made from twigs - are gradually being taken over by more commercialized decorations and non-Dominican images like Santa Claus, elves, reindeer and snowy scenes.

The 'thirteenth salary' paid to most Dominican employees in the state and private sector unleashes a major spending spree in mid-December. This shopping frenzy involves food and drink as well as gifts. Bosses may give their workers small presents at Christmas time, and business associates exchange tokens, usually food baskets or bottles of wine or spirits. Many Dominicans help poorer relatives, employees or acquaintances with a donation towards the Christmas Eve meal, in the shape of a gift basket or money. The *Angelito*, or Secret Santa gift exchange is popular at schools and workplaces.

EASTER – *SEMANA SANTA*

Easter week starts on the Monday before Good Friday and lasts until Easter Sunday. Church services and religious processions are held during the week, but for most Dominicans Easter means a few days at the beach. Schools are on holiday all week, and most businesses wind down mid-week as the exodus from the cities gets under way. A traditional *Semana Santa* dish is *habichuelas con dulce* – made with beans, spices, condensed milk, coconut milk and sweet potato.

OTHER CELEBRATIONS

Valentine's Day (*San Valentín, Día del amor y la amistad*) in the Dominican Republic celebrates both friendship and romantic love. Friends as well as lovers exchange gifts, flowers or chocolates. Mothers Day (last Sunday in May) is a major occasion: motherhood in general is celebrated and the custom is to congratulate all mothers, not just one's own. The run-up to Mothers Day is almost as busy as the Christmas shopping season. International Women's Day (March 8th) is a date celebrating women's achievements and their contributions to society, and the custom is to congratulate all women. Secretary's Day gives employers a chance to reward their admin staff, usually by taking them out for a meal. Halloween has been embraced by many Dominicans, although some criticise it for being a foreign import while others condemn it as a pagan or even satanic ritual. Dominicans also mark *El Día de los Muertos* (All Souls Day, 1st November) by visiting the graves of their loved ones, but none of the above are public holidays.

Religious occasions include *La Altagracia* and Mercedes Day as well as other Catholic holy days like Corpus Christi and national dates include Restoration, Independence and Constitution Days, all public holidays. Sometimes when a holiday falls in the middle of the week, it is moved to the following Monday to create a long weekend.

OFFICIAL PUBLIC HOLIDAYS

- **1 Jan** New Year's Day
- **6 Jan** Epiphany
- **21 Jan** Our Lady of Altagracia
- **26 Jan** Duarte's Birthday
- **27 Feb** Independence Day
- **22 Apr** Good Friday
- **2 May** Labour Day
- **23 Jun** Corpus Christi

- **16 Aug** Restoration Day
- **24 Sep** Our Lady of Las Mercedes
- **7 Nov** Constitution Day
- **25 Dec** Christmas Day

The official list is updated every October and can be downloaded from:
www.set.gov.do/legislacion/descargar_dias_feriados.asp

BIRTHDAYS

Even the poorest Dominican families will push the boat out to celebrate their children's birthdays, especially the first birthday party. This may well be a legacy of a country in which mortality in early childhood used to be high, and in some cases is still a reality, so a child surviving to see its first birthday is a genuine cause for celebration. At the very least this will consist of a cake (*bizcocho*), drinks and a few balloons, though more lavish celebrations may include children's entertainers, a large buffet and party favours as well as the cake. Most middle class families will include beer for the adults and 'grown up' buffet food (usually *kippes* and *pastelitos*) and pizza or hot dogs for the children. The custom is that the cake is served just before the end of the party, and as well as 'Happy Birthday' in its Spanish and English versions, a traditional Dominican birthday song '*Celebro tu cumpleaños*' is always sung. At the age of fifteen, girls celebrate their *quinceañera* where they are formally presented to friends, family and society in general as young women for the first time.

SOCIALIZING

When arriving at a social gathering, you are expected to greet everyone personally, introducing yourself with a handshake and a kiss if appropriate. Dominicans do not adhere to the rule of bringing a bottle of wine to a dinner party, but wine, a box of chocolates or some other contribution is always welcome. In informal gatherings especially, a guest can take it upon himself to call the nearest *colmado* and order a few beers. Music is almost always played at social gatherings, often at the expense of conversation, and it is common for people to get up and dance whether at someone's house or a public venue like a *colmado*. As in many Latin cultures, it is common for friends to turn up at your house unannounced, or to call just before they arrive, giving you little or no warning. This is when *colmados* really come into their own. Another quirk is that while you may have invited one person or a couple, they could well turn up with a larger entourage. At parties, food is never served until the very end, and this is considered a cue for departure, although not before you have eaten your fill.

Dominicans are enthusiastic drinkers, especially of beer, rum and whisky, but while many think nothing of cracking open a beer mid-morning, the practice of drinking to get drunk is not viewed with approval. Strangely for such an otherwise hedonistic culture, Dominicans in general do not smoke.

Weddings

Weddings range from unbelievably lavish banquets held at the country's top hotels to small backyard celebrations. There is a best man (*padrino*), and a maid of honour (*madrina*) who is expected to provide the cake. The actual marriage ceremony can be civil or held in a church, and the party will always include music and dancing.

Baptisms

Baptisms are mainly religious, family services, sometimes followed by a small party for the guests. It is customary for the godparents to foot the bill.

Funerals

When someone dies, the family holds a *velorio*, usually in a funeral parlour, which is a wake or vigil the day and night before the funeral. Funerals are almost always held on the next day. The *velorio* is when most people are expected to go and express their respects and condolences to the mourners; closer friends and family attend the funeral. After the funeral, mass is said every evening for nine days, and the final service is an opportunity for people who didn't make it to the *velorio* or the funeral to express their condolences to the relatives.

Demographics

Ethnically, Dominicans are above all a blend of African and European, with some indigenous ancestry found to still be lingering in many people's DNA. When the Spanish arrived with Columbus's first voyage in 1492, the island was inhabited by *Taíno* Indians. Overwork at the hands of their new Spanish masters combined with massacres and disease ensured that that the *Taíno*s ceased to exist as a culture within a generation or two, but inter-marriage with the colonists allowed their genetic heritage to endure.

The sixteenth century saw the arrival of African slaves to replace the *Taíno*s as labourers and, once the island became an important sugar producer, as cane cutters. Over the centuries, immigrants from other parts of the world have added their influence, both cultural and ethnic, to the mix. Spain continued to send colonists in large numbers, mainly from the traditional émigré regions of Galicia and the Canaries as well as other parts of the Iberian Peninsula. Migration also took place from other parts of the region, like the freed African-American slaves who settled in *Samaná* in the early 19th century and the *cocolos* from the English-speaking Caribbean who migrated to the southeast in the late nineteenth and early twentieth century.

They were joined in the late 19th century by immigrants from the Middle East, Italy and China. The Italians and Middle Easterners have since made their mark both economically and politically and are prominent among the rich and powerful sectors of Dominican society. The Chinese influence can be seen in Santo Domingo's newly renovated Chinatown district.

A few hundred Jewish refugees from Nazi persecution in Europe were brought in by the dictator Trujillo to curry favour with the Allies during the Second World War. It is also claimed that Trujillo's ulterior motive was to bring in more white immigrants in the hope that they would intermarry with the locals and 'whiten the race'. Although Trujillo's original aim was to allow as many as a couple of hundred thousand to settle in the Dominican Republic, only a few hundred ended up actually arriving. They were settled in the north coast town of Sosua and built up a successful dairy and meat processing business, *Productos Sosua*, which still exists today.

However, most of the original immigrants and their descendants have since left the area but their story is commemorated in a small museum, next to the synagogue, which still holds regular services for the remnants of the community and visiting Jewish tourists. There is also a small Jewish community in Santo Domingo, with a community centre and synagogue.

There is a large presence of migrants from Haiti, some say as many as one million, living in the country. They have migrated or have been brought over to the country over the years to work in farming, mainly sugar cane harvesting, and construction, as well as many other low income, low status jobs.

In the late twentieth century North American, British and European expatriates began moving to the DR. More recently, the DR has seen Russian and other East European arrivals, settling predominantly in tourist areas like Punta Cana, Sosúa and Juan Dolio.

So whatever your nationality, rest assured that in almost every case your compatriots may well have preceded you.

Culture

MUSIC AND DANCE

Music and dancing are a central part of everyday life and are intertwined and inseparable for most Dominicans. The main homegrown musical genres are *merengue* and *bachata* – used to describe both the musical style and the dance that accompanies it, while other traditional Latin styles like *salsa* and *son* are also popular.

Merengue is said to have originated when African slaves observed their European masters dancing at parties, and adapted these sedate ballroom styles to a more rhythmic beat. Classic *merengue* is accompanied by a basic accordion, *guira* (metal grater) and drum trio known as a *perico ripiao* and standards such as *Compadre Pedro Juan* are still much loved by purists. Contemporary *merengue* is much more produced and orchestrated and can be wild and frenetic. Top *merengue* artists include Juan Luis Guerra, Chichi Peralta, Kinito Mendez, Fernando Villalona, Johnny Ventura, La Banda Gorda and Los Hermanos Rosario.

Bachata consists of melancholy, guitar-dominated ballads and is danced much slower than *merengue*. It is basically the Dominican Republic's equivalent of country music – or *Tango*. Originating in the seedier bordellos and taverns, the lyrics are tragic and sentimental and the vocals nasal and plaintive. Frank Reyes, Antony Santos, Zacarias Ferreiras and Raulin Rodriguez are some of the most popular stars of *bachata*. The male-female duo Monchy and Alexandra, and Dominican-American band Aventura have given *bachata* a more international flavour - and in the case of Aventura, massive success. Over the last few years *bachata* has crossed over to the mainstream and can be heard practically everywhere in the Dominican Republic, from the corner shop *colmado* to the top entertainment venues.

Perico Ripiao - merengue roots musicians

Son is a melodic, sophisticated Cuban musical dance style revered especially by older Dominicans who can be found dancing the night away at special venues like El Monumento al Son in Santo Domingo's Zona Oriental, the small but lively El Sartén bar in the Colonial Zone and El Secreto Musical in Villa Consuelo. Even if you are not a dancer yourself these places are great for people watching and soaking in the incredible atmosphere.

Salsa is not as popular with Dominicans as with other Latin nations but it is still danced in many discos and venues, although it will invariably be overshadowed by the more popular *merengue* and *bachata*.

Many younger Dominicans are fans of *reggaeton* and Latin rap, both with roots in Puerto Rico and urban Latino communities in the United States. Dominicans of all ages are also followers of international rock and pop music, and in the last few years dance music D.J.s have attracted massive crowds at large indoor and outdoor venues.

Since the 1960s a generation of musicians comparable to the Cuban *Trova* and other Latin-American left-leaning, socially aware musicians has been active. The latest exponents are young singer-songwriters like Pavel Nuñez and the more veteran folk singers include Victor Victor and Sonia Silvestre. In a more ethnic/experimental category are Xiomara Fortuna and Roldán who have blended western rock styles with Dominican 'roots' music like *Gagá* and *Palos*, in innovative collaborations with traditional musicians from the deep *campos*.

Art

The island's original inhabitants, the *Taíno*s left their religious artwork in the shape of cave drawings or petroglyphs, which in turn have influenced contemporary artisans and artists who make use of the imagery in their work.

The colonial period was characterised by European art of the time, and religious images like the portrait of the Virgin of Altagracia fall into this category. One nineteenth century Dominican who made his mark on the art world was Theodore Chasseriau, who was born in El Limón in Samaná and moved to France with his French father and Dominican mother as a child. He grew up to attain fame as one of the Romantics and several of his paintings hang in the Louvre alongside Ingres and David.

Twentieth century artists: Yoryi Morel painted the realities of Dominican life in a post-impressionist style. The mid twentieth century saw many public buildings with epic murals, the most prominent of these by Spanish exile Vela Zannetti. Other artists whose work has a particular Dominican flavour include Guillo Pérez, Ramon Oviedo, Plutarco Andujar, Cándido Bidó and Belkis Ramirez.

A younger generation of artists that has enjoyed acclaim and success beyond the shores of the Dominican Republic as well as within the country include names such as Raquel Paiewonsky, Jorge Pineda and German Pérez.

Good places to get an overview of the Dominican art scene are the Museo de Arte Moderno in Plaza de la Cultura and private collection at Museo Bellapart on Avenida John F Kennedy in the capital, Centro León in Santiago, smaller venues like Casa de Teatro in Santo Domingo's Colonial Zone and provincial cultural centres around the country.

Folkloric art includes carnival masks and faceless dolls. Much of the craft selection on sale in the country is mass-produced and globalized, but it is possible to find some authentic examples. Santiago has an eccentric but enjoyable Folkloric Museum which is definitely worth a visit.

LITERATURE

The Dominican Republic, despite having a consistent active literary tradition, has not produced a writer of the calibre of Colombia's García Márquez or Argentina's Borges. One exception is Ramon Marrero Aristy's *Over* about life in the sugar cane communities in the middle of the last century, which is generally considered to be a Latin American classic. But like the fictional works by most of the country's best-loved authors such as Juan Bosch, it has not been translated into English. On the other hand, some of Juan Bosch and Joaquin Balaguer's political writings may be available in English.

More recently there has been a small explosion of Dominican-themed literature in English from second generation immigrants to the United States: leading this young and talented pack is Junot Diaz, whose first novel *The Brief Wondrous Life of Oscar Wao* won the 2008 Pulitzer Prize and whose breakthrough publication of short stories, *Drown*, came out to widespread critical acclaim in the mid 1990s. The other big name in Dominican-American literature is Julia Alvarez, whose novels deal with Dominican themes and include *In the Time of the Butterflies*, *When the Garcia Girls Lost their Accents*, *Yo*, *In the Name of Salome*, *Saving the World*, a series of novels for younger readers, and poetry collections.

Other notable names include Angie Cruz whose novels narrate the urban émigré experience in the United States (*Soledad*, *Let It Rain Coffee*), and Nelly Rosario who combined magic realism with the generational epic saga genre in *Song of the Water Saints*.

FOOD
(ADAPTED FROM DOMINICANCOOKING.COM)

Dominican cuisine is the result of the intersection of crossroads of many continents and several countries. Before the Spaniards arrived on the island of Hispaniola in 1492, the indigenous *Taino*s ate food that reflected the resources found in their natural habitat as well as their technological limitations. Unlike the *Taino*s themselves who all but died out in the first fifty years of Spanish conquest, many of these dishes and ingredients have survived and today are an important part of the rich Dominican culinary culture. With the arrival of the Spaniards, many new species of animals, vegetables, fruits and grains found their way to the island. The Spaniards also introduced many foods typical of Mediterranean cuisine and others that had been passed down to the Spaniards by the Arabs during their 700-year domination of the Iberian Peninsula.

The introduction of African slaves in 1503 presented yet another new (and important) gastronomic imprint on Hispaniola. It is worth noting that the African influence is almost as strong as the Spanish influence in the Dominican culture – and the cuisine is no exception.

Dominican fare is very similar to that found in other Latin American countries, especially Cuba and Puerto Rico – the only two other Spanish-speaking countries in the Caribbean. Some of the dishes are almost identical and only the names change.

Other countries and influences have also found their way into Dominican kitchens. Pasta is a fundamental part of Dominican cooking; spaghetti was once called "the meat of the poor'. Other ingredients like salt cod and salted smoked herrings are also common in Dominican kitchens.

The base of Dominican cuisine is the *sofrito*, which is a mixture of spices and herbs, sautéed until the flavours are set free. Typically a *sofrito* includes thyme, salt, crushed garlic, parsley, onion (finely diced), green pepper, coriander/cilantro, tomatoes, tomato paste and vinegar. Many Dominican dishes are prepared using this mixture. Sometimes, to shorten the preparation time, people blend these ingredients and keep them in the fridge for a 'ready-to-use' seasoning.

A typical Dominican breakfast could consist of *mangú* – puréed plantains, cassava or *yautía* - accompanied by scrambled eggs and topped with sautéed onions. A few pieces of boiled cassava or another root is a good substitute for the *mangú*. This can also be accompanied by a few slices of deep-fried Dominican cheese (its consistency and taste similar to Greek *feta* or Indian *paneer*, but it is made with cow's milk). You may also accompany it with a couple of slices of deep-fried salami. A cup of cocoa, or coffee with milk is a suitable ending to this breakfast.

La comida (lunch) is the most important meal in the Dominican Republic. The family will gather around the table to share *La Bandera Dominicana* (the Dominican flag), the typical lunch. This consists of a combination of rice, beans, meat (or seafood) and salad or a side dish, and when prepared correctly, it becomes a meal that includes all food groups. The fresh ingredients provide for a meal that is not only delicious but also healthy and nutritious.

Accompany your lunch with a glass of iced water and end it with dessert, followed by a cup of coffee (*un cafecito*).

Dinner is a lighter affair, usually something made with tubers, a sandwich, eggs or soup.

Making casabe or cassava bread is an ancient tradition dating back to pre-Columbian times

Language

Like most other Latin American variants of Spanish, Dominican Spanish is different in accent and vocabulary to the Castillian Spanish spoken in the Iberian Peninsula. It does have a certain amount in common with the Spanish spoken in Andalusia, the Canary Islands, Puerto Rico, Cuba and the Caribbean coasts of Venezuela and Colombia.

Dominican Spanish is spoken very fast, with dropped Ss and characteristic slurring of the *ado* and *ada* endings, thus *pescado* (fish) becomes *pecao* and *cansada* (tired, f.) becomes *cansá*. The most striking Dominican regionalisms are the practices of pronouncing Rs as Ls in the capital, Ls as Rs in the south west and Rs as Is in the central Cibao region. Another typical Dominican speech pattern is the inversion of the question structure: ¿*cómo estas?* becomes ¿*cómo tu'tá?*. Several newcomers have taken a while to realise that *'ta bien* is *está bien* (that's right, OK) and not *tambien* (also).

Combined with the speed of delivery, it is enough to make a newcomer's head swim. Non-Spanish speakers who have made the effort to learn some Spanish before arriving in the country should take comfort in the following: even native speakers from other parts of the Spanish-speaking world find Dominican speech difficult to follow at first, and it does not take too long to adjust.

As in most cultures, body language plays an important part in communication. While many gestures are universally understood, some take a while to decipher. Two typically Dominican gestures are the nose wrinkle, indicating puzzlement, and the mouth pointing, where the lips are pursed while the head jerks in the indicated direction. It can also express silent disapproval or wry amusement when directed at a person.

Vocabulary includes several Dominican specific words and expressions with roots in *Taíno*, African languages, English and others:

Un chin meaning 'a little bit' is said to come from *Taíno*. Then there are all the *Taíno* words that became known universally, like tobacco, hammock, hurricane and cassava. African words survive mainly in food names like *mofongo* and *mondongo*. English influenced words are common, like *zafacon* for rubbish bin, said to derive from safety can, *suape* for mop, and *guachiman* for watchman. These words are believed to have stuck during the first United States invasion of the country in 1916. Since then the global influence of English has made an even stronger mark, especially in areas like baseball where practically every term is an adaptation of its English equivalent – *jonrón* for home run being the preferred term to *cuadrangular* in more correct Spanish.

As with many other colonial situations, words and terms that were in use at the time of colonisation and emigration from the old world and since fallen out of use in their countries of origin still survive in Dominican Spanish, with archaic words such as *acechar* (to look) and *apearse* (get down from) still in everyday use.

Otherwise Dominican Spanish is standard Latin American Spanish, with terms like *carro* rather than the Iberian *coche* for car, *manejar* rather than *conducir* for drive, and the complete absence of *vosotros* as the second person plural familiar form of address, apart from in church services. *Ustedes* is used in all situations.

SPANISH DOMINICAN-STYLE: A CRASH COURSE

Greetings

Saludos	Greetings – can be used at all times of day and night
Buenas	Dhort for *buenas tardes* (good afternoon/evening) but can be used at all times
Adios	Goodbye
Hasta luego	See you later (usual reply is "*si dios quiere*" God willing)
Hasta mañana	See you tomorrow (usual reply is "*si dios quiere*" God willing)

Hola	Hello (less formal)
Bye	bye-bye (less formal)
Buenos días	Good morning
Buen día	Good morning
Buenas tardes	Good afternoon/evening
Buenas noches	Good night
¿Cómo estás?	How are you? (informal address, usually expressed as *Como tu 'ta*)
¿Cómo está?	How are you? (formal address)
¿Qué tal?	How're things (informal)
Bien (gracias a dios)	Fine, thank God.
¿Y tú?	And you?
¿Y usted?	And you? (formal).
Encantado/a	Pleased to meet you
Un placer	A pleasure to meet you

SOME RANDOM SITUATIONS

At the gas station

Expat: Hello, I have a problem with my car. My engine will not start.
Hola, tengo un problema con mi carro. El motor no prende.

Mechanic: You have run out of gas?
¿Hay gasolina en el tanque?

Expat: No there is plenty of fuel
No, el tanque está lleno.

Mechanic: It'll be your distributor then.
Entonces sera el distribuidor.

Expat: Why do you say that? You haven't looked at it yet?
¿Como lo sabes, ni lo has mirado?

Mechanic: The car I repaired yesterday had that problem.
El carro que reparé ayer tenía ese mismo problema.

Chit chat with neighbours

Neighbour: When you lived in New York, where did you work?
Cuando vivías en Nueva York, ¿dónde trabajabas?

Expat: I'm not from the United States, I'm from England.
No soy de Estados Unidos, soy de Inglaterra.

Neighbour: Oh! That is far away.
Oh! Eso está lejos.

Expat: Yes, it's in Europe.
Sí, es en Europa.

Neighbour (to husband): Come here Manolo, I want to introduce you to our new neighbour, she's American.
Ven aca, Manolo, te quiero presentar nuestra nueva vecina, es Americana.

Fast talking banter

Dominican friend: How're ya?
¿cómo tu 'tá?

Expat (checks to see if has arrived in Japan by error): what?
¿que?

Dominican friend (slowly): How Are You?
¿cómo estás?

Expat: Ah, OK, Very well, thanks.
Ah, OK. Muy bien, gracias.

At the disco

Tiguere: Hello beautiful.
Hola linda.

Expat (indifferently): Hi...
Hola...

Tiguere: What's the matter? Are you angry?
¿Que pasa? ¿Estás guapa?

Expat: I thought you already decided I was 'linda'.

Tiguere: *No, enojada* – angry. (No, angry)

Expat: Oh, no, now I am very pregnant.
Oh, no, ahora estoy muy embarazada.

At the restaurant

> Expat: What's for breakfast?
> *¿Que tiene para el desayuno?*
>
> Waiter: We have fruit salad, eggs on toast, mangú with salami…
> *Tenemos ensalada de frutas, tostada con huevos, mangú con salami…*
>
> Expat: Does the fruit salad have plantain?
> *¿La ensalada de fruta tiene plátano?*
>
> Waiter: No, but the mangú does.
> *No, pero el mangú sí.*

SOME LANGUAGE PITFALLS

Embarrassed – do not say *embarazado/a* in Spanish – it means pregnant. Say *tengo verguenza*.

Introduce – do not say *introducir* which means "to insert" – say *presentar*

Beautiful is *lindo/a*. *Guapo/a* means angry or tough in DR Spanish.

Plátano is plantain. *Guineo* is banana.

Coche is cart (as in horse and cart), *carro* is car.

Preservativo is not jam, jam is *mermelada*. *Preservativo* is contraceptive.

A good indication of fluency in a language is the ability to read the local newspapers. The main Dominican papers are the venerable *Listín Diario, El Caribe, Hoy, El Día* and *Diario Libre*. The last two are free daily newspapers and the articles, especially in *Diario Libre*, are fairly succinct and reasonable well written. The writing in the other main newspapers tends to be more long-winded and not as accessible to a learner of the language. A more highbrow newspaper was the weekly *Clave* and its sister publication the online daily *Clave Digital*, but they ceased publication in August 2010 following their exposure of alleged links between a senior public figure and a major drug smuggler.

Listín Diario – www.listin.com.do
Hoy – www.hoy.com.do
El Caribe – www.elcaribe.com.do
Diario Libre – www.diariolibre.com
El Día – www.eldia.com.do

There are also several online publications focusing on national and regional news.

HOW?

What The...?

'Only in the Dominican Republic'

Thus far the information provided in this book has been in the main factual and pragmatic. However, there is only so much that can be absorbed without information overload, plus there are likely to be readers who get a better picture about the country from the anecdotal, the quirky and those downright head-scratching incidents which make up much of the expats' life in the DR. So we have gathered a series of real-life happenings, which have occurred either to Ginnie and Ilana, their expat friends and others who share the same sense of humour.

We begin with two cautionary tales for new and would-be residents as to exactly how long it can take to achieve a fairly simple task, the first with a commercial organisation and the second with the electricity company for the area in question. This is otherwise known as the *Mañana* Syndrome. For advanced level purists there is the closely associated *Ahorita* Syndrome; literally the diminutive form of 'now', in the DR *ahorita* is used to mean 'sometime soon'. And the difference? *Ahorita* is like *mañana* but without the same sense of urgency!

New residents who come from cultures where provision of goods and services is but a 'phone call away are easily identifiable here in the Dominican Republic during their first few months. They can appear frustrated, short-tempered and wear an incredulous look. Yes, getting even simple things achieved can take a lot longer than you are used to. It is part of the charm of the country. No neurotic 100 miles per hour lifestyle here, accompanied by cries of 'I haven't got time'. Dominicans always have time... for people. It is just tasks that take a little longer. A hint. Never let your frustration show for real. Be laid-back about all of this; demonstrate that you, too, understand the mysteries of the term *mañana*. And smile.

CAUTIONARY TALE ONE

One expat decided that instead of manually writing raffle tickets and the like, she would purchase a stamp (the sort you press in an ink pad) with the appropriate information. So on Monday 20th September (this all happened in 2004) she went in search of a producer of same. The stationers in Puerto Plata were unable to supply but advised of a company nearby which did. She duly went to this company, provided her information, the exact size required (to fit a raffle ticket which she provided) and was told it would be ready 22nd September. At that stage she had lived here nearly thirteen years; things are never 'ready' when you are told they will be. Things take time here in the Dominican Republic. You learn to stop overstressing like a Westerner and become laid back.

She let 22nd, 23rd and 24th go by and visited the office on 25th. It wasn't ready. Friday was a holiday, said the *jefe* (a Spanish word meaning boss and pronounced 'heff eh' or 'hay Fay' depending on where in United States you come from). Indeed it was, but Friday was 24th and this should have been ready on 22nd. Not to be picky she desisted from pointing out the obvious. "It'll be ready Monday 27th," he said.

Our intrepid expat called by on Monday – everyone in the whole place is wringing their hands. *Jefe* having conniptions. The air full of "*Ay, Dios MIO*", "*caramba*", "*ay, ay, ay*" and so on. The electricity company, *CDEEE*, has just sent a surge, computers busted, data collected over a ten year period, destroyed. The expat empathised... at length. It would have been churlish to enquire the connection between this act of God and the non-production of the stamp. Monday was the day for *simpatico*. Lots of it. Tomorrow, said the *jefe*, Tuesday 28th. It will be done.

As a side note, such electrical surges are not uncommon here in the Dominican Republic. If you are a foreigner building a house you allow for this by using surge protection. And if you are in any doubt you employ low-tech devices such as earthing yourself via wellington boots and rubber gloves.

Tuesday 28th. "The man who makes the wooden base for the stamp hadn't finished it, because he had no power." Expat empathises... at length. Life isn't fair, is it; you either get no power or 300 volts rocketing through exploding everything.

"Tomorrow for sure," said *jefe*. Although this print office is now rapidly becoming this expat's social centre, she deprived herself of the opportunity to visit on 29th and 30th.

When expat arrives at the office on 1st October *jefe* is beaming. The stamp is *ready*. Looks impressive, if a little large. He proudly demonstrates... it goes right off the page. *Jefe* and expat both scratch their heads (for the uninitiated this is a DR ritual, it denotes *simpatico*).

Jefe once more presses stamp in inkpad, gets up, goes away... and comes back with five sheets of raffle tickets. It appears this company prints them. So not only had expat left a sample ticket and the exact size required, they have thousands of the things.

She enquires as to why the error. New man is making stamps. New man is summoned and he and *jefe* have a discussion. New man says he will make another stamp immediately. "Not so fast," expat interposes. She asked new man, in Spanish, to explain to her why the error. Shoulder shrugging. Silly expat, wrong question. Rapidly correcting her mistake she asked if he understood what the error was. *Jefe* sat forward on his chair, all agog, to listen to new man. New man mumbles through his embarrassment that he knew what the error was. "Good," said expat. "What is it?" New man looks beseechingly at *jefe* for help. *Jefe* sits even further forward. By this time the rest of the workforce have downed tools and assumed the role of audience participants. "I'm waiting for your answer," expat intones, a trifle imperiously. Eventually new man looks at his boots and mutters that the stamp is too big.

"Splendid," expat roars, clapping him enthusiastically on his arm. "You are correct. Indeed it is. Now, *señor*, one more question... why is it too big when you had the ticket size provided by me, nay, when you print the tickets, every day, for weeks?"

Silence.

Well, it went on a bit and eventually new man scuttled away, vastly relieved that expat wasn't going to damage his marriage prospects, on top of having made him lose face. *Jefe* was most understanding and told expat that she had every justification for being annoyed. Not that she was annoyed in the slightest; she was performing what is known in the DR as *el show*. This led into a discussion of how *jefe* could make his staff accountable for their work, during the course of which, the new plate was made (it is a ten minute job).

But, you've guessed it; we now need a smaller wooden base to put it on... "Monday 4th," he said.

Anyone prepared to place a bet on Monday 4th?

It wasn't ready.

The man who made the wooden bases didn't want to work at the weekend. *Jefe* said there is only one man in Puerto Plata who makes these bases. Last March *jefe* bought 300 bases of different sizes from a man up from Moca, but he hasn't been up again since March. *Jefe* and expat have an empathic 'where do you get the staff these days' chat.

We will pass over the 5th, 6th and 7th October!

Finally, Friday 8th. It is ready. It is attached to its base. It is the correct size. It works! "*Caramba*", "*Ay Dios Mio*" etc., this time in tones of exultant joy.

Moral of the story: Expat was of a sunny disposition throughout because she didn't actually need the stamp until Christmas. Forward planning. Damage control. There was no urgency for her. That would not have been new man's understanding, of course and he was not there on Friday 8th for some inexplicable reason. So, a ten-minute job took some two and a half weeks. By Dominican standards, that is not bad. Bad would have been three months. It is all a matter of perspective.

So the moral of this 100% true story for new and potential residents is to start early; it will get done eventually. Never lose your cool, or if you pretend to, let them know afterwards that it was 'pretend'. Expat made a new friend in *jefe* and his wife, he hopefully learned something about staff management, and his wife assuredly learned something about being assertive. And it was all done observing local norms and not falling into the colonialist, imperialist trap of 'expat knows better'. Of course *jefe* thought that expat was totally knowledgeable about the print business. She actually knew squat but it doesn't do any harm...

There is a follow up to all of this. Expat and her husband pondered the shortage of these wooden bases and the somewhat casual work practices of the one and only person in Puerto Plata who made them. Expat's husband is an avid golfer and recent changes made by the new management at the golf club meant that prices have gone up noticeably for players, who are no longer obliged to take a caddy with them when they play.

The result, inevitably, is fewer players and less use of the caddies. So the caddies sit around at the caddy shack, hopefully waiting for a punter and in the meanwhile doing... well, nothing. These wooden bases for the stamps are handmade and very low tech. All that is required is a piece of wood, a knife, and later some sanding and varnishing. Something that caddies sitting around a caddy shack could easily manage.

Expat and her husband went with one of the caddies for an impromptu visit to *jefe* in his print shop. In fact everything is impromptu here. You just turn up. If they're not there you go back later. Expat introduced her other half to *jefe* and he explained his idea of piecework for the caddies, making the wooden bases, so they could earn some money whilst they weren't caddying. He then left the caddy with *jefe* to sort out payment details. You don't want a *gringo* interfering in a business negotiation between two Dominicans! Hopefully this would meet both *jefe*'s need for bases and the caddies' need for some cash.

If both follow through, of course, and in this culture you can't take that for granted!

The footnote is, they didn't.

CAUTIONARY TALE TWO

The second cautionary tale happened to a friend of ours, another British expat who lives in Juan Dolio on the south coast. We'll call her Matilda. In October 2006 Matilda was having a problem with her electricity supply (beyond the usual one of power outages): when the pump for the well water kicked in, her air-conditioning went off, likewise when her swimming pool pump went on, her TV went off, and at 7pm each evening all of her power went off. This she attributed to the TV viewing habits of the twenty or so Dominican and Haitian families who were illegally hooked up to her supply of power and who probably all sat down to watch the same *telenovela* (soap opera) at the same time. Matilda realised that never needing to look at her watch at 7pm was a plus but it was overcome by the other minuses and so she decided to go independent and acquire her own 7000-volt transformer. So that no one could hook up illegally she was going to position the transformer inside her garden on top of a thirty-five foot concrete post.

Matilda reflected that in the UK such an installation would take place in the daytime. In the DR it takes place at night. Matilda's Dominican husband patiently explained that it was because there was no sun so it was cooler for the workers.

"Thank you, dear," said Matilda. "Silly me, I thought they needed to see to fix 7000 volts of electricity thirty-five foot up a pole." She also reflected that in the UK a team of well qualified electricians would be running the show – in Juan Dolio it was two electricians and five *motoconcho* drivers; in the UK a mechanical hoist would elevate the heavy transformer – in Juan Dolio it was a piece of rope and now you know what the five *motoconcho* drivers were for; in the UK workers would have refreshed themselves with water and coffee (7000 volts can have its dangers) – in

Matilda's garden expected refreshments were two litres of *Brugal* (rum!); in the UK the well qualified electricians would have produced an appropriate array of suitable tools – in Juan Dolio they asked for Matilda's kitchen knives.

However, the job was done and by midnight the experienced electrician was unconscious on Matilda's patio (the *Brugal*, not an electric shock) and two of her kitchen knives had been left up the thirty-five foot pole probably due to alcoholic amnesia. The installation job was done but the next job was to connect the transformer to the power supply. The electricity company promised to come the next day and didn't, then the next and didn't but three days later Matilda's electrician returned and started to put in cable which eventually reached her house. He also told her to put six pounds of salt in the ground next to the transformer (to draw the moisture and keep it grounded but he didn't tell her that – in the UK they would have used a copper bar for grounding). The next day the electrician returned but a bit fell off the transformer so the electrician had to take this away to find a replacement bit. He also took the old transformer away and did not return for two days so Matilda was without power for two days and beginning to get a little cross. She naturally complained to the electricity company who sent an Inspector who told her that if anyone touches the wires in an attempt to steal them they would die (7000 volts remember), and that Matilda needs US$6,750 worth of insurance to cover for this and without it they will not connect her brand new transformer.

A week later Matilda had negotiated the price for the insurance down to US$1,750 which included replacing the wooden posts she had previously been swindled into having for her Cable TV and internet connection (long story), with concrete posts which were deemed less of a danger to marauding thieves intent on stealing her wires. The following week work on installation of the concrete posts began, but it was not all plain sailing even then as she had to purchase yet another concrete post and various replacement parts for things that had fallen off, gone wrong or otherwise malfunctioned.

Eleven months after the process started the electricity company finally connected Matilda's transformer to the power supply. Her stepsons took down the old wire which they could sell and the twenty or so Dominican and Haitian families illegally hooked up to her old wires were no longer able to do so to her new ones. Matilda had 7000 volts all to herself and the explosion she had anticipated at the time of connection did not materialise. Of course she had to buy a watch.

So is that the end of the story? Not quite! Fifteen months later the earth moved for Matilda. In fact the earth moved for almost the whole of Juan Dolio. Mr Matilda on a fitness kick? Not exactly. The inventive twenty or so Dominican and Haitian families had not let the transformer being thirty-five feet up a pole interfere with their favourite *novela*. Matilda does not know how but they found a way to reconnect. Matilda's husband disconnected them and then a couple of days later they tried again and BOOOM. The explosion plunged the whole of Juan Dolio into darkness, fried Matilda's television and most of her light bulbs, and probably gave an added curl or two to the hairstyles of the usurpers.

So Matilda bought another transformer, and went through roughly the same procedure getting it fitted! This time it was February so the electrician could work in the daytime and this time refreshments were of a non-alcoholic nature. But some things in the DR never change – they still used a rope to haul this exceedingly heavy object aloft. Matilda has promised to notify us of any further developments that might occur before publication…

Understanding DR bureaucracy

BUREACRACY TALE ONE

We now turn to two tales about a subject that often confronts and challenges new expats – that of finding one's way around the Dominican Republic's bureaucracy. Expats can be forgiven for thinking that bureaucracy in the DR is deliberately so engineered as to make life difficult for foreigners. Nothing is further from the truth; Dominicans suffer the slings and arrows of outrageous pettyocracy just as much, if not more than foreigners do. Two suggestions might help the new expat: suspend any notions you might have of logic and think of it as a game, something similar to charades or better still, chess. Your mission, should you choose to accept it, is to outsmart the other player by accurately predicting his moves before he makes them and taking action which will render those moves futile and self-defeating. Above all, enjoy the game and keep your cool.

Nine years ago Ginnie bought a second-hand 4x4 in the DR and this is the strange saga that followed:

"It wasn't the first vehicle I had bought: thirteen years ago I bought a VW Beetle from the same vendor whose house in the centre of Puerto Plata we had purchased. At that time I went through the process of getting the car's *matricula* (log book) registered in my name. It was a cumbersome, lengthy and somewhat arcane process in those days, involving publication of intent to change ownership in a newspaper advert and a visit to Santiago for the police to issue a certification of the chassis and engine numbers. Plus lots of official stamps appended to reams of official paper. Delays occurred due to misplacing of the documents which had to go to the capital, Santo Domingo, plus the usual breakdowns of computers and/or computer systems and/or the electricity supply but... eighteen months later I had my *matricula* in my own name!

The next vehicle I purchased turned out to be a piece of junk. Knowing I would not be its proud owner for eighteen months I decided to sell it as quickly as possible. This was achieved despite the fact that the *matricula* was not in my name. The third vehicle I purchased is my current one, the SUV bought nine years ago which was and still is providing sterling service. The owner was an Irish mechanic who was working in the DR at the time and who had professionally and lovingly nurtured this 1988 vintage vehicle. What he hadn't done, however, was to get the *matricula* transferred to his name when he had purchased it. Neither had the person from whom the Irish mechanic bought it – a US citizen who ran a safari tour company. In fact the name on the *matricula* was that of the Dominican dealer who had imported the car and sold it to Mr Safari.

I happily drove my SUV for several months before presenting myself to the *Dirección General de Impuestos Internos* to apply for the vehicle to be put in my name and pay the transfer taxes. This was neither a good example of procrastination nor a lack of funds so much as 'other priorities'. We were heavily involved with assisting a fellow expat who had been wrongly jailed at the time and his need for assistance was of greater immediacy than my need to get my car documentation correct. However, when things had quietened somewhat at the jail (read: a period free from riots) I duly got all my paperwork together and along I went to pay the taxes and transfer the document, confident in the knowledge that I had done this before with the VW Beetle so I knew what the procedure would be.

Wrong! Apparently the VW transfer with all its stamps, paperwork and visits had been the simple version! This was because the vendor of the vehicle had her name on the vehicle's *matricula*. The SUV vendor, on the other hand, did not, nor the person he had purchased from. Without a copy of the *cédula* (ID card) of the person named on the *matricula*, the transfer could not take place. Mistakenly, I thought that it would be relatively easy to track down the dealer to ask for a copy of his *cédula*.

The dealership was in Santiago, a town about seventy-five minutes drive from Puerto Plata where I live so I naturally telephoned first. This was where the fun started. For the purposes of this article I shall call the dealer Cesar Brito. Cesar, it transpired, had sold the dealership and retired a few years before my call. The last known address the new dealership had for him was in Santo Domingo, the capital of the Dominican Republic and some four hours drive distant. Undaunted (you need to be undaunted if you live in the DR) I asked a friend living in the capital to track down Sñr. Brito and get a copy of his *cédula*.

Weeks later I discovered that poor Cesar had not enjoyed a very long retirement: according to my friend in the Capital he had died. And dead men don't have *cédulas*. Back I went to the *DGII* (the tax office) and explained that there was no way I could get a copy of the *cédula* of the person named on the *matricula* because its owner was no more. Now, I thought, they will find a way to let me pay the taxes and get the *matricula* put in my name. Wrong again! This time I was told that since Cesar had inconveniently died I would need the *cédula* of his heir, his eldest son.

Back to my friend in the Capital. And after a few weeks, "He doesn't have family here; they all moved to the US years ago." So back to the *DGII*, "He doesn't have family here; they're all in the US."

"Can't you contact them in the US?"

"I don't even know which state they live in. Where would you suggest I start?" Much shrugging of shoulders, followed by discussion with supervisor.

I suggested that maybe payment of an extra fee would ease the difficulties (you don't talk about bribes here, but 'extra fees' often smooth seemingly insurmountable problems). But, without the *cédula* it couldn't be done, extra fee or no extra fee. So, that was that. The *matricula* remained in Cesar Brito's name RIP and I happily continued to drive the vehicle whilst keeping a copy of the bill of sale from the Irish mechanic to myself in the glove compartment in case I was ever stopped.

In 2000 we had a change of Government and by 2002 it was becoming clear that their political platform **was** 'extra fees' and since the tax office was staffed by at least some political appointees, I thought a return visit might be worthwhile. By this time I had a new *matricula* and a different number plate (they are issued every four years as a method of obtaining tax revenue) but the new *matricula* was still in the deceased's name. So I returned to the tax office feeling I should have brought an audio version of the story with me so I could just plug it in and play… but even stereo would have made no difference.

"Can't be done without a copy of the *cédula*."

We had read this particular chapter before! I continued to happily drive the SUV apart from the three weeks when it was off the road having a new chassis fitted. The frame had basically succumbed to the salt in the sea air, and was a series of holes held together by rust such that our mechanic was concerned that one day the whole thing would just collapse in the road. He did a splendid job and after his ministrations my SUV drove like a Sherman tank.

Fast forward to 2004 when we had another change of Government. This one, however, promised Governmental austerity and a full frontal assault on corruption – hardly fruitful ground for 'extra fees' or so I thought, so I didn't return. Not until November 2007 when I read in a newspaper of a Governmental push to claim back taxes on car transfers and an amnesty period until January 2008. The supervisor at the tax office, a political appointee of the 'austerity, anti-corruption' Government, told me confidentially that she could get me a copy of Cesar Brito's *cédula*... for an 'extra fee'. I was ecstatic and so would Cesar have been had he seen his photo ID on the *cédula* because, given the circumstances, he really looked very well indeed!

This, however, was only the start of the circumvention. The supervisor had explained to me that I would need a lawyer who was a 'friend' (nudge, wink). What he needed to do was to make out a new contract of sale whereby the vehicle was sold directly from Cesar Brito to me, thus removing both Mr Safari and the Irish mechanic from the line of succession. We had lived in Puerto Plata for sixteen years at the time so we certainly had lawyers who are 'friends' and when I went to one he certainly needed little explanation of what was required, so the supervisor at the tax office must have had an endless supply of dead men's *cédulas*.

The following week I collected the contract which the friendly lawyer had also arranged to be signed by a Notary Public as required by law as well as by the dead vendor, Cesar Brito... don't ask! The friendly lawyer's colleague had been wonderfully helpful because she had paid over the stamp money for me when going to get her own chassis and engine numbers looked at. So the next part of the procedure was similar to that of thirteen years ago – a visit to Santiago for the police to issue a certification of the chassis and engine numbers.

My other half volunteered for this task and probably wished he hadn't. When he arrived at the police certification centre he found it had moved from where it had been thirteen years previously. Intrepidly, he tracked down the new office where he discovered that one more piece of bureaucratic paperwork was required: a slip from the *DGII* in Santiago. This would mean leaving the certification centre and…who knows? They could move it again in his absence. So he enquired whether by some remote chance the certification centre happened to have a spare copy of the bureaucratic paperwork and lo and behold for 100 pesos they did! Then all proceeded swimmingly until the police went hunting for the chassis number. The sharp amongst you will recall that years back the SUV was off the road for three weeks whilst the mechanic made and fitted a new chassis… to which he had neglected to attach the numbered chassis plate.

"Can't be done without a chassis number plate?" Fortunately, no. Living here sixteen years helps with the instantly plausible stories. That and mangling the Spanish tenses so that it was a little uncertain exactly when this work had taken place. Don't forget the late Cesar had sold me this vehicle last December, not nine years ago!

So, all done and dusted? Not quite. Surely you weren't expecting instant gratification? This is the DR after all. Unfortunately the certification centre had insufficient staff to process the paperwork that day.

"Come back to Santiago tomorrow."

Fine, but that's another whole day spent on this task. However, as stated above sixteen years of residence in the DR brings certain advantages one of which is having friends in towns other than where we live. My other half paid a quick trip to a lawyer friend in Santiago and she agreed to collect the certification *mañana*. Of course first he had to authorise her to do so by giving her a copy of his own *cédula*.

The following day we checked and friendly lawyer had indeed collected the certification, which she duly dropped off at the home of other half's golfing partner, also in Santiago and finally the next weekend, after golf, my other half came away triumphantly clutching the certification. We cheered!

So now it is time for me to spring into action. Back to the tax office I went carrying all the required documentation...or so I thought. I had the police certification, the contract of sale between Cesar and myself, the original *matricula*, my *cédula*, Cesar's *cédula* and untold copies of all of these documents. Our friendly supervisor (the specialist in dead men's *cédulas*) proceeded to authorise my documentation when all of a sudden her face fell. She pointed to the back of the *matricula* and said in a disappointed voice, "You didn't get Cesar to sign the back of the *matricula*."

It would probably have been a tactical error to point out that Cesar, six feet under, wasn't exactly up to signing anything. But what a bi-polar experience – this good lady who had got me the fake *cédula* on payment of a bribe... er fee now believed that Cesar actually lived. I thought maybe we were being overheard so I responded with, "So sorry, I must be getting forgetful now I'm getting older." The age card works wonders here, playing the little old lady with arthritis is even more likely to elicit respect and help. So the supervisor 'helped' me. She took a cursory look at the *cédula* she had produced and faked Cesar's signature. She also worked out what the transfer taxes were – 1200 pesos (about US$34). Then all I had to do was line up in a very long queue and wait to pay it. This is where the arthritis came in: I gave my sob story and supervisor passed all the paperwork to Junior, the clerical officer responsible for receiving payments. He was all of five feet distant the other side of a cramped partition. She even told him to hurry up about it. So I waited seated whilst the reams of paperwork were minutely examined one more time, the tax payment was accepted, a receipt was issued and voila... a new *matricula* in my very own name!

It only took nine years. But you have to set these things in perspective. Some of the local population who lost their homes to Hurricane David are only now having housing made available to them. And Hurricane David was in 1979. And the current registration plate number on my (note "my") *matricula*? 007007. Oh indeed, James Bond is alive and well and hunting down dead men who DO sign *cédulas* in the Dominican Republic!"

BUREAUCRACY TALE TWO

"The second bureaucracy story happened recently and stars a character very familiar in Dominican Governmental offices – a medium-ranking administrative clerk with delusions of grandeur. Not clinical delusions as such, you understand, but control issues – "this is *my* office, where things will be done my way, and you all need to be aware of my position and dust yourselves off after bowing and scraping to My Presence." Advice for new expats: do not attempt to confront, aggress or reason with such a character. You will lose the game. Instead, try getting his underlings on your side by facilitating group sniggers, use the group (or mass of people waiting for the same 'service') and above all use humour to get Mr. All Powerful smiling. Of course you can't do this in English.

In 2008 I was due to renew my *cédula* and since it is currently not possible for foreigners to do this in Puerto Plata, it is necessary to make the journey to the *Junta Central Electoral (JCE)* in Santo Domingo. My other half (the golfer) needed to renew both his residency and his *cédula* and, as it so happened, went the day before I did. I thus heard in advance that the *JCE* office for foreigners had a Trujillo-style *jefe* who had struck confusion and impotence into some of the new expats applying for their first *cédulas* by not permitting their accompanying lawyers to be present in the office with them. Okay so it was crowded and there wasn't really room for extraneous individuals but he could have let the lawyers in when their clients were actually called to the desk to be processed. Imagine these people with little or no Spanish trying to understand what they were being asked to do – in previous years the lawyer has always been the interpreting intermediary.

Forewarned by my other half that Trujillo employed techniques of intimidation I was thus prepared. I was also cognisant of the fact that the staff running the desks were quite human with good senses of humour – they just happened to be women and my partner had used a mixture of male flattery and humour directed against *jefe* to get the women tittering.

The first hurdle was actually getting into the room. I arrived with a Dominican friend with whom I had intended lunching afterwards – another example of how much I have internalised Dominican 'optimism' since the procedure this year was about to take far, far longer than on previous occasions. Trujillo said there was no room inside; my Dominican friend immediately disappeared and I was allowed in. Round one to Trujillo who had Proved His Power to control entry to his chamber. I was ushered to a space on a sofa next to a couple who happened to be from Korea. It was now a question of sitting and waiting. And watching. Because what transpired after observing for twenty minutes was that there were in fact two lines (a loose description) moving anti-clockwise. One was for first time *cédula* applicants and the other was for renewals. From the sofa one moved to the right to a row of chairs against the wall as a space became available.

The entry door was strategically placed between the sofa and the row of chairs thus meaning that if a new person entered and spotted an empty chair they would, naturally, sit, thus taking a place before those waiting on the sofa. The Korean couple were fluent in both English and Spanish but they were not very assertive. Trujillo had told them to sit and that he would call them. And meanwhile on the sofa they stayed whilst new entrants entered and sat in the next empty seat in the row of chairs and thus usurped the place of the Koreans. The Koreans had not been alarmed by this because they had believed that Trujillo really would call them. By the time I started up a conversation with the Koreans they had already been there well over an hour.

Realising they had been forgotten, the next time Trujillo passed the sofa the Korean husband explained the problem in fluent Spanish and a very reasonable tone of voice. Trujillo's response was that for them the procedure was 'different'. This is called 'not admitting responsibility'. I discovered they were in fact renewing their *cédulas* as were the other people on the chairs; the procedure for the Koreans would be no different from the rest of us. The Koreans and I communicated in English having first established that Trujillo did not understand it. Korean husband, before I could stop him, then took issue with Trujillo's 'your procedure is different'. Sharp intake of breath by *El Jefe*, forward projection of chin and drawing of self up to his full height of 5 foot 4 inches. Absolute power had been challenged!

The Korean husband was applying reason and he was doing so in a calm, polite fashion but if you meet an official here with control issues it is better not to point out that he had committed an error by forgetting to call this couple because you will never get him to agree with you. He would lose too much face by so doing. It is better to throw yourself on his mercy, admit the error is yours and beseech his goodness in magnanimously doing what he can to correct your error. You can even ham it up and still appear credible here.

Basically, that is what I did when I intervened in this situation. Having told the Korean in English to play along with me and not argue with Trujillo I then launched into: "Of course the procedure is different for them; you'll need to forgive them, they don't understand. But they were here before all those other people on the chairs so if you could work some sort of miracle and slip them in when the next person at the desk is finished, that would be great and meanwhile I'll explain to them where they got the procedure wrong."

I thus assumed the role of 'mediator for the cerebrally challenged' and Trujillo actually half-smiled. Someone else was agreeing with him (oh yeah), acknowledging his authority and placing the fault at the feet of the Koreans. He duly became Miracle Worker and they went to the next available desks for processing thus recouping some of their place in the line. Unfortunately, when they were processed they turned to thank me. Wrong! I nearly yelled at them, "NO, you thank him. Effusively." But I couldn't have done so without causing more problems so instead I smiled at Trujillo and shrugged my shoulders in a 'what do they know' fashion. Trujillo and I were beginning the tortuous process of bonding. Should be good for skipping one or two places in the line I thought. If the Korean couple ever read this book: I am not insane, it is a game, a charade but it needs to be played by charade rules right to the end.

The Koreans left and all this while more and more foreigners (minus lawyers) were entering the room. Trujillo decided to have a roll call so that Everyone Knew Their Place in the line. He did this by calling the numbers from one to sixteen and pointing to each of us in turn in such a way that one felt like standing and saluting, or clicking one's heels together smartly. Course, it might have been a good idea had he done this while the Koreans were still in line and then the problem might not have arisen. Noticeable was the fact that he only roll-called the renewals; the other line, the contra rotating first timers, were left to fend for themselves.

He started his roll call at the chair nearest the desks and proceeded uninterrupted until he got to number four. An empty chair! He beckoned to number five to move up but number five said that the young lady in number four had gone outside and would be back.

"Outside?" intoned Trujillo loudly and in disbelief. "She has no business going outside. She cannot keep her place if she goes outside. Where has she gone? I will put someone else in her place."

Faced with this onslaught number five, a mild-mannered Haitian man, looked at the floor. Silence. And Trujillo was still waiting for an answer.

Trujillo's tirade had been in Spanish. I did the only thing I could think of – I took a straw poll of the rest of the room in as many languages as I could muster: English, French, so-so Spanish, abysmal German and sign language. "The boss here wants to know where the young lady in seat number four has gone. Does anyone know? Can you all understand me? Should I do it in body language? Any ideas where she might be? What about you, sir?" to some inoffensive Belgian. He just stared at me like I had landed from Mars. The Croatians, however, had a good sense of humour and mercifully spoke English.

"She gave up and went home," offered one Croatian with a twinkle in his eye.

"No, no, she go outside to make phone call," interposed a German in English.

"She went to get some lunch," an overweight Colombian suggested.

"She went to check if the date had changed yet," the Croatian was really getting into the spirit of things.

There is nothing quite like audience participation. As well as calling out answers the foreigners began to chat among themselves. The girls at the desks were grinning ear-to-ear and Trujillo was beginning to realise that he was losing his floorshow. Eventually I called for a group consensus answer to be put to Trujillo, "Could we agree she might have gone to the bathroom?"

"Agreed."

"I agree."

"I'll go along with that," and such-like from those who were playing the game. As for the others, ditto the comment above about Mars.

By this time I had got close enough to Trujillo's badge to see that he was called Tito. Really! I think the Croatians found it as funny as I did but it passed over the heads of the other nationalities present.

"Don Tito, the group consensus seems to be that number four has gone to the bathroom," I said very loudly in a helpful fashion in Spanish. One of the Croatians, the one with the evil sense of humour, also spoke Spanish.

"But did number four go for a number one or a number two?" Screams of laughter from those who understood the significance. The Croatian was on a roll now; clearly a performer he started to use body language to signify for non-Spanish speakers the difference between number one and number two.

"Yes, yes, yes, thank you, thank you. That is a good reason for going outside." Don Tito had zero appreciation of music-hall comedy. But I couldn't have had a better co-conspirator.

Round two to Croatia and the UK. At which point number four re-entered the room and was somewhat surprised when she received a group round of applause accompanied by winks and smiles. A confidential question elucidated that she had been to the bathroom – good guess.

Round three went to the newly forming group cohesion which of course was a trifle threatening for Don Tito. It is impossible to intimidate a group of people who sit and grin at you.

The dénouement came when number five was given his biometric details on paper to read and check. He stared at it for a long, long time such that it became obvious he was having some difficulty reading. Eventually the girl behind the desk cottoned on, helped by the Croatian and myself gesticulating from behind the Haitian. She proceeded to call number five's details out loud for his verification: "Is your name xxxx? Is your date of birth xxxx? Is your sex male?"

I smiled and she said it was important to check any changes from the last *cédula*. So I asked the room in as many languages as I could muster how many *gringo*s had had a sex change since their last *cédula*. And the Croatian, bless him, minced his way around the room to cover the languages I couldn't. At that we discovered that even Don Tito had a sense of humour...

Eventually I, too, was processed and left but not before congratulating Don Tito on his splendidly well-run office and telling him how it would feature in the next book I wrote. He positively glowed and was extremely gracious. Probably glad to see the back of me. Don Tito, if you're reading this, well you were forewarned."

AND ANOTHER STORY

There is another category of anecdotes that have you smiling at the sheer inventiveness of the Dominican population. It starts at an early age for many, where poverty means that toys do not come from the toy-store but from discarded household items, such as the space gun which is really a washing-up liquid plastic container; or the night shift of Edenorte (the electricity company) who eschew the use of flashlights when working on-high to repair blown transformers – they use their truck, rev the engine, make sure the headlights are blazing, put rocks under the wheels, pull a piece of broken mirror from inside the truck and one worker will sit in the road in front of the headlights and use the mirror to direct a huge beam of light right up to the man working at the top of the pole. Or the car repair shops where 'new' exhaust pipes are beaten out using earth pushed inside to hold the shape during the hammering.

Nor should it be assumed that all authority figures either have an axe to grind or are uncaring. Every town has its *locos* and Puerto Plata is no exception; one of these used to walk the streets pretending he was driving a motorcycle: knees bent as if sitting, arms out holding the handle bars, making motorcycle noises as if switching gears - brrrrmmm, brrrrmmm, brrrrmmm. One day he was the centre of a huge commotion, horns honking and people yelling. The imaginary motorcycle had imaginarily broken down and was blocking a busy street. *Loco* stood on one leg, while trying to kick-start his imaginary motorcycle with the other leg and working the throttle like a man possessed. Finally two police officers arrived and it could have been assumed that an arrest was imminent. But no. The first officer motioned for the drivers who were honking to take it easy, while the second asked the *loco* to step aside. The second cop then calmly grabbed the imaginary handlebars and moved the imaginary motorcycle off to the side of the road so that the cars could pass. Who says that the DR police don't have an understanding of people and mental illness well above their training (or pay grade)?

Finally, a story (again 100% true), which illustrates how differently things are done in the DR. In March 2009 an expat friend of ours was driving from the north coast of the DR, having spent the weekend with friends, back to her home in Juan Dolio on the south coast. At the start of the track that leads to her home she was suddenly surrounded by six men, all armed, who wanted to take her car. Our friend needed to get home urgently to use the bathroom so she persuaded the men to follow her back to her house rather than take the car there and then. In fact she told them they could shoot her if they wished but she really did need to get to a bathroom! This admirably cool behaviour in the presence of potential danger was doubtless conditioned by the fact that our expat friend has been shot before, at home, and against heavy odds lived to tell the tale. Once home she went to the bathroom whilst her Dominican husband dealt with the six men.

These men were not standard thieves, it should be understood, although our friend did not know that at the time. It transpired that four years earlier her husband had stood guarantor for a loan for a friend of his who needed the money so that his son could have an operation. The sick boy's father had paid back most of the money borrowed but not in the correct time period and thus the outstanding amount had been augmented by interest and penalties so that it now reached US$8,380. As the father had gone missing and could not be contacted by the loan company, they did not use telephone or mail notification to alert the guarantor of the loan as to his debt; instead they sent six heavies to sequester his vehicle. This is fairly standard practice here so if you are ever held up by six armed men it is worth enquiring whether they are normal robbers or whether they have just cause. That way one can avoid panicking unnecessarily.

The loan company's 'staff' duly took the vehicle and our friend set about finding ways to raise the money required so that she could get the vehicle back – the vehicle being worth more than the sum outstanding on the loan and interest. Meanwhile her husband went to the Fiscal and got an arrest order for the father, found him and had him locked up. But this family have no money which was why they needed the loan in the first place to pay for the operation, so apart from agreeing to sell the family pig for about US$270 the rest of the payment had to come from the expat and her husband.

Four days later the expat had called in debts owed to her and borrowed the balance from friends, so armed with the required cash, her husband went to the loan company to hand it over and reclaim their vehicle. When he got there he discovered that their vehicle had been totalled. Hard to believe that this could happen in the repo yard of a Savings and Loan company. In fact it hadn't; the man driving it back from the expat's home to the loan company had apparently driven into a fork lift truck which was mending the road. As you do.

The Savings and Loan Company had written off our friend's car as irreparable so her husband decided to let them substitute one of the vehicles they had already repossessed that had remained in one piece. In order to achieve this he had to use a veritable army of lawyers, Fiscals, police, plus the *National Intelligence Department* (don't ask!). However, all's well that ends well and our friend's husband drove home in a pickup truck which was in far better condition than theirs had been. The 'new' vehicle is a manual which is not a problem for our expat friend who is a British woman brought up on manual vehicles, but for her Dominican husband only familiar with automatics, there will probably be some interesting times ahead. The next day he was going to work and in order to get out of their drive he had to call for his wife to put it in reverse…

We hope that these true anecdotes have given the reader a window on life in the Dominican Republic for expats. Or at least a rear-view window. The expat's life can be simple and enjoyable or it can be fraught with difficulties. The determining factor is the expat; Dominicans for the most part will remain the same. Openness to the new culture, the ability to both learn and laugh at oneself, and to have a quiet but firm self-confidence sprinkled with a dash of humility will lead to the simple and enjoyable life. The absence of these will lead to a life fraught with difficulties and the Dominican 'entrepreneurial spirit' will ensure that the difficulties persist; there are so many tales we could tell you… perhaps in the next book; fictionalised to ensure the authors continued ability to write.

HOW?

Resources

Non-Fiction Books

Something to Declare (essays) - Julia Alvarez, Plume, 1999

Dominican Republic – Culture Smart! The Essential Guide to Customs and Culture – Ginnie Bedggood and Ilana Benady, Kuperard, 2010

Quisqueya – Mad Dogs and English Couple – Ginnie Bedggood, Best Books 2007

The Washington Connection and Third World Fascism – Noam Chomsky and Edward S. Herman – *The Dominican Republic: US Model for Third World Development*. South End Press, 1999

The Dominican Republic: A National History – Frank Moya Pons, Markus Wiener Publishers; 2nd edition (August 1, 1998)

Trujillo – the Death of a Dictator – Bernard Diederich, Markus Wiener Pub; 1ST edition (April 1, 2000)

Aunt Clara's Dominican Cookbook – Clara González and Ilana Benady, Lunch Club Press, 2007

When the Cocks Fight – Michele Wucker, Hill and Wang; First Edition edition (April 3, 2000)

Fiction Books

In the Time of the Butterflies – Julia Alvarez, Algonquin Books 1995

When the Garcia Girls Lost their Accents – Julia Alvarez, Algonquin Books 1992

Yo – Julia Alvarez, Plume 1997

In the Name of Salome – Julia Alvarez, Plume 2001

Soledad – Angie Cruz, Simon and Schuster 2002
Let It Rain Coffee – Angie Cruz, Simon and Schuster 2006
The Farming of Bones – Edwige Danticat, Penguin 1999
The Brief Wondrous Life of Oscar Wao – Junot Díaz, Riverhead, 2007
Drown – Junot Díaz, Riverhead, 1997
Over – Ramon Marrero Aristy, 1939
Song of the Water Saints – Nelly Rosario, Vintage 2003
The Feast of the Goat – Mario Vargas Llosa, Picador 2002

Video/DVD

La herencia del tirano: Balaguer y el poder – Rene Fortunato, 2002
Other documentaries about Dominican history by Fortunato are:
Trujillo: El Poder del Jefe I, 1991
Trujillo: El Poder del Jefe II, 1994
Trujillo: El Poder del Jefe III, 1996
Balaguer: La Herencia del Tirano, 1998
Juan Bosch: Presidente en la Frontera Imperial, 2009

Reports

Human Development: A Matter of Power – United Nations Development Report on the Dominican Republic, 2008
English summary downloadable from:
www.pnud.org.do/sites/pnud.onu.org.do/files/Resumen_Ingles.pdf

PNUD June 2010 *Política social: capacidades y derechos Volumen I: Marco teórico; La política social: capacidades y derechos; Educación; Salud. Volumen II: Empleo; Seguridad social y asistencia social; Asentamientos humanos. Volumen III:*

Justicia y derechos; Inmigración haitiana; Cohesión social; Hacia una política social basada en derechos. Downloadable here: *odh.pnud.org.do/politica-socialcapacidades-y-derechos*

Articles by Ginnie Bedggood

Glitz, Bling and Merengue – Britishexpat.com 2006
britishexpat.com/americas/dominican-republic/glitz-bling-and-merengue

Can I count your vote? – Britishexpat.com 2006
britishexpat.com/americas/dominican-republic/can-i-count-your-vote

Culture Shock Revisited – Groping Toward a More Useful Conceptual Framework - Offshorewave.com, 2007
www.offshorewave.com/offshorenews/culture-shock-revisited-groping-toward-a-more-useful-conceptual-framework-by-ginnie-bedggood.html

Mobilising For Change In The Dominican Republic – Offshorewave.com, 2008
www.offshorewave.com/offshorenews/mobilising-for-change-in-the-dominican-republic-by-ginnie-bedggood.htm

CULTURE SMART!

DOMINICAN REPUBLIC

Occupying the eastern two-thirds of island of Hispaniola, the Dominican Republic has something for almost everyone – except perhaps obsessive perfectionists. If you can relax and go with the flow you will experience a land of great environmental diversity with a rich and varied culture, a turbulent history, some infuriating idiosyncrasies, and a people whose friendliness is legendary.

The Dominicans are flamboyant, irrepressible, generous, headstrong, and resilient. Their culture is a distinctive mix of an easygoing Caribbean nature coupled with Latino verve and showmanship.

For those who choose to break out of the confines of all-inclusive tourist resorts, *Culture Smart! Dominican Republic* offers a tantalizing insight into this warm, vital, and intriguing people. It takes you on a journey from the unspoiled coastline to the agricultural interior, to the imposing mountains and to the hamlets where time appears to have stood still. It then catapults you into the twenty-first century, through poverty and opulence, to the hustle and bustle of the large cities and the lifestyles of the luxury coastal tourist resorts.

Culture Smart! Dominican Republic offers practical advice on what to expect and how to behave in a Dominican home, or in social and work settings.

It will help turn your visit, whether it's for business or pleasure, into a memorable and enriching experience.

ISBN: 978 1 857 33527 9

Price: £6.95

by Ginnie Bedggood and Ilana Benady

"The standard Dominican lunch is known as la bandera (the flag), as its three main components supposedly represent the red (beans), white (rice) and blue (meat!) that make up the country's flag."

Find information like this and much more about what makes a place tick in Culture Smart! guides for over 80 countries. Available from all good bookshops or online at **www.culturesmart.co.uk**

Published by

·K·U·P·E·R·A·R·D·

Publishers & Distributors
59 Hutton Grove, London N12 8DS, UK • Phone: +44 (0)20 8446 2440 • www.kuperard.co.uk

Lightning Source UK Ltd.
Milton Keynes UK
UKHW012109131020
371517UK00014B/220

9 781907 498725